HISTORIC DART

HISTORIC DART

Eric Hemery

David & Charles
Newton Abbot   London   North Pomfret (Vt)

For Sibyl Penty

British Library Cataloguing in Publication Data

Hemery, Eric
  Historic Dart.
  1. Dart River region(Devon)—History
  I. Title
  942.3′592   DA670.D5

  ISBN 0-7153-8142-3

Phototypeset by Keyspools Limited, Golborne, Lancs
and printed in Great Britain
by Redwood Burn, Trowbridge
for David & Charles (Publishers) Limited
Brunel House Newton Abbot Devon

Published in the United States of America
by David & Charles Inc
North Pomfret Vermont 05053 USA

CONTENTS

Appendices

FOREWORD

It was with more than just personal pleasure that I accepted Mr Hemery's kind invitation to write this Foreword to this his latest book on the river Dart and Dartmoor.

The Dart has played and still continues to play an important role in the life of Buckfast Abbey. The early monastic communities did not choose the sites for their monasteries to suit romantic notions of idyllic surroundings. They were, on the contrary, hard-headed realists who carefully reconnoitreed the ground before establishing any foundation. This was especially true of the Cistercians of the twelfth and thirteenth centuries. That there was a monastic site at Buckfast before this time is certain, but it was the Cistercians who carefully surveyed the site before building Buckfast according to the classic, almost rigid, plan which they adopted in this country.

A glance at the map of the Dart shows what a perfect spot Buckfast was for a monastic foundation. The curve of the river provides a tongue of land which serves admirably for draining from the hills above. For a large community of people, water was of course a prime necessity and the streams running into the Dart provided fresh water, a source of power and a sewerage system. During the course of building in modern times, we have come across the culverts which were built for all these purposes.

Buckfast then was not just a beauty spot on the Dart to which men could retreat from the world. Monasteries were busy centres of the local community and of national significance. Buckfast, Buckland and Tavistock were all strategically situated and the crosses on Dartmoor indicate that there was constant travel between the three houses.

Mr Hemery in this present book shows what the economic value of the Dart has been for this part of Devon. As we at Buckfast know, this is no matter of past history; it is a feature of the present. For Dartmoor has played an important part in the development of one of the activities of the modern Abbey of Buckfast. The development of the Buckfast strain of bees, which has been the life-work of Brother Adam, would not have been possible without the seclusion afforded by the Moor. In 1921 the isolation apiary was established at Sherberton on the left bank of the river Swincombe which joins the West Dart just upstream from Huccaby. The fact that the site at Sherberton is so protected from any marauding drones gives us the opportunity to carry out the carefully planned cross-mating of the different races of bees. The 1,000ft contour line passes through this apiary and so provides the conditions for testing the stamina of the young queens. Winter on the Moor can be harsh. In the late summer the ling heather on the higher parts of the Moor furnishes the source of nectar for the delicious flavour of Dartmoor Heather honey.

All lovers of England must be grateful to Mr Hemery for the painstaking research apparent in all his writings. He has opened up to modern readers the manifold riches of this unique part of our country. The river Dart leads us to a glimpse of the wonderland of Dartmoor, for:

There's piskies up to Dartymoor,
An' 'tidden gude yew zay there bain't.

Dom Leo Smith OSB, PhD,
Abbot of Buckfast

PREFACE

The rural crafts, light industries and enterprises situated on the banks of this beautiful river, some dependent utterly upon its waters, make a list of surprising length and variety and encompass a period in time of almost 10,000 years. From the flint weaponry of Mesolithic man to the late twentieth century AD the list includes activities as diverse as tourism, monasticism, steam passenger railways, speleology, carpet pile manufacture, film-making, specialist training in Music and the Arts, the training of officers for the Royal Navy and, four decades ago, training of assault troops for the invasion of Nazi-occupied Europe.

If an account of such human industry is to be coherent it needs, like a large-scale musical work of several movements, thematic cohesion. This is here provided by the river: a long, silver thread of impelling motion that creates its own variations and releases its volume in majestic climax into the restless waters of the English Channel in Start Bay.

It should perhaps be made clear that the river's tributaries are omitted from this study. Not only would the inclusion of even the moorland tributaries necessitate a much larger book (they are described in the author's *High Dartmoor: Land and People*) but would deflect from the book's main objective, which is to focus attention on the pageant of people and events in the Dart valley proper.

Names of many Dartmoor features as marked on OS maps represent mistranscriptions. Authentic spellings are used here (see *High Dartmoor: Land and People*).

By her green hills and delights of woods and valleys, by her many voices, Dart is all Devon and so incomparably England.
Eden Phillpotts, 1939, in *Storm in a Teacup*

Yet—

In the minds of men the useful has succeeded the beautiful. But Society has a soul as well as a body.
Benjamin Disraeli (1804–81)

INTRODUCTION: *GENESIS ET SEQUENTIA*

In the Beginning, when the Andes and the Alps were yet to be uplifted, the region where the great granite upland of Dartmoor was eventually to dominate the landscape of South-West England lay beneath a vast inland sea. Then, during cataclysmic earth movements at the close of the Carboniferous Period some 290 million years ago, there came about a series of mighty upthrusts of fluid, molten magma. This magma solidified into granite, and the older country rock on its perimeter, which it so drastically altered upon contact, became metamorphic rock. Existing peaks and rocks overlying the granite were uplifted, cracked, weathered and crumbled, their debris swept down the moulded valleys of the ultimately unroofed, exposed granite. The immense granite bed, or 'batholith', resulting from these upthrusts extends from the Teign valley within a few miles of Exeter to the seabed a hundred miles west of Land's End—including, and extending beyond, the Isles of Scilly. Like the back of a monstrous serpent, the apices of the batholith form a series of humps, or bosses, declining in elevation westward; the highest and greatest of these is Dartmoor.

The ravages of the last Ice Age—we are now in an 'interglacial' between one Ice Age and another—had yet to lay waste Dartmoor's granite peaks and the valleys had not then attained their present depth. After the Ice Age the upland, following the recession of the ice sheets, became gradually covered by heath vegetation and began to assume the appearance it bears today: this heath, or moorland, was eventually named Dartmoor because the principal river of the region came to be named Dart. During the 4,000 years which man has lived on the banks of Dart, he has created many and varied rural industries, leaving relics to fascinate us to this day.

It is commonly accepted that Dart, one of twelve main rivers pouring from the Moor to vitalise Devon, is so called from the swiftness of its current. None, certainly, is more beautiful. Twin sources initiating lengthy branches east and west; a moorland river system of fifty-five distinct and distinctive tributaries, and a remarkable granite gorge downstream from the confluence of the twin rivers at Dartmeet, create a course on high Dartmoor of unique interest.

Below the Moor is a secondary gorge, also remarkable, in Holne Chase; there follow lush meadows and fertile lowlands between Buckfast and Totnes and a 12-mile estuary guiding the river to the Channel in Start Bay 46 miles from its main source on northern Dartmoor.

Not for nothing is the estuary referred to as 'the English Rhine', though the scenic attractions and historical associations of both Dart and Rhine are very different. Dart, too, possesses features physical and historical which distinguish it from all other British rivers. The celebrated historian Professor W. G. Hoskins writes of it as 'unquestionably the loveliest river in England' and geologist Dr J. F. N. Green, in *History of the River Dart* (Proceedings of the Geologists' Association, Vol 60) describes it as:

> ... very steep, falling over 1800 feet and, draining one of the wettest districts in England, ... rapid, violent and often dangerous. According to R. H. Worth the volume in flood may be 3900 times as great as summer normal.

Homo Sapiens

Although not Dartmoor's swiftest river—that is Tavy on the western moor—Dart is full-bodied and swift on reaching the Moor's central basin, in which oasis for twelve centuries the moormen, the true farmers of the Moor, have lived and worked. Saxon settlers were perhaps first to name the darting river near their homes, a name preserved by their Danish and Norman successors in the form 'Derte', recorded in 1086.

As long ago as 8000 BC, Mesolithic nomads hunted the Moor but did not live upon it. To us they appear as a shadowy people from the border-country and coastal caves such as Kent's Cavern, Torquay, who left upon the Moor nothing more enduring than the tiny worked flints found at Postbridge and elsewhere. Somewhat nearer our own time, in the Early Bronze Age *c* 1800 BC, came Celtic immigrants from the Continent. Known as the Beaker people because of their well-fired, patterned pottery, they came chiefly from the Loire and Seine valleys. Crossing the Channel with families, livestock and belongings, a feat in itself, they sailed up the inviting estuaries of south Devon: Tamar, Tavy, Plym, Yealm, Erme, Avon, Dart and Teign—all but the first, Dartmoor rivers. But the banks of these estuaries were covered by beast-infested forest, and the pioneers moved upstream to the foot of the great heath-land of Dart rising imperiously above the surrounding countryside, its outline punctuated by ruined, jagged peaks of granite to which they gave the name *twr*—a tower: hence our word 'tor'.

At the foot of the Moor the immigrants found their progress virtually barred by V-shaped gorges through which the rivers rushed headlong in quitting the high hills, occupying in times even of normal flow the width of the valley floor, and in times of spate presenting a frightening appearance, in contradistinction to the wide, glaciated U-shaped valleys of the northern British fells and mountains which adequately accommodate both rivers and settlers—and thus, so long ago, became tamed.

Above the gorges on either side they saw huge, elevated tracts of open moor, rising high above the tree-line and offering an often steep, rocky and boggy way forward. Gaining the escarpment, they discovered an environment beyond their dreams: turf soft as lambswool, heather, bracken, peat, building stone in abundance, vast, empty ranges of tor-crowned ridges above wide river basins, mountain tarns—not yet for many centuries to be drained by tinners—mountain air, pure, sparkling streams and panoramic views ranging up to 100 miles. Truly a land of milk and honey!

To a people colonising an unknown land, however, safety and security seemed compatible only with remoteness and height, so that tribe after tribe pressed onward and upward until they had penetrated the mysterious, outer ranges of heights. There they settled, masters of their own new world, looking down upon woodland groves in valleys on the Moor's perimeter which were the habitat of wolf, bear and boar. They were overlooked in their new-found territory only by heights yet more remote where, they quickly discovered, immense carpets of wet peat—later to become the great, deeply fissured peat-bogs we know today—lay upon the high hills, where no man could survive or grow his crops, and where the rivers took their rise.

On the slopes of the broad, dry heather-moors, they built protective 'town walls' of moorstone to enclose their circular stone huts, roofed with a thatch of rushes laid upon a conical timber frame, the whole overlaid with turves. Impounding their stock by night against predators, and farming and hunting by day, they and their descendants lived out a pastoral existence of enviable simplicity and peacefulness for over 1,000 years, until a deteriorating climate from about 500 BC onwards drove them down to the lower, drier edge of the Moor—and finally, *c* AD 50, to the lowlands. The communities gone, the great moorland fell silent.

The Romans, sternly practical, had no need to penetrate the wilds of Dartmoor. They shipped their lead supplies from Somerset's Mendip Hills and their tin from Cornwall, not suspecting the existence of mineral fields in Devon. Saxon and Dane in turn were to break the great silence, 700 years to pass before the Saxon farmers made their *worthigs* ('worthys'), clearings in forest or scrubland on the lower slopes of the Moor; such land reclamation was less necessary in the central basin—there are very few worthys there—where a few bold spirits had already ventured to settle at Sherwell, Sherberton and Hexworthy.

What follows is a pageant of the centuries, its opening scenes set around the twin rivers of East and West Dart, and the closing scene the passage of the waters between the twin castles of Dartmouth and Kingswear, watching over the river's entry into the English Channel.

William Browne, a Devon poet of Tudor times, wrote of the

Dartmoor streams, and the riches of the countryside they water, in words which are especially appropriate to the earlier parts of the present work:

> Show me who can so many crystal rills,
> Such sweet-cloth'd vallies or aspiring hills;
> Such wood-ground, pastures, quarries, wealthy mines;
> Such rocks in whom the diamond fairly shines.
> (From Song Two of *Britannia's Pastorals*, Book II)

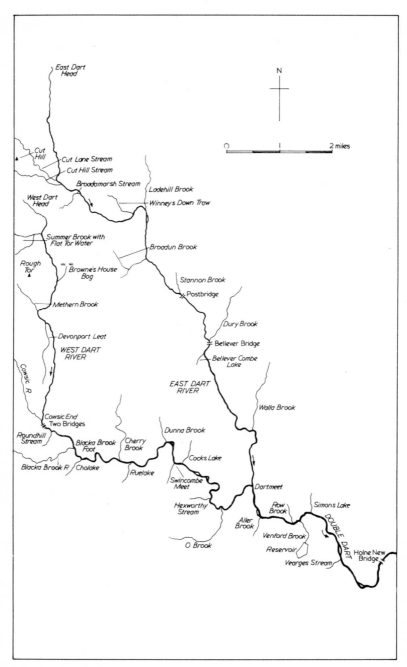

The Moorland Dart

I

THE MOORLAND DART

East Dart: Upper Reach

At East Dart Head, Time has stood still. Fox, badger and otter cross the huge, elevated boglands as they did long before the Iron Age immigrants arrived on the lower, peripheral heather moors. The head-basin is rimmed by deep, fissured peat-bog extending in all directions to cover an area as large as Torbay; here, in Dartmoor's great northern fen, Dart falls from deep peat into a well-like, natural hollow in the underlying granite, 1,840ft above the sea. Also in the fen are the river heads of Teign, Taw, Ockment, Tavy, Walkham and West Dart: Tristram Risdon wrote in his *The Chorographical Description or Survey of the County of Devon* in 1714 that:

> ... its fountain is to be fetched from Dartmoor hills, the mother of many more; but this the first-begotten hath its appellation from thence.

A bog that gives rise to seven main rivers—where in Britain is there another?—inevitably possesses uncommon properties, botanical, atmospheric and spiritual. The vast expanse of fen, rising almost to 2,000ft at Cut Hill, is like no other. So serious an impediment has it always been to the movement of flocks, herds and mounted moormen that, perhaps as long ago as the thirteenth century, man created the artificial pass known as Cut Lane between the upper reaches of East Dart and Tavy, to facilitate long-distance herding between the central basin and north Devon. Since then, others have been cut, one connecting Dart with Teign country and mid-Devon. These passes—'cuts' the moormen call them—provide glimpses of a strangely primeval world.

High on the east valley-side of the upper reach at 1,765ft, is the ruin of a small granite building, one of several in the vicinity likely to puzzle the walker who reaches this lonely place: 12½ft long by 6½ft wide, it is built with rounded ends and contains a fireplace, and beside it, a cupboard recess in the wall. The doorway, now collapsed, was intact twenty years ago; like that of a Bronze Age hut, it was built small and low to minimise the effect of adverse weather conditions, and had to be entered on all fours. This was the 'house' of Stat the peat-cutter, and the wind-swept height upon which it stands is Stats House Hill. During the mid- to late-eighteenth century there began the large-scale cutting of peat as marketable fuel for mines and lowland towns; this necessitated remoter, more extensive peat-beds than those traditionally used by the moormen for their domestic peat. It was imperative that peat-workers ensured for themselves warmth and protection from the elements during their working hours in such wild solitudes. Peat was cut during the early summer, stacked to dry in piles called 'stooks', and transported by packhorse to civilization before the autumn rains began. Highest of these isolated houses is Moute's Inn, not far from East Dart Head, at only 30ft below 2,000ft. Thus, while still in its upper reach, the river flows near the pass of the medieval stock-farmer, the 'houses' of the Georgian peat-cutters and, discussed next, the workings of the tinners of Tudor times.

As Dart emerges from this fastness and the peat recedes from its banks there are seen beside it the spoil heaps of the tinners, searchers for *cassiterite*, tin ore, in the distant days of Henry V, and here and there the scant remains of little buildings, the 'tinners' houses', in which they lived during their working week in this forgotten place. The heavy, tin-bearing stone in the heart of the granite had been wrenched out by the elements and deposited by the streams as alluvia on their flood-plains. There, over some five centuries, the tinners burrowed, dug, and diverted the very rivers in order to search the bed for the prized ore. The centre of these operations, remotest in the Dart valley, lies below the picturesque and ancient crossing place known as Kit Steps, where the wide basin of Broada Marsh (literally, 'broad marsh') shows signs of extensive working by tinners (*see plate 1*).

Looming above this ancient working is the mountainous Cut Hill, while into it pour the waters of mires and tributaries that greatly swell the river's volume—to an extent, in fact, that in 1516 (8 Henry VIII) precipitated an event destined to cause a stir in far-off Westminster. A great quantity of silt and gravel resulted from the tinners' operations and its disposal was essential to their progress. The common method was to heap it in mounds about the flood-plain where the work was in progress; the swiftness and volume of Dart below Broada Marsh, however, suggested an easy alternative: the basin is closed on the lower side except for a narrow defile known as Sandy Hole, through which the river escapes with some velocity; here the tinners excavated the river bed, walling up the banks on either side to create a narrow, steep channel to further accelerate the current. Into this they proceeded to tip their waste, a measure which, only too successful as it transpired, carried it from the workings and greatly reduced their toil.

There can be little doubt that the tinners held the convenient theory that the river, with some nine remaining miles of moorland course, would adequately disperse the waste before it reached the lowlands. That this did not work out in practice is shown by the complaint made in Parliament by Richard Strode, MP for Plympton, to the effect that the harbour of Dartmouth, rather than intermediate parts of the Dart valley, was receiving the tinners' waste.

> And now is supposed by certayne inhabitants of Dartmouth ... that the Ruble, Gravel and Sandes, descendeth by Reason of the great Floodes ... whereby in Continuence it should greatly hurt and quirt the said Haven, which God forbid.

Such was the power in those days of the stannary authority, the vigorous medieval trade union whose hold over its members was absolute, that the Stannary Parliament at Crockern Tor (West Dart) imposed a fine of £160 on Strode for, it was alleged, interfering with the rights of the tinners. Strode, as a Member of the Imperial Parliament, chose to ignore the impeachment, whereupon his person was seized by stannary officials and

incarcerated in the 'annoious, contagious and detestable' Lydford
Castle Prison, where:

> In the morn they hang and draw
> And sit in judgement after. (William Browne)

Such unexpected ramifications of the tinners' skill in hydraulics at
Sandy Hole led to the personal intervention of the King, Henry
VIII; Strode's appeal from prison that the stannary judgement
which had committed him should be declared 'utterlie voide' was
allowed, and his release at once effected. The sequel to all this was
the redundancy of the granite water conduit at Sandy Hole, for
under the presidency of Sir Philip Champernowne—his family was
shortly to purchase the Dartington Hall estate—the stannary
assembly on Crockern Tor of 1533 decreed, under the pressing
thumb of Westminster, that the tinners should:

> ... every of them Convey and Carry ... the Gravel, Ruble and
> Sandes into old Hatches, Tippetts, miry Places or other conveneient
> Places, from the said great Rivers, so that the said Gravel, Ruble or
> Sandes be not conveyed to the said Havens of *Dartmouth* and
> *Plimouth*, or any of them hereafter shall be decayed or hurted.

Along the western edge of Sandy Hole (a 'hole' in Devon is a small
gorge) runs the ancient north–south trans-Dartmoor track, now
known to comparatively few people. From it the prospect of the
valley is rewarding, both up and downstream: north (upward), Cut
Hill still dominates the lonely waste through which East Dart
flows; south (downward), the river makes a spectacular display in
descending from upper to middle reach. The granite bed is much
exposed at the edge of the upper-reach peneplain, and this Dart has
cut and eroded at the beautiful place called Waterfalls, where the
water is impelled towards a hidden defile between Broadun and
Lade Hill and descends 400ft to the middle reach in the central
basin.

East Dart: Middle Reach

Signs of Bronze Age man appear here: a large burial chest, or
kistvaen, stands well back from the river's right bank beside the

wall of a circular enclosure known as Roundy Park, where the valley is overlooked by the shapely Hartland Tor. Near the kistvaen runs the north–south track, here a stony road approaching an attractive fording place on Archerton Brook, a right-bank tributary of the river. On the south side of the track descending from the bold mass of Broadun, are the homes of those who cremated their dead and deposited the ashes, within pottery beakers, in kistvaens such as that at Roundy Park.

This stretch of the Dart valley near Postbridge saw the establishment, beside the river, of that most ancient of industries, the production of flint arrowheads, knives and scrapers for the Mesolithic hunters of 8000 BC. Discoveries were made between 1901 and 1950—the early ones by Robert and Olive Burnard—of microliths now exhibited at the Royal Albert Museum, Exeter. Flint is not indigenous to granite country, so supplies for the manufactory here had to be imported from the chalk-lands of east Devon and west Dorset. These remarkable finds of worked flints indicate that non-resident Mesolithic man hunted the area on a wide scale long before the arrival of the Bronze Age immigrants whose homes are the earliest domestic ruins on the Moor.

Below Broadun Ring runs the dry channel of a leat cut in 1844 to conduct water from East Dart to Powder Mills, the old gunpowder factory west of Postbridge. Prior to the invention of dynamite in 1867, the powder manufactured here was used by miners and quarrymen in blasting. The manufacture of gunpowder needed a copious and never-failing supply of water, and, as a potentially hazardous undertaking, a site removed from any habitation, yet where existing roads would facilitate transport by large wagons. Such conditions were met ideally in Dartmoor's central basin, which was crossed by two trans-moorland roads based on ancient trade routes, one from Ashburton to Tavistock (south-east to west) and the other from Chagford and Moreton-hampstead to Plymouth (north-east to south-west), the roads crossing at Two Bridges in the West Dart valley.

Much of the gunpowder was delivered over long distances by horse-drawn wagons, but with the opening in 1883 of the Great Western Railway line between Yelverton and Princetown, large quantities were carted to Princetown and put on rail for more distant parts. Albert, Prince Consort, took a personal interest in the establishment and granted an interview to its founder, Alderman Frean of Plymouth. The gunpowder was tested and graded by the firing of a projectile over a measured distance from a mortar, which relic remains today still bolted to its granite bed at the mills. The wheelhouses and certain buildings of the old works may be seen from the B3212 road west of Postbridge.

The immense central basin, an elevated oasis, forms an unusual topographical feature. All other British highland regions have a central apex; Dartmoor, however, has two apices, these rising to the north and south of the central depression. This depression, or basin, has consequently dictated a historical pattern of settlements and tracks like no other. Because the great blanket bog areas of the apices long ago forbade penetration by packhorses or mounted parties, the transbasin tracks had necessarily to climb the escarpment of the Moor on both east and west sides and descend into the basin to cross it; but Dart and its tributaries pour across the basin floor, compelling the traveller to cross six rivers, three of them—East and West Dart and Cowsic—dangerous when in flood. A Dartmoor river in spate is both unfordable and unforgettable, and the advent of 'clapper' bridges in the Middle Ages represented the first step towards ensuring a regular flow of traffic between border towns then attaining commercial importance. The bridges were constructed of drystone piers and imposts consisting of huge granite slabs. The East Dart clapper bridge at Postbridge, a fine example and noted tourist attraction, dates probably from the early thirteenth century. It is obvious that care was needed during high winds to ensure the safe tread of heavily laden packhorses, for there is no evidence that these bridges were at any time provided with parapets; such parapet clappers as still exist belong to the nineteenth century, by which time the old packhorse routes had been superseded by the new turnpike roads with their high arch bridges. Merchandise carried consisted chiefly of wool, tin and peat; and a good deal of what may be termed executive travel also took place. A journey from Exeter, Devon's capital, to Tavistock and into south-east Cornwall was far more direct and clean under hoof, as well as less fraught with dangers from waylaying thieves, than one below the edge of the Moor through border-country lanes.

Regional trades and activities so far reviewed in East Dart country have brought us, at Powder Mills, to within a century of our own time. A step of fifty years forward, to the formation by the Government of the Forestry Commission, will take in the serried ranks of dark green conifers now ubiquitous in our highland regions. Though often badly sited from the aesthetic viewpoint— as are those in East Dart country mentioned below—they contribute vitally towards national timber needs. The view from the river's high left bank just below Bellever Bridge underlines three markedly different periods in time: first, the river displays three modes of crossing—stepping stones (likely to be pre-medieval), clapper bridge (medieval) and, between them, the ford; second, the arch bridge, having a different (and later) origin from the turnpike bridge upstream at Postbridge, was built soon after the Napoleonic wars; third, the mid-twentieth-century environmental blunder of tree-planting above the opposite bank, reaching as it does to the very foot of two fine skyline tors beyond—but this at least has led to the establishment of a busy forestry centre at Bellever offering steady employment, with new houses built for foresters and their families in 1944.

The clapper bridge once served a noted historic track, the Lych Way—the 'way of the dead'—from the central basin to the church of St Petrock in Lydford, under Dartmoor's western escarpment. The Sacraments of the Church were administered at St Petrock's to the forest dwellers, so that the dead had to be borne over many miles of wild moorland for burial in parochial consecrated ground. Such journeys, often made under terribly adverse weather conditions, and with the corpse carried on a litter between bearers, must have been harrowing indeed; there even arose from time to time the need to salt down the corpse against decay when floods or snow made the Lych Way impassable. An atmosphere of the 'long ago' still somehow pervades the old track, but much of the funeral traffic had ceased by 1260, when Bishop Bronescombe of Exeter granted a petition from the forest dwellers of Brimpts, Huccaby and Hexworthy, in the east sector of the central basin, to be allowed to take their dead to the closer parish church of St Pancras, Widecombe-in-the-Moor. The petition was based mainly on this plaint:

Et quod loca predicta a matrice ecclesia de Lideford sereno tempore per octo, et tempestatibus exertis in circuitu per quindecim, distant milaria.

This is to say that those tenement dwellers found the journey to Lydford of 8 miles in fair weather to become one of 15 in foul.

Among the conifers on the hill-crest are several kistvaens, one having an associated monumental stone row. Downstream from Bellever, East Dart passes through the deep, high-sided valley known as Lough Tor Hole to enter the land of the Ancient Tenements, oasis group-settlements with attendant privileges granted by the Crown to medieval stock-farmers, together with the use of huge tracts of pasture ground in the high hills, in return for certain duties of range supervision. The tenement holders were the first true moormen, the stock-farmers whose wool, beef and packhorse-power led to the development of a large trading network with Dartmouth, Plymouth, London and the Continent. Old drift ways and fording places occur below Lough Tor Hole and at Walla Brook Foot, where once great herds were driven before the advent of mechanised road transport.

In Lough Tor Hole, resting in silent decay beneath the conifers on the left bank, is the ancient farm of Whiteslade where, a century and more ago, lived two spinster women who were said to have existed on a diet of pickled slugs gathered in their garden: hence the ruin has entered the annals of Dartmoor's history as Snaily House. The very large stepping stones long ago manoeuvred into position in the river nearby are consequently known as Snaily House Steps. A short way downstream the valley opens and the ancient crossing place of Win Ford connects the Commons with the Forest of Dartmoor. This reach of East Dart, Babeny Rit, is altogether more secluded than the geographically equivalent, Hexworthy area of West Dart and possesses a pastoral atmosphere all its own.

Downstream from Babeny Rit, on an ancient way of the central basin, once stood a large clapper bridge, since destroyed by flood. Several original stepping stones remain of the series known as Babeny Steps, while the old way they and the bridge once served follows the right bank and, passing above the ruin of Dolly's Cot, climbs to the Ancient Tenement of Brimpts. The intriguing name of the ruined cottage stems from its one-time occupant, Dolly Trebble, a damsel whose attractions did not escape the attention of the Prince Regent over a century and a half ago during his visits to Tor Royal near Princetown, as the guest of Sir Thomas Tyrwhitt. This astute man built the war prison at Princetown and the Plymouth & Dartmoor Railway—a tramroad for horse-drawn trucks—and was for many years Gentleman Usher of the Black Rod in the House of Commons.

At Babeny Steps the river swings southward to approach Dartmeet under the splendid mount of Yar Tor and a Bronze Age village overlooks the valley from the lower slope of the tor. Downstream, another pair of bridges bring a picturesque touch to the valley and cameras click all day as children add colour to the old grey stones of the Dartmeet clapper where once packhorses crossed. Although no longer intact, the bridge offers a safer perch than the Georgian structure nearby, which lacks the refuge bays of earlier packhorse (arch) bridges and has a confined width calculated to cause hair-raising moments for a pedestrian as a forty-seater coach lurches over its hump.

Downstream is the meet of the Darts, East and West, below which a great force of water enters a hidden valley of dramatic depth, beauty and legend: Double Dart Gorge.

West Dart: Upper Reach

Below the skirts of the mountain Cut Hill in the northern fen, West Dart springs to life from a 12ft peat cliff, its fountain head linked to upper East Dart country by the peat pass known as Johnson's Cut. Flowing through a shorter upper reach than its sister river, it passes two tinners' houses and the mellifluously named Summer Brook, Summer Hill, Wildbanks Hill, Browne's House Bog and Rowter Moor before reaching the edge of its peneplain and dropping through a steep-bedded transitional passage—there are no waterfalls like those on East Dart—to its middle reach.

West Dart: Middle Reach

The river, ending its transitional passage, adopts a direct, southerly course into the central basin. Flowing across Wistmans Wood Ford, the traditional crossing place of the Lych Way, it reaches the weir of Devonport Leat Head, from where water is taken in by the remarkable 33-mile-long, granite-lined channel constructed in the late eighteenth century and conveyed to Dock, as Devonport was then called. Powers to leat water from West Dart and its tributaries Cowsic and Blacka Brook were obtained in 1793 by the Company of Proprietors of the Plymouth Dock Waterworks and the channel was cut in 1793-4. The further cut of 6 miles to West Dart was delayed for a time and water was initially taken in over a 27-mile course from Blacka Brook. It is altogether a notable piece of hydraulic engineering of its time—over sixty years earlier than Brunel's famous Saltash Bridge—including, as it does, a 700yd-long tunnel near Siward's Cross driven through granite to penetrate the water-divide westward into Mewy country, where it cascades over granite steps in descending to the valley and is carried across the river by aqueduct.

On the lower valley-side opposite the leat, as it gains height above the river, is Wistmans Wood, the most remarkable of Dartmoor's three primeval oak groves; growing well above the normal tree-line, they are the highest placed of any in Britain. Wizened, misshapen trees cling to life, sheltered by huge boulders ice-transported down the hillside from Longaford Tor; in advanced age—up to about 500 years—they bow their trunks and project branches earthward before the force of the tearing north-west winds that rake this valley and prune their canopies to a mean height of about 15ft above the ground. The conditions promoting the rejuvenation of all three woods are shelter from the easterly winds and the presence of a clitter, or boulder-field, at the foot of a west-facing slope, where seedlings are safe from grazing animals. There is an abundance of bird and small mammal life here.

As the tor-crested ridge above the wood declines southward to the central basin, its final feature is a tor recorded in history before the oldest surviving tree in Wistmans Wood lay in embryo. Mention was made earlier of this rockpile, Crockern Tor, where the tinners' assembly, the Stannary Parliament, met intermittently and for which records exist for the period 1494–1703. Devon was divided into four stannary districts, each with an appointed Stannary (tin-market) Town, the boundaries meeting at Crockern Tor: the towns were Chagford, Ashburton, Plympton and Tavistock. Each district was represented by twenty-four jurats, and tremendous noise and bustle must have attended their arrival on horseback and assembly at the tor, where legislation enacted sometimes occupied several days. The parliament was presided over by the Lord Warden of the Stannaries, an office held by some noteworthy sons of Devon: Sir Philip Champernowne in 1533, and in 1600 Sir Walter Raleigh. The Lord Warden, or in his absence the Vice Warden, traditionally occupied a granite settle before a huge moorstone table beneath the summit rock; the ninety-six jurats, their horses tethered below the tor at long-vanished corrals, could hear clearly the voice from the Chair, for the great rock above serves (as simple experiment proves) as a sounding board. The constituent parts of the 'Judge's Table' and 'Judge's Chair' were later removed to Dunnabridge.

Near the south-west foot of Crockern Tor passes the line of another important trans-Dartmoor packhorse track from east to west, the original packhorse way, in fact, between Exeter and Tavistock. By this means, access to the tor was easy, even when the Moor was mist-shrouded. The track crossed West Dart at a ford and clapper bridge, since destroyed by flood, and ascended the steep west valley-side to run above the Cowsic gorge and cross that river at Beardown clapper bridge. The bridges, about half a mile apart, are unlikely to have given the locality, Two Bridges, its name, which almost certainly is a corruption of the early-sixteenth-century *Tobrygge*, meaning 'at the bridge'—that is, the since-vanished West Dart clapper. Several cottages stood here in earlier times and the great clapper that stood with them would have made an ideal rendezvous for travellers, packhorse drivers and moormen. The role is now filled by the Two Bridges Hotel on the left bank of West Dart, to which patrons are motor-borne rather than mounted.

Swelled by the waters of Cowsic from the next valley, Dart flows beneath the modern road bridge, past the hotel and through the graceful arches of the turnpike bridge. Downstream are Prince Hall Rocks, two opposing small rockpiles overlooking the river's junction with its tributary Blacka Brook, as it enters what is probably the oldest pattern of still-worked farmlands in Britain, for here begins Ancient Tenement land, the eastern area of which was referred to earlier. The now wide river winds through these medieval settlements in the order: Prince Hall, Broom Park (part of Sherberton), Dunnabridge, Brownberry, Sherberton, Hexworthy and Huccaby. There are ancient buildings, ancient family names—Caunter, Hext, Coaker, French, Hannaford—packhorse lanes between field hedges, and, despite tractors, cattle-lorries and riding establishments, an overall atmosphere of a time long-past. The duties formerly undertaken by the moormen in return for privilege pasturage and peat-cutting in the Forest of Dartmoor included assisting at the annual stock 'drifts', when animals belonging to unlicensed owners and found grazing on the heights of the Forest were driven down to the central basin and impounded at Dunnabridge Pound, its massive wall proof against breach of pound. It was to Dunnabridge that the relics of the presidential seat from Crockern Tor were brought late in the eighteenth century; the Judge's Seat was erected as stocks for would-be pound-breakers and the Judge's Table as the protective canopy for the dipping well in old Dunnabridge Farm court.

Although many British estates and highland zones were drastically stripped of standing woodlands and conifer plantations at the outbreak of World War I, the most unusual form of timber transport to the railhead was reserved for that of Brimpts (south-east central basin), from where an aerial ropeway stretched westward across the basin to Princetown station, terminus of England's only true mountain railway—unwisely closed by British Railways in 1956—and thence to the port of Plymouth. The ropeway straddled West Dart and its tributaries and the moor people were delighted to discover the ease with which timbers could be persuaded to fall from the travelling cradles. Beside the lonely upper reach of a little tributary, Cholake, is a concrete engine-bed; upon it, over sixty years ago, worked the power-plant that motivated the cradles, for this desolate spot is half way between Brimpts and Princetown, the machine thereby providing a balanced thrust on the ropeway for cradles travelling in both directions.

Below Huccaby, last of the Ancient Tenements, the river speeds over a rocky bed to accompany the by-road to Hexworthy, which is carried across it by a high arch bridge of some elegance. This replaces a large clapper swept away in a 'freshet' towards the end of the eighteenth century. Here, Dart is impelled rapidly towards the bridge by a steep bank. A cloud-burst over West Dart country had brought about the freshet, a mass of water resembling a tidal wave, the full force of which was hurled at the bridge. Two men were crossing at the time; one pressed on and survived, but the other, tragically illustrating the old adage 'He who hesitates is lost', hesitated, started back and indeed was lost, together with every stone of the great medieval clapper bridge. The experience of this awesome event prompted local people to demand a new county bridge with a centre arch high enough to clear the worst spate.

As the river leaves Huccaby the valley opens upon a flood-plain where an ancient track crosses at Week Ford. Massive stepping stones and a wide ford lie amidst the plain near the confluence of O Brook with the river. Above the right bank upstream from the confluence are two medieval tinners' blowing houses, that is, mills equipped with blast furnaces for the smelting of tin ore and the production of ingots for the stannary markets. Furnaces and ore-crushing drop-stamps were actuated by waterwheels supplied by gravity leats from streams, the water being conducted from the banked-up end of the leat, the 'launder bank', through a wooden launder to overshoot the wheel. At the Week Ford blowing-houses may be seen the leat from O Brook, the high launder banks above both houses and the waterwheel pits, ore-crushing tables (known as 'mortar stones'), here used beneath triple stamps, a fine mould stone, one remaining furnace and a storeroom in the lower house.

All tin ingots produced here were marketed at Ashburton Stannary.

Below Week Ford appears the tree-clad, V-opening of Huccaby Cleave, where West Dart enters a secret valley harbouring a persistent tradition of pixies—the Little People. An impressive cavern known as Pixies' Cave, formed by the natural movement through weathering of granite masses, lies in Pixies' Wood near the head of the strange little Beehive Combe. As the Cleave opens, the river approaches its junction at Dartmeet with East Dart.

Double Dart: Lower Reach

Almost 4 miles of serpentine, heavily wooded and precipitous-sided cleave, the Double Dart Gorge, close upon the river as it flows from Dartmeet: Cumston Tor, Vag Hill, Benjy Tor, Sharp Tor, Mil Tor, Hockinston Tor overlook the great defile; Aller Brook, Row Brook, Venford Brook, Simon's Lake, Vearge's Stream enter the river, the last two from hanging valleys. Pink granite bedding, in places massive, lies below the swift river, whilst no nobler rockpile rises in Double Dart country than Looka Tor, towering like a ruined fortress from the very (left) river bank. Near it lies Langamarsh Pit where farm-worker Jan Coo of Rowbrook Farm—an English Peer Gynt—was said to have been lured into the underworld by the pixies, a disquieting tale.

On Vag Hill, high above the east valley-side near Rowbrook Farm, is a tiny combe, strange in its darkness and seclusion, known as Warren House Pit, containing the ruins of the rabbit warrener's house that gave it its name. The establishment of the warren was recorded in a lease of 1613 and the warreners, Richard Reynell and Walter Furseland, set about constructing the adjuncts of a commercial warren, in particular the pillow-mounds, or 'buries' colonised by the rabbits for breeding, and granite vermin traps to capture the predators which nightly emerged from setts among the valley-side rocks to raid the buries. Two types of vermin trap were used at Vag Hill; one, resembling a small granite tunnel, is common to the Dartmoor warrens; the other, unique in my experience, is a vermin-drowning trap.

At the foot of the hanging valley of Simon's Lake is the mass of bedding known as Broada Stones, where certain physical features of the gorge combine acoustically with the elements to produce an uncanny moan, traditionally the 'Cry of the Dart' (and described by a twentieth-century Widecombe-in-the-Moor authoress, Beatrice Chase, in her book *From a Dartmoor Window*).

To have clambered over the east gorge-side on Midsummer Day, up to some thirty years ago, would have been to risk being run over by a stray wagon wheel, for the old custom of 'rolling the wheel' down the side of the gorge from Mil Tor was a popular one, and it would have been disconcerting, to say the least, to have heard one of these huge wheels hurtling through the undergrowth above one. (*See plate 2* for the impressive scene of this rustic festivity.)

The crags of Benjy Tor rise above the western brink of the gorge, while above the eastern brink is Dr Blackall's Drive, named after the nineteenth-century owner of Spitchwick Manor, who had it made. A well-defined track, it runs between Bel Tor Corner ($1\frac{3}{4}$ miles east of Dartmeet on the Ashburton road) and Newbridge Hill, and provides a scenic walk or pony ride of outstanding beauty. From it are seen all the gorge-side tors and beyond them the great, sweeping line of southern Dartmoor, while from the depths of the gorge comes the sound of Dart's rushing waters and the occasional sight of a fishing heron.

What has been written and illustrated here of Double Dart— indeed, of the entire moorland Dart— is little more than a sketch, yet it may help the reader to form some conception of the river's remarkable character. At the mouth of the gorge, between the declining slope of Newbridge Hill (the very foot of high Dartmoor) and the perpendicular cliff of Holne Wood above a right-bank flood-plain, the river divides at Long Island. Flowing over Hannaford Stickles, past Deadman's Corner and sweeping round Wellsfoot Island, it passes swiftly under the medieval New Bridge (carrying the B3357 road), past the (in summer) capacity-packed car park beside it, and into the border-country. It has left its birthland.

THE BORDER-COUNTRY DART

High Dartmoor is surrounded by a characteristic belt of country which provides a transition from high moor to lowlands. This belt varies in width from 2 to 3 miles in most areas but stretches across 7 miles on the north-east fringe, where the River Teign emerges from Fingle Gorge at Steps Bridge. Rivers and tributaries descend rapidly through gorges; packhorse lanes drop steeply from moor-gates to border-country farms, villages and towns; cornditches—a combination of ditch, wall and bank to keep deer out of the enclosures but to allow them to leap out should they somehow have gained entrance—stand at the head of the enclosed lands; buildings, gateways, stiles and bridges are constructed of granite moorstone sledded or carted down from the Moor; handsome, crocketted church towers of granite rise above clustered villages in which vicarage, cottages, shop and sub post office (the last two usually one and the same) and an inn satisfy the spiritual and material needs of the inhabitants. This peripheral belt, in places as beautiful as may be imagined, is the Dartmoor border-country. Through it, Dart flows in a great northward loop after leaving New Bridge, so putting between it and the road the wooded height of Holne Chase. Recrossed by the road at the foot of the loop, the river again plunges away from it, this time into Holne Park and Hembury Woods, before coming to the end of the reach at Buckfastleigh.

Horseshoe Falls to Buckland Woods

Hannaford House and Lower Hannaford Farm on the north-east side, and Kinghurst on the south-east, face across the valley under

1 The wilderness of Broada Marsh. Everywhere blanket bog ('fen') covers the hilltops and higher sides. The tinners' spoil-heaps mark the basin floor, where the expanse of marsh is threaded by the East Dart River. The elevation of the valley floor is 1,600ft

2 Double Dart at Black Pool. Notice the swirl of the current. Mil Tor rises beyond, with Miltor Wood on the slope. The elevation of the valley floor is 800ft

3 One of the adits of Southwood Copper Mine in Holne Park. Bottom left is the remaining iron rail of the tramroad. Note the lichen and hardfern (*Blechnum spicant*) on the right

4 'Buckfast Abbey and the Valley of the Dart' by William Turner. Artist's licence shapes the distant background, but Hembury Castle (left) and Auswell Rocks (right) are authentically shown. Also topographically accurate are the plain between the mansion and the river (now the Abbey lawn), the steep bank (right) and the road to Dart Bridge and Buckfastleigh (left of the mansion).

Holne Woods where Double Dart leaves the gorge to approach New Bridge. Holne Cot, to which a private drive branches from the road to Holne Moorgate, nestles on the hillside above the woods and provides magical views in autumn. Almost a century and a half ago, in 1846, a copper mine was working at Lower Hannaford, where the Dartmoor granite terminates abruptly at the level of the culm slate, though nearly all traces of the mine have long since vanished. It was known as Great Wheal Elizabeth and the large, water-filled hollow on the river's left bank below Hannaford, Salter's Pool, was one of its workings. The tail-race of the mine leat appears to have reached the river at the lower end of a flood-plain below Hannaford Stickles.

Dart arrives at Horseshoe Falls and divides at a midstream mass of slatey rock, formed from shales violently affected by contact with molten magma 290 million years ago; here water-smoothed pebbles of fine-grained granite have been deposited on slate banks by the river in flood. Granite occurs not only in pebble form but also as fine sand ground by water action and lying in a man-made channel opposite Horseshoe Falls, where water was once taken in and leated to the former Holne Chase Tin Mine, known simply as Chase Mine, north of the high road. Following the abandonment of the workings soon after 1875, the leat was for a time used to supply fish-rearing ponds belonging to Chase House (now the Holne Chase Hotel). These ponds were originally the mine reservoirs. On nearing the road, the leat received a streamlet falling from Kinghurst Down and passed beneath the road at a point marked by still-surviving bridge parapets. From here, the channel is seen following the right bank of the river to terminate among swampy, overgrown pits.

The B3357 highway in the locality of New Bridge is based upon an ancient track; it joins the arc points on the river's 3½-mile bowed loop at New and Holne Bridges—by road only 1½ miles apart. As the road descends Newbridge Hill in a series of sharp bends, it affords fine views of the Dart valley. Crossing the river where once stood a massive clapper, it mounts the east valley-side before descending Chase Hill to recross at Holne Bridge, a fine example of a packhorse bridge with two large semi-circular arches and

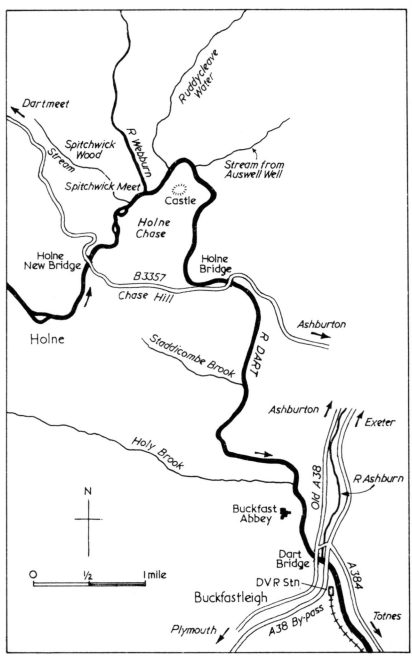

The Border-country Dart

pedestrian refuge bays, built in 1413; like other ancient Dartmoor bridges, it now has to bear the tremendous weight of modern coach and animal-transport traffic, surely a tribute to the building skill of our forefathers! In 1645 it was surveyed by Sir Thomas Hare, Bart, and fellow Justices, who, it is recorded, 'viewed the decayes of the Bridge called Holne New Bridge' and ordered the sum of £13 to be raised for necessary repairs. On the river's right bank near New Bridge is a small lay-by; the stream flowing here is the one from Kinghurst Down, crossed by a footpath to Holne via stepping stones and an antique stile consisting of slotted granite posts and wooden cross-bars.

A wide flood-plain stretches below Newbridge Hill Corner, connected by a narrow strip of land to another above the bridge at the car park. The upper one, now drained, was once called Newbridge Marsh, and the lower, larger and partly drained one, Deeper Marsh, a name still used today. Its bracken-patched turf is marked also by the crumbled prehistoric walls of Higher Corner Pound and the upper edge of the plain is crossed by the road from New Bridge to Lower Town and Leusdon. Rising finely above all are the clustered quartz-schorl rocks of Leigh Tor, adorned by oak and ash. This represents the heart of a tourmaline dyke which, twice crossing the valley, runs through Holne Chase to Auswell Rocks. Leigh Tor is the first of several crags of metamorphic rock above the river in the border-country reach which, together with the wild appearance of the river in Holne Chase, give the valley an aspect of some grandeur.

The Deeper Marsh plain is a favourite playground and picnic area for visitors, who, as National Park notices make clear, are literally wearing away the riverside here. Downstream are Higher Corner, Higher Corner Pool, an island, and Lower Corner Pool and Stickles, where the river enters the scenic confines of Holne Chase.

The Leusdon road above the left bank passes the lower entrance to the ancient manor of Spitchwick before branching off to Buckland-in-the-Moor. Spitchwick Manor is of pre-Norman origin and there can be little doubt that successive houses have occupied the site since Saxon times. The present building shows signs of some antiquity as a manorial hall farm, but occupants in later time have made extensive alterations, and it has evolved solely as a residence—the working of the land and animal husbandry being undertaken at nearby Spitchwick Farm. In Georgian times Lord Ashburton owned the house, and later the mid-Victorian Dr Joseph Blackall, who cut the scenic carriage drive on the eastern brink of the Double Dart Gorge.

Lord Ashburton was a distinguished son of the Dunning family whose roots lay at Gnatham in the parish of Walkhampton, under the western skirts of Dartmoor, in the reign of the Stuarts. John Dunning later settled as an attorney at Ashburton and lived for a time at Gulwell, in Staverton parish, where his son John was born in 1731. John Jnr was called to the Bar in 1756 and in 1774 and 1780 stood as a Member of Parliament for Calne in Wiltshire. He was a member of a literary club founded in 1764 by Dr Samuel Johnson, whose personal friendship he won. In 1769 Dunning negotiated for the purchase of the manors of Widecombe-in-the Moor and Spitchwick, and largely rebuilt the latter house. He was accorded a mark of favour in 1773 when Sir Joshua Reynolds painted his portrait, whilst public recognition of his services to the Law came on 8 April 1782, when he was created Baron Ashburton. One of Dunning's many successful cases was his defence of Captain Edward Gould of Pridhamsleigh against a murder charge at Exeter Assizes in c 1786 (see Appendix). As a direct consequence of this case, Lord Ashburton became the owner of Pridhamsleigh and other properties in Staverton parish.

An impressive extension to the entrance hall at Spitchwick was added a century later by Dr Blackall in the form of a granite porch large enough to admit a carriage, so that the gentry might board and alight in inclement weather without inconvenience. Panelling on walls and beams under ceilings are also latter-day additions, but none the less tasteful for that, the ceilings being low enough to induce a sense of cosiness in this manor house perched 700ft above sea level in the high border-country. At the rear of the house in the stable yard is an unusually fine specimen of a granite drinking trough, the water supply entering through a large duct with stepped bed.

The picturesque by-road east of Spitchwick Lower Lodge, not so long ago a dusty white track, accompanies the river and crosses the incoming River Webburn at Buckland Bridge. The confluence, Spitchwick Meet, lies a few yards below the road and is an inviting water-sport place, though not one recommended for young children. The Revd Dr John Keble (1792–1866), Professor of Poetry at Oxford from 1831–45, in whose memory Keble College was founded, once stood here and recorded his impressions in two verses of whimsical lines that begin:

DART   Wild Webburn, wild Webburn, why rush on so fast?
            Your speed is so reckless, it never can last.

WEBBURN   Indeed, Mrs Dart, I must own it is true.
            But then, pray consider, I'm younger than you!

East of Buckland Bridge is the quaintly named Mistresses Piece—the personalities once involved having faded anonymously into history—where a riverside path branches from the Buckland road at the picture-book Buckland (Lower) Lodge, and passes through a gateway. The by-road, meanwhile, bends abruptly northward and climbs through the sheltered Buckland Woods—where whortleberries have been picked in December—to reach the tiny, high-border-country village of Buckland-in-the-Moor; set amidst romantic scenery, with its Georgian mansion, Buckland Court, and granite church of St Peter, it is of rare attractiveness. Over all looms Buckland Beacon, where Dartmoor makes its first rise from the valley below Auswell Rocks.

A little apart from the houses of Buckland village stands Buckland Court, now unfortunately in a semi-derelict condition, though its quiet dignity of half a century ago is evident from existing pictures. The Court was for long the seat of the Bastard family, who were so active in planting trees and laying down the Buckland Carriage Drives. In the roadside wall bounding the grounds of the Court is a maltreated, medieval granite cross, first noticed by William Crossing and described in his *The Ancient Stone Crosses of Dartmoor*.

St Peter's Church still contains relics of the first stone church built here in the late twelfth century which, like other Dartmoor churches such as St Pancras at Widecombe-in-the-Moor, was not at that time provided with a tower. The late fifteenth to early sixteenth century saw the addition of towers at Widecombe and Buckland, whilst in more recent times, a former parishioner, William Whitley of Wellstor, was inspired to donate a tower clock-face as a memorial to his mother, with numerals represented by the twelve letters spelling out MY DEAR MOTHER. The relevant Report of the Rural Dean of Ashburton gives the date of the faculty granted for the installation of the clock as 13 October 1930, on which occasion the peal of bells in the tower was increased from five to eight. The fragment of another ancient cross lies near the south gate of the churchyard, where it has been used as a coping stone of the wall and consists of the upper portion of an octagonal shaft with head and one arm. An octagonal pedestal outside the gate could have been the base of the cross. Yet another cross, this time a modern one at the west corner of the churchyard, is of interest in marking the resting place of several members of the Bastard family—of William Pollexfen Bastard, Priest, of Kitley and Buckland Court, 1832–1915, and his wife and daughters. William was the son of Edmund Pollexfen Bastard, who erected bond-stones on Dartmoor bounding his Buckland manor lands. Bearing his initials, 'PB', they are to be seen in the locality of Blackslade Mire.

In his scholarly, privately published book *Tore Abbey*, Deryck Seymour quotes from a mid-thirteenth-century charter specifying a gift of land to the 'Canons of Torre by Roger de Bokelonde', so giving us the medieval version of the name. Like other parishes so named—there are seven in Devonshire—Buckland (all were originally Bokelonde) means the 'book-land' or land detailed in a charter. In the village is Southbrook Farm, where Mr David Perryman has farmed for forty years. The farm is mentioned in several charters examined by Deryck Seymour as 'Suthbrok' or 'Southbrok' and was anciently important as a manor court. In one charter, for instance, William de Baldryngton refers to 'my court of Southbrok'. Seymour writes:

In (charter) 85 John Gobet refers to the close he retains as 'south of the courthouse'. The present house is obviously a rebuilding of something far older, but no doubt stands on the same site as the medieval house.

On the edge of a wood on David Perryman's land near Auswell Cottages is a derelict barn containing, of all things, two Plymouth Corporation horse-drawn road-sweeping machines—likewise derelict. Sold by the Corporation as redundant shortly after World War I, they were purchased by William Whitley (donor of the church clock) after he had acquired the Buckland Court estate, for sweeping the Buckland drives—the scenic carriage drives running high above the river in the Chase. But too late. The time for wagonette and landau travel had passed, the unromantic internal combustion engine was shattering the silence and churning up dust on the Ashburton road and sweepers and barn fell into silent decay. It is astonishing to come upon them, below the modern house known as Buckland Hall, and to read still decipherable words on the front board of the less decayed cart.

A track runs south-westward from Southbrook Farm and enters Combe Wood. Undoubtedly of great antiquity, it passes below the ruined barn and once served a number of cottages nearby, now merely overgrown walls in the wood; continuing through Auswell Wood above Raven Rock it joins eventually with the higher drive already described. It is possible that the cottages, forming a kind of Buckland Lower Town, represent a small settlement of miners' houses. The ruins deserve more careful inspection than their present buried condition allows.

Opposite Southbrook Farm the village post office and school stand beside a swift stream leated from Ruddycleave Water, which rises in Blackslade Mire on high Dartmoor. Emerging at the roadside through a granite portal, it fills a dipping trough once in constant use by thirsty horses. 450ft above the church and 1,000ft above the winding river is the brink of high Dartmoor, where the land sweeps down south-eastward to the undulating plain of Ashburton.

Rounding the great hill under Auswell Rocks are the Buckland drives, once celebrated for scenic excursions undertaken in horse-drawn carriages and not to be missed by well-informed tourists. This pleasant mode of admiring the Dartmoor country was long in vogue, indeed, the author's wife's grandfather once plied a hackney carriage west of the Moor near Yelverton. Subject to the closure of gates, the drives may today be traversed on foot, and without doubt the two most satisfying are the riverside drive from Buckland Bridge and that branching from the Ashburton road near Auswell Cottages. The latter is said by some to have been anciently the Buckland-Ashburton road, though I doubt this, as it has the appearance and carefully graded level of the other Buckland drives and is lined by pine trees, which are not indigenous to the Moor. It is, of course, possible that the drive was made by surfacing an ancient track, though it has to be said that the Buckland-Ashburton road running east of Auswell Rocks past Druid Cross has been in existence for a very long time and must be regarded as the true road. It is clearly identified as such in a portion of one of the medieval charters reproduced in his book by Seymour. The drive, meanwhile, curves round the high slope of the hill and enters Auswell Wood to follow what becomes a 600ft escarpment about the wonderful glen of Holne Chase, one of the most beautiful places in rural England.

It is interesting, too, that a Ward Lock *Guide to Dartmoor* of eighty-one years ago should stipulate one-way traffic in the Chase on certain days 'as the road is only wide enough for one coach to travel safely through it', thus underlining its popularity at the turn of the century.

In Auswell Cottages live Mrs Marshall and Mr and Mrs Hillhouse, who have described to me some interesting nearby remains. According to Mrs Hillhouse these had been almost totally destroyed some years ago by the giant caterpillar-track machines of a forestry company. The remains appear to me to be those of an Iron Age settlement not unlike others on the eastern fringe of Dartmoor, in particular Roundy Pound on Teigncombe Common, near Chagford. An inner circle of slabs with a diameter of at least 30ft is enclosed by another circular wall separated from it by an area about 15ft wide. Within the area so enclosed, but nowhere outside it, Mr Hillhouse had obtained positive results in a sweep with his metal detector, suggesting that iron smelting could have taken place, as it did at Roundy Pound. Near the outer pound on the north side runs a wide ditch, possibly a droveway, terminating in a primitive wall of slabs and large stones—the east boundary of the Iron Age farmer's field-system. The site is characteristically similar to that of Roundy Pound, which occupies a shelf between Kes Tor and the steep side of the gorge of the North Teign river under Batworthy. In this case the shelf is above the River Dart in Holne Chase, whilst behind it, north of the nearby Buckland-Ashburton road, the land rises to the frontier tor of Buckland Beacon. One fine stone, 4½ft above present soil level and 2ft 10in wide, is the only remaining vertical one in the ruined field-system wall, though the Hillhouses can remember others.

Immediately below Auswell Cottages, in a field belonging to Southbrook Farm and connected to the cottages by an ancient path, is Black Well. The ruined walls enclosing the well are traditionally those of a butter house, or dairy; this could have belonged to the ancient manor house said to have stood on the site of Buckland Hall, the cool waters of the spring being available to manor and cottage alike. It is a sequestered place, from which one may look beyond the surrounding woodlands to the heights of southern Dartmoor.

Holne Chase

The Anglo-Saxons had a word, *hole*, meaning a deep valley. It occurs frequently on high Dartmoor and is almost certainly the origin of the name Holne, which parish includes not only a part of the Double Dart Gorge, but also the borderland reach below New Bridge now being described. Holne is still often pronounced as 'Hole' on Dartmoor today and appears as 'Holle' in a document of 1564.

The great glen, formed by the Chase proper on the river's right bank and Buckland and Auswell Woods on the other, can be reached on foot by tracks, or drives, branching from the following roads: from Buckland Bridge—obtain permission from Mr or Mrs Elliott at Lowen Lodge (properly Buckland Lower Lodge) to pass through the gate marked 'Private'; from the Buckland-Ashburton road at Water Turn (obtain permission at Higher Auswell or enter at the Buckland end at the higher junction of drive and road at Auswell Cottages); from the B3357 highway at Holne Chase Hotel's lower entrance drive (obtain permission from the hotel to proceed beyond); and from the north end of Holne Bridge. In all cases it is wise to keep to the path.

Downstream from Buckland Lower Lodge the river passes over a series of stickles (a steep course, or rapids) that impart a glistening sheen to the normally dark floor of this deep valley. Ruddycleave Water comes swiftly from high Dartmoor to make a beautiful fall above the riverside drive, which is carried across it by a small Victorian stone bridge of two openings known as Warren Bridge.

Dart now approaches the head of its great loop where the scenery is at its finest and impressive by any standards: Raven Rock protrudes from the north hillside and Eagle Rock from the south, indicating the former presence there of those great birds: re-entrants in the north hillside create massive spurs between which nameless streamlets fall to the river, one, uncharted, passing beneath the drive through a duct. This is the stream that flows from Black Well near Auswell Cottages.

On the high, wide shoulder or shelf of Chase Hill above the right bank, and overshadowed by the foliage of scattered deciduous trees, are the ramparts of Holne Chase Castle, an Iron Age earthwork. Its circumference is given by William Crossing in his *Guide to Dartmoor* as 550yd, and P. F. S. Amery wrote in *TDA* 6 of 1873:

> In 1870 Sir Bouchier Wray's gamekeeper, whilst digging out a rabbit from a clitter of rocks between the camp and the river, came upon about a dozen iron weapons, resembling heavy spear-heads, twenty-four inches long and two inches broad, tapering to a point at one end, whilst the other was bent round to receive a shaft.

In 1871 Prof. Church of the Agricultural College, Cirencester, identified them as 'unfinished straight swords', adding that 'whether they are Roman or not is a question of great difficulty'.

Following a lapse of thirty-three years, Amery again wrote about this discovery (in *TDA* 38 of 1906):

> The bars resembled heavy spear-heads, were twenty-four inches long and two inches broad, tapering slightly to a flat point at one end, while the other was bent round as if to receive a shaft or form a handle. Unfortunately the man broke most of the bars against the rocks, but carried two or three back to the house, where the gardener used them for supports under a cucumber frame.

Similar discoveries mentioned by Prof. Church in other parts of England include 150 bars, rusted in a solid mass, in a dingle on the east side of the Malvern Hills near The Wych, seventeen on Hod Hill and two at Spettisbury Camp, both in Dorset, and others on smaller earthwork sites known as 'camps'. Miss Susan Pearce, Curator of Antiquities at Exeter's Royal Albert Museum, confirms that:

> ... they are Early Iron Age currency bars, usually thought to be sword blade blanks, of a kind relatively common in Western Britain. The bars are currently in the Torquay Museum, Babbacombe Road, Torquay.

Returning to the Buckland side of Dart, where rocky declivities and varied woodlands embellish the steep hillside from the river to the quartz-schorl crags of Auswell Rocks, we learn from the Revd Samuel Rowe, writing in *A Perambulation of the Ancient and Royal Forest of Dartmoor and the Venville Precincts*, of planned afforestation in very early Victorian times. He describes the prospect as:

> ... a succession of fine woods and plantations, belonging to Mr J. P. Bastard of Buckland Court, with Holne Chase full in view on the opposite side of the Dart. The ancestor of the present owner—the late Col. Bastard—early in this century, purchased Auswell Manor, and planted the waste lands with fir, larch, and other forest trees, on so extensive a scale, that the thanks of the House of Commons were given him for what was designated his patriotism.

Beside the stream from Black Well ducted beneath the drive is a Buckland Manor bond-stone marked 'March 4 1887'. Another, to the north-east and higher in the wood, is known as Kingshead.

The boundary is of some antiquity and it is not unlikely that 'Kingshead' is a corruption (as occurs elsewhere in the Dartmoor country) of 'King's Seat', denoting the site of a medieval hunting lodge. Above the streamlet looms a fine, perpendicular crag of schorl, the drive bending to pass beneath its face, another crag forming its foot and falling sheer to the river. This is dramatically known as the Lovers' Leap. An iron stake has been driven into the head of the rock and later adopted as the support for a wire fence forming a flimsy protection against the 200ft drop below; the stake has, however, a less mundane association. William Crossing writes in his *Guide*:

> ... an upright iron bar ... was placed here to mark the spot on which the Prince Consort stood when he visited the woods, by George Sparks, a former well-known whip of Ashburton, who drove his royal highness on that occasion.

Crossing, in his little known book *From a Dartmoor Cot*, was the first author to relate the story from which the crag gained its name. It concerns Wilfred, a young monk of the pre-Reformation Buckfast Abbey, who was ready to renounce his monastic vows in favour of his love for the beautiful Rosine. Pursued to this spot by Rosine's violent guardian, Ronald Brandram, with drawn sword, the lovers escaped by a leap of death 'into the rolling waters of Dart beneath them'.

It appears that Ronald Brandram had given liberally of his wealth to Buckfast Abbey, no doubt to gain for himself divine indulgence for his sins, of which, like the fits of tempestuous rage that from time to time possessed him, the Cistercian brothers knew nothing. Following the awful moment of the tragedy, Brandram rushed down the valley, crossed the river under Hembury Castle and turned to go up the hillside. Suddenly, a storm which had for some time been threatening burst upon him and a shaft of lightning took his life. The blackened corpse was found at Hembury and the monks laid it to rest in their hallowed ground. But, wrote Crossing:

> ... when the night of the third of July, the anniversary of

Brandram's death, again arrived, the brothers of the abbey were startled at beholding the apparition of the departed standing over the spot where they had laid his body ... The years rolled on ... and the home of the Cistercians on the Dart passed into the hands of aliens, and became in time a ruin. But ever on the night of the third of July the apparition appeared on the foundations of the ancient church.

From the Lovers' Leap, the drive descends to regain the riverside. Crossing another streamlet it turns towards the south-west with the river, which here is parallel with its north-eastward course at Ruddycleave Foot. A quiet deep, Foster's Pool, is succeeded by stickles and a long island which cause sudden and great agitation to the river, accentuating the wildness of the glen. Below the island, another unnamed stream reaches the river's left bank some 400ft below the brow of Raven Rock; near it is visible an old leat bed, leading to an area which in former times was mined for copper and iron ores.

The overgrown ruins of buildings lie on the left bank below the last great spur, Cleft Rock, and between them and the river a quantity of slag resembling green glass lies on some spoil heaps. Mr Tom Greaves of Exeter's Royal Albert Museum, a mines historian, has confirmed that this is slag, not from glass-making, but from iron mining. It is fortunate both for historian and writer that the Commissioners in a legal action of 1605 should have given instructions for the drawing of a map of the area under litigation and that it should have been studied and described by a contributor to *TDA* 56 of 1924, J. S. Amery. From him we learn that approximately $\frac{2}{3}$ mile above Holne Bridge, on the east bank of the river, are two buildings marked on the map as 'Iron Mill', that the bases of two furnaces remain, the stones of which are vitrified by heat, and that large heaps of slag occur between buildings and river. Specimens of the slag were analysed by Dr Satterly, then Vice-President of the Devonshire Association, and declared to be the result of iron smelting. Amery observes that some ore could have been obtained from Cleft Rock, an interesting pointer to pre-copper mining activity on the hilltop. The leat, of large capacity, is well marked, as are the outlines of the higher mine building.

A short way downstream is the second building, the smelting house or Iron Mill, with wheel-pit, tail-race and furnace revealing pieces of vitrified stone, a large, isolated lump of which also lies near the furnace. All are relics of iron smelting during the reign of Elizabeth I.

The head of Cleft Rock, as its name implies, is deeply split, though this was not by natural forces. The miners of Auswellwood have cleft its head in order to sink a shaft: this, in such a position, presents a rather alarming appearance. Two adits and a gunniss, also dangerously open, lie near the rock and show that a great deal of labour went into the mine. Properly known as Auswellwood Copper Mine it was working in 1809, though lack of production records implies a limited output. Several trenches appear on the brink of the precipitous hillside 300ft above the brawling river, and, in addition to the shafts, indicate the punishing labour undertaken by those men of the late eighteenth century in their search for copper ore, and all for a return likely to have been insubstantial. The ore raised was loaded into donkey baskets, the donkeys being shod at a smithy near Auswell Cottages of which traces still remain. Sabine Baring-Gould observed in 1900 in *A Book of Dartmoor* that the workings 'occur at a junction of the granite and the sedimentary rocks' and that they 'are very primitive and deserve inspection'. This would now be dangerous on two counts: first the nature of the workings and, second, their location within a private shooting lease. The relevant entry in *The Metalliferous Mining Region of South-West England* states that:

> The very small dumps contain only a few fragments of veinstone which consist of quartz and olive-green chloritic peach with pyrite, chalcopyrite, generally iridescent, and traces of mispickel.

Charles Vancouver wrote, in his *General View of the Agriculture of the County of Devon*, in 1808 of the 'copper mine working in Buckland-in-the-Moor with considerable expectations of success'.

Downstream from the iron mine are the private grounds of Holne Bridge Lodge. Immediately outside the (upstream) fence of the grounds are further relics of mining activity, which I would associate with Auswellwood Copper Mine. These, in a jumbled and now overgrown heap, include the masonry of a razed building, large wooden beams, a wire mesh sieve and lengths of iron tramroad rail. Mr G. E. Wyatt, owner of the Lodge, pointed out to me the visible track across his lawn of the old tramroad, which ran from the building to the river at a point directly opposite a very large adit opening upon the bank. The adit was for the extraction of copper ore, and a means of transporting it direct to the stamps without involving the lengthy diversion via Holne Bridge was apparently in use here; a masonry platform has been built at the mouth of the adit from where it is probable that an aerial ropeway carried the ore baskets to the opposite bank, where it was loaded on to horse-drawn tramroad trucks. The ruined building is likely to have housed the stamps, a supposition strengthened by the existence of a leat leading to it from the river, and the large, decaying beams which would have formed the support frame for the waterwheel-powered stamps. Several adits exist in the locality, two of them in the hillside directly behind Mr Wyatt's house.

It becomes important again at this point to stress the consequences of private ownership of the land where the relics lie. Economic Forestry Ltd of Exeter own the land where the old iron mine is situated; this means that no right of way, *per se*, exists on the river's left bank at the time of writing. The track, passing behind Holne Bridge Lodge, is that already described as running past Buckland Lower Lodge to Buckland Bridge.

Mining for tin on the Holne Chase side of the river has already been mentioned as accounting for the leat from Horseshoe Falls. The site lay some way down-stream, where three large adits open upon the riverside drive. Near them is the ruin of a small square building; although not obviously connected with the mining, it probably had such an origin. A dangerous shaft of the mine, which must have had severe flooding problems, opens among trees on the south side of Chase Wood, and the sole output record is of 5 tons of ore in 1875. Subsequent minerological examination of the ground revealed that little remained to be raised. The mine was recorded as working in the *Mining Journal* of 1849.

Peter Hannaford of Sherwell, a Dartmoor man in his late eighties, can recall the reminiscences of his uncle Roger, who worked at Chase Mine. Apparently a shaft sunk in the Chase hillside was later extended by a gallery running beneath the river bed, through which a good deal of ore was extracted. It happened that no authority had been obtained by the mine owners to make any drivage beneath the river, and Peter remembers his uncle referring always to this operation in the words, 'Us wus poachin', U zee.' When the lode was exhausted, the roof of the tunnel was breached to flood the illicit drivage and forever drown the evidence; with it, says Peter, were drowned some fine tools—sledge-hammers, pick-axes, shovels—and no man has since been near the place. To this day, he declares, a whirlpool in the river below Lower Spitchwick Lodge pinpoints the position of the breached tunnel roof. He is right. It is no place to swim, or capsize a canoe!

A riverside drive (on private land) follows the river's right bank between New and Holne Bridges. The now barricaded gateway at the higher (New Bridge) end is seen beside the parapet of the leat bridge; at the lower end, the drive climbs from the riverside to reach a pleasant Victorian house which, built on the site of a hunting lodge, remained a private residence until 1932, when its occupants were named Scott. Since then a private hotel, it is now owned and managed by Mr and Mrs K. Bromage. It is a place of character and peace pervaded by the atmosphere of a country house home, the result of the outlook of a proprietor and wife absorbed in their environment. The unique setting of the Holne Chase Hotel and its commendable service make it my first choice among Dart valley hotels.

Between the drive and the spur opposite headed by Cleft Rock, the river passes two flood-plains; on the Buckland side, a green and open sward is crossed by the lower end of the drive from Buckland Gate which joins the B3357 road at Holne Bridge. Dart emerges from the Chase to bend between the flood-plains, due east to Holne Bridge, approaching it through a deep, slatey trough in which green slates of Upper Devonian origin are visible on the south side and dark culm shales on the north, while 50yd below the bridge lies a fault where the culm measures actually pass into the Devonian.

A winter visit here enables one to avoid the flow of tourist traffic

5 The Right Revd the Abbot of Buckfast, Dom Leo Smith OSB, standing before the wrought-iron entrance gate bearing the Abbey coat of arms. The central tower, north transept and west front of the Abbey church appear in the background

6 A barrel plating unit used for zinc plating, at the works of the Buckfast Plating Company

7 Buckfast spinning mill. Director D. J. Hitchcock stands before a carding set, inspecting the sliver on a spool

and appreciate the setting of the bridge; erected, like New Bridge, in the year 1413, its high arch resembles that of Hexworthy Bridge (West Dart) and was built for the same reason, a great spate in August 1413 having carried away the previous bridge. Bishop Stafford of Exeter granted Indulgences to those who contributed money for the new bridge, which has one segmental and three semi-circular arches. Ashburton Parish accounts for the year 1564–5 contain an entry of 'VIIIs. IIId. for making III beams for the bridge called the Holle Bridge', though it is by no means certain what the purpose of the beams might have been.

Holne Bridge provides a convenient division between the upper and lower parts of Dart's borderland reach, the previous alternation of gorge and open plain giving way to an extensive left-bank flood-plain and an escarpment above the opposite bank. The latter rises from the riverside less than a mile below Holne Bridge, the intervening space being laid out with the drives, lawns and gardens of Holne Park House. At this point, we make a digression away from the river. Downstream from Holne Bridge, road and river continue together for a short way before diverging west of Lent Hill. From here it is road rather than river that is our guide, for, in the remote past when earth movements and advancing and receding seas were still shaping the land, Dart, yet to excavate the striking depths of Holne Chase, may have flowed eastward instead of entering what is now Holne Park. At a series of flats at 490ft north of Staddicombe, as Dr J. F. N. Green wrote in his paper *History of the River Dart, Devon*, in 1951:

> The river turned north-eastward across the present line of the Dart, here flowing south to Druid Cross, where a terrace bears a spot-level 482.
>
> The ancient valley of the Dart can be mapped with considerable accuracy from this point.

Perhaps, passing almost at the summit level of Bowden Hill, below which now lies Ashburton town, the river entered the present-day 'Ashburton dry valley'. Turning south-eastward at Bickington, it could have received the River Lemon and occupied its valley as far as the confluence with Teign, where began an estuary lying higher upstream than that now occupied by Teign below Newton Abbot, for the sea level was higher and the coastline nearer, being some way inland from present-day Teignmouth. To stand upon any of the little hills on the south side of the Ashburton dry valley is to be tempted to reason that its shaping was the work of a considerable river, its volume progressively swelled by streams from the south-east escarpment of Dartmoor beyond.

Recently, Dr Denys Brunsden, a geographer at Kings College in the University of London, has taken a particular interest in the Ashburton valley and re-examined Green's theory. He wrote in *TDA* 100 of 1968 that 'the evidence in favour of occupancy (of this valley) by the Dart is not strong and that such evidence as exists must be regarded as inconclusive'. Yet it is a romantic theory, and if true would be fascinating. Dr Brunsden obviously has respect for Green, and at no point in his appraisal allows himself to become dogmatic. I talked recently with Professor Allan Straw of the University of Exeter on this subject and was assured by him that the presence of river gravels, including granite waste and water-worn pebbles, could alone prove Green's theory—and it must be admitted that these, so far, are lacking.

The earth movements that subsequently tilted Dartmoor towards the south would certainly have diverted an east-flowing Dart into its present lowland course, as well as initiating certain southern Dartmoor rivers and releasing Ashburn, Lemon and Teign to follow the courses they now occupy.

We now return to road and river under Lent Hill, where a divergent south-eastward bend of Dart takes it into the heart of Holne Park.

Holne Park to Buckfastleigh

Until comparatively recently water was taken from a weir at the river bend into a deep, stone-lined channel that fed ornamental ponds. Canoeists on the river customarily 'shoot' the weir with loud impacting thuds on the hulls of their boats. The leat was cut in 1850 to conduct water to Southwood Copper Mine. The ponds were created at the end of the century, when the Dawson family occupied the mansion; later, during the 1930s, a turbine was installed, giving a further lease of life to the leat, which drove the turbine and an electricity generator for lighting the house, cottages and outbuildings.

The entrance gate to the park near Holne Bridge, together with a handsomely built lodge and drive to the mansion are above the right bank near the weir. Although pedestrian access is unrestricted, it should be realised that the park is not a public pleasure ground; indeed, it has a particular challenge to offer the adventure seeker. Before me as I write is a well-produced booklet containing these words:

> The River Dart Country Park Limited is a private, family-run company, formed in the early part of 1976, with various management objectives in mind. The first of these was to form and manage a Country Park recognised and financially aided by the Countryside Commission, for the Public to enjoy informal recreational activities.
>
> The second reason for our existence is to provide residential courses for children and adults covering a wide range of subjects, many of which cannot take place elsewhere.

The Country Park succeeds the Outward Bound School, which in 1960 followed upon the closure of the Holne Park Hotel. The hotel had opened after the death of the last private resident, Mrs Norah Dawson, in 1932, but the expense of upkeep, aggravated by closure during the war years when the RAF commandeered the building, finally brought the business to its knees. The managing director of the Country Park, Patrick Simpson, is the son of a local landowner who has done much to maintain employment and serve the community, and whose family has owned the property since 1932. The list of activities that can be enjoyed at the Country Park is comprehensive.

Holne Park contains its own Dart bridge, a sturdy, arched structure built in 1940. Known as Waterworks Bridge—for it carries the supply main from Venford Reservoir on Dartmoor to Paignton Waterworks—it spans the lower stretch of the long reach of river from New Bridge (some $4\frac{1}{2}$ miles of the border-country Dart) much favoured by canoeists as a training water; indeed, winter activity by canoeists when the river is in full flow introduces a bustling activity to Holne Park unimagined by summer visitors. The valley below the bridge, overlooked by the spur of Hembury Woods and Castle, possesses a more pastoral aspect: Devon closewool sheep browse in meadows on the bank, while gentle hills and downs beyond, speckled by the roofs of farms and cottages, proclaim the end of the border-country reach and the approach to the lowlands.

Riverside paths and drives in the park provide good walking; two steep combes channel right bank tributaries, one from Staddicombe and the other, densely wooded, from Hembury Woods. The Staddicombe valley is a pretty, hidden, green combe watered by a clear streamlet, where cold winds are eliminated and spring sunshine smiles on new-born lambs—crows and magpies strutting among them with the insolence of their scavenging kind. An old longhouse stands near the head of the combe, its existence unsuspected by the traveller on the Holne road above, from where a track of uncompromising steepness leads to the old farm.

Below Staddicombe, on the verge of Southpark Wood, are the remains of Southwood Copper Mine. Downstream from the artificial ponds the Holne Park leat was aqueducted across the river and its continuation on the right bank is a leaf-filled trench that suddenly appears from nowhere, so to speak, at some height above the river, the aqueduct having long ago disappeared. Below the trench are several adits driven into the hillside, one having a forked channel within the entrance, and a remaining iron rail of the tramroad used to bring ore out for loading on to waiting packhorses (*see plate 3*). The difficulties encountered in driving the leat along the steep, rocky hillside were in places overcome by constructing wooden launders—as Sir Francis Drake did when driving the Plymouth Leat through Burrator Gorge—and in others by banking up the channel beneath overhanging rocks.

On the opposite, east bank of Dart, Shere Wood clothes the valley-side as it closes in to form, with Hembury Hill, a dark and narrow defile for some distance. At the head of this is a pre-World War II bungalow bearing the impressive name, 'Queen of the Dart', so preserving the name of a small copper mine that worked on the flood-plain here 125 years ago. Mining records show no plans of underground working and state that 'the recorded output is 408 tons of 4 percent copper ore in 1856'. The mine is mentioned in copies of *Mining Journal* between 1858 and 1862. The ore was loaded on to wagons, trundled along the lane to Summerhill and from there to iron-smelters at Buckfastleigh.

A pleasant woodland path climbs gently from 'Queen of the Dart' between Shere Wood and fields nearer the river, which, here bordered by Blackmoor Wood, are used by Buckfast Abbey Farm; emerging at Blackmoor Cottage, it joins a narrow lane leading to the A38 road near Priestaford. Blackmoor Wood, dense and unthinned, is a private shooting lease fenced by barbed wire, so obliterating a riverside path that once led from 'Queen of the Dart' past Black Pool Island to Buckfast. Two river terraces run through the wood and emerge in the field downstream, the lower retaining its original steep, slatey side, where many water-smoothed granite pebbles lie, indicating clearly the former passage of the river that had carried them for at least 9 miles from the edge of the Dartmoor granite.

As I contemplated this scene on a cold afternoon under the brow of Hembury Woods opposite, the Abbey bells began to ring, their sonorous peal borne upwind through the valley to where, perched on my seat-stick, I was writing. It was almost spring and cock-birds were waxing aerobatic in pursuit of eligible females, water fowl rose from the river, the March sun warmed fields and woodland and all seemed so right in this beautiful world: it was, mercifully, a far cry from the troubled haunts of warring men and terrorists. Are we who live in the West Country truly alive to the abiding privileges?

Hembury Woods, rising steeply above the west bank, is a naturalist's wonderland. 'Please do not pick the daffodils' reads the plea on a notice board, from which may be imagined the beauties of Hembury Woods in April, when the new buds of spring wave about a carpet of yellow trumpets and the sound of Dart at the foot of the steep. This fairyland lies at the first rise of the Dartmoor borderland hills, where the river divides at Long Island, then re-unites to form its final series of stickles. Here on the lower valley-side are seen water-smoothed lumps of granite deposited by Dart in flood in an earlier age when the slate valley was less deep. An adit of perhaps 150 years ago penetrates the western hillside and opens upon the river bank opposite the lower portion of Long Island. It appears to have been a drivage for copper and, as such, an outlying working of Southwood Mine—or even of Brookwood Mine in the Mardle valley, for which lodes were also worked both in the Holy Brook valley north of Mardle and midway between Mardle and Dart. It seems unlikely that it belonged to the Queen of the Dart mine, records of which indicate no underground working.

The river is wide and swift in the defile under Hembury Woods and formed a natural barrier against invaders from the east with designs on the Iron Age fortress of Hembury Castle, 400 steep feet above its right bank. This fine, but unfortunately overgrown, hilltop fort, located on a spur between Dart and its tributary Holy Brook, was one of many in the south of England constructed during the Iron Age by Celtic immigrants from the Continent, one of a series fringing the eastern border-country of Dartmoor. Others were Holne Chase, Wooston, Cranbrook and Prestonbury, all purpose-built for repelling raiders from the already established moorland settlements of large Iron Age huts on eastern Dartmoor, who were seeking lower, drier pastures. Unlike the fort dwellers of east Devon, it is improbable that the guardians of these places had to contend with Roman attack, the nearest known Roman road being some 20 miles east at Exeter, where the Roman fortress of *Isca Dumnoniorum* was founded at the termination of the Fosse Way in the reign of Nero (AD 54–68). Professor Hoskins writes in *Devon*:

> Despite many attempts to prove the existence of Roman roads west of Exeter (and attempts *inter alia* to establish Totnes as a Roman town) there is as yet no evidence of Roman occupation beyond the Exe.

The Romans, exhibiting practical sense in avoiding physically difficult country where the occupants presented no special menace to the movement of their troops and supplies, by-passed Dartmoor and its border-country. Hembury Fort must not be confused with another so named near Honiton and described by Hoskins as 'the grandest earthwork in Devon'. Dart's Hembury is striking, too, despite the concealment of lines and proportions by trees and scrub. Entrances and double ramparts are massive, and glimpses through the winter trees of Dartmoor's lofty skyline give some idea of the magnificent prospect formerly commanded by the fort, when any approaching force from the west would have betrayed itself, even from a considerable distance, to a watching sentry.

J. W. Lloyd Page, in his *An Exploration of Dartmoor and its Antiquities* writes that:

> There are those that think that Hembury was a Danish fort. According to a local legend, it was won from the invaders by the strategy of women, who, allowing themselves to be captured by the pirates, cut their throats during the night.

Page quotes the Devon antiquary Spence Bate as stating that 'Hiarnbury' is still the popular pronunciation, and as early books and maps give 'Henbury', it is certain that 'Hembury' represents a corrupt derivation. R. Hansford Worth, a noted Devon antiquary whose special subject was Dartmoor, and who died in 1950, wrote in his notes of the 'pollution of the speech of the country folk by literary English'. The results of this pollution are all around us, used by the Ordance Survey and adopted as official spelling by bureaucratic bodies. Hembury Woods are owned by the National Trust and, together with the fort, easy of access from the Holne-Buckfast road, where ample car-parking spaces exist.

South-east of Hembury Fort, Dart sweeps from the defile between Blackmoor and Hembury Woods, receives Holy Brook at the foot of the borderland hills and enters the Buckfast Abbey grounds to approach the pastorality of the lowlands. Holy Brook, once a very considerable stream but long ago robbed of its head-waters through cutting-back by the river Mardle, approaches Dart through a wide and pretty wooded vale and is crossed by the Holne road at the single-arch Hembury Bridge, its parapet crested by a coping of flat slabs cramped together with irons. In *TDA* 108 of 1976, Miss Theo Brown records of Holy Brook:

> The Holne W. I. stated that this was not an old name. But the stream obviously had some antiquity for its numinous reputation since it

runs through two fields known as 'Paternoster'. It has been proved that the water is slightly radioactive, and it is firmly believed to this day that it has curative properties. If you have strained a muscle, bruised yourself, or suffer from rheumatism, etc., you have only to walk right in the brook and the trouble will be ameliorated.

'Vales of Bliss'

At the confluence of Holy Brook and Dart, and just within the Abbey enclosure, is Buckfast Weir, from where water is leated through the Abbey grounds to the Buckfast spinning mills. The green and pleasant flood-plain below Holy Brook Foot is, and for over nine centuries has been, holy ground. The Dartmoor poet Noel Carrington, who died in 1830, wrote:

> ... The arrowy Dart,
> Fleetest of river. Though the desert lifts
> Awhile its tors above him, yet he sweeps
> Full soon impatient down to vales of bliss.

The late Dom John Stéphan OSB, a Buckfast monk who died on 2 May 1976, and had been President of the Devonshire Association in 1963, spent the greater part of his life researching the origins and history of the great abbey, and his findings have been published in two works, *History of Buckfast Abbey* and *Buckfast Abbey: A Short History & Guide*. The ancient coat of arms of the Abbey—an abbatial pastoral crook surmounting a Dartmoor stag's head — is reproduced on the front cover of the *Guide*. The emblem was carved in pre-Dissolution times upon the pulpit of Holne Parish Church, where it may be seen today; more recently it has been wrought in the ironwork of the Abbey's main gateway (*see plate 5*).

The Christianised Danish king Cnut in 1018 granted property and land for the newly established monastery, which is referred to in the *Domesday Book* of 1086 thus:

The abbot has a manor called BULFESTRA [Exeter Domesday reading] and *it is the seat of the Abbey and never paid geld*. There the abbot has 1 smith and 10 serfs, who have 2 ploughs; there the abbot has also 3 swine, and woodland one league in length by one half league in width.

The several manors of the Abbey include extensive areas of grazing land on Dartmoor. Stéphan remarks in his *Guide* that:

> 670 sheep were numbered on the estates by the surveyors, to the great scandal of the writer of the Anglo-Saxon Chronicle, who did not spare his criticism of the 'Invaders' rapacious methods: 'So diligently did King William have the land surveyed, that not a single hide or virgate of land, and not even (though it is a shame to say what he thought it no shame to do) a single ox or cow or pig was omitted and not returned in the reckoning' ... Later historians are grateful to William for his thorough-going inquisition, which has supplied them with such valuable information. The 670 sheep mentioned above, as being reared on the abbey estates, afford an indication of what was for centuries an important source of revenue to Buckfast Abbey and the County of Devon, the woollen industry.

The ancient trans-Dartmoor track linking the monasteries of Buckfast, Buckland and Tavistock (the last two situated in the western border-country) passes across grazing land once used by all three communities and is marked by a series of medieval, rough-hewn granite crosses. Some way to the south is another track, also ancient and properly known as the Jobbers' Path; though unmarked by guide-crosses, it is persistently mislabelled 'Abbots' Way' by the Ordnance Survey.

Observance of the Benedictine monastic rule at Buckfast was, as in many other houses in the late eleventh century, undergoing decline and corruption, a state of affairs due to be remedied within a decade or two by the monastic Reform initiated in 1098 by the Abbot of Citeaux in Burgundy. As a result, the Abbey of Our Lady of Buckfast was affiliated to Citeaux in 1148 and the 'Grey' Brothers became the 'White'. Stéphan writes:

> Besides changing the colour of their habits, the monks also gave up some of their own traditions, e.g., preaching missions and other external pastoral work. As Cistercians their life was to be exclusively *monastic*, concentrated on Prayer and Work within the cloister, or at least the Abbey estates ...
> ... The second of the charters issued by Henry II and dated 1165, was witnessed by Archbishop Theobald of Canterbury and St. Thomas Becket, who was Chancellor at the time. This coincidence must have intensified the horror and consternation felt by the

monks, when the news reached them a few years later (1170) of the murder of St. Thomas, who had succeeded Theobald as Archbishop of Canterbury. Add to this the fact that one of the actual murderers, Sir William de Tracy, was one of their own neighbours, as he owned a manor at Bovey Tracey, only a few miles from Buckfast.

The crosses on the true Abbots' Way are likely to have been the work of one of the early Cistercian abbots of Buckfast: Nicholas, Michael, Peter, William, Howell, Henry, Simon, Robert—it would be historically satisfying to know which of these mitred abbots first determined on the sensible step of erecting cruciform guide-stones to help the traveller.

In course of time the minions of Thomas Cromwell, Henry VIII's commissioner for the dissolution of the monasteries, Viking of the abbeys, descended upon the great house beside Dart, and on 25 February 1539, at which time its yearly income was valued in the *Valor Ecclesiasticus Henry VIII* at the then considerable sum of £406 11s 2¾d, obtained the deed of surrender. No story here of brave opposition and abbatial martyrdom, such as with Abbot Whytinge of Glastonbury, but of reprehensible Cromwellian scheming. Until 1535, Simon Rede was Abbot of Buckfast; upon his relinquishing office—whether through his death or externally imposed persuasion is not known—Sir Gabriel Donne was intruded by Cromwell, rather than constitutionally elected by the monks, to succeed him. Thus surrender was implemented without opposition.

Sir Thomas Denys, squire of Holcombe Burnell, inherited the Abbey property and vandalised and stripped the buildings, so hastening their ruin. The ultimate sacrilege came in 1806 when a local woollen manufacturer bought the land, razed almost all that remained standing and built himself a new house and mill upon the relics. These appear in the picture (*see plate 4*) of 1829 by William Turner (1775–1851), 'Buckfast Abbey and the Valley of the Dart'; that they scarcely strike a discordant note is due to the remarkable impressionist technique of our great English painter. The point where Turner placed his easel is now overgrown and dangerous of approach.

Many people know the marvellous story of faith, determination and pluck that transformed this scene. How one monk, Brother Peter, trained the handful of brethren that would assist him, over an unbroken period of thirty-one years, in building the Abbey. It was designed by F. A. Walters, the architectural supervision being continued after his death by his son Edward Walters. How that abbot of strong mind, Anscar Vonier (Abbot of Buckfast 1906–38) was inspired by the Golden Altar of Coblenz to have the Buckfast Golden Altar modelled upon it, as well as to produce the *Corona Luces*—'the Crown of Light'—the great candelabrum suspended above the sanctuary before the high altar.

There was a strange yet reconciliatory twist of fate in the name of the Superior of the community from which French monks came to re-colonise Buckfast in 1882; like that of the despoiler of 1535, it was Denis—in this more auspicious case, the Very Revd Dom Etienne Denis OSB. Monks of the Order of St Benedict occupy modern Buckfast and fulfil realistically the old maxim of monastic life: *Ora et Labora*—'Pray and work'. Worship in the Abbey church and corporate and private prayer form the power-house wherein the brethren find guidance and strength to fulfil their vocations, each one to his own calling. The community is led today by the Rt Revd Abbot Leo Smith OSB, PhD (*see plate 5*), whose quiet courtesy has so helped my brief researches at Buckfast.

The Abbey School was opened in September 1967, the foundation stone having been laid in 1966 by the Apostolic Delegate on the Feast of the Assumption of the Blessed Virgin Mary. The headmaster, Dom Cuthbert Smith OSB, MA, worked with architect Francis Pollen to produce an unusual but successful and attractive plan.

That education at pre-Reformation Buckfast was also highly thought of is clear from this story, taken from Vol 10 of *The Buckfast Abbey Chronicle* (1940):

One day, so we are told, the Countess of Devon was taking her walk in the direction of Hensleigh, when she met a tailor descending a hill, laden with a large covered basket. As he passed, a cry came from the hamper. She stayed her steps and asked what he was carrying. 'Only seven puppies that I be going to drown in the Exe', was his reply. 'I want a dog', said the Countess, 'open the hamper'. The tailor tried to excuse himself, but the Countess insisted, and on the lid being raised, seven little babes were revealed. 'Alas, my lady', said the tailor, 'I am as poor as a church mouse. My wife gave them to me all at once. What could I do but rid myself of them? See, they are all boys.' The Countess charged herself with their education, and when they were old enough sent them all to Buckfast Abbey, to be reared for the Church. Four became Rectors of Tiverton (for Tiverton had four rectors)—the others their curates!

Wine is imported by the monks from vineyards in the Herault region of southern France; with it they blend vanillin, caffeine, potassium phosphate, sodium phosphate and sodium glycerophosphate to produce the vintage now famous as Buckfast Tonic Wine—for which, let it be confessed, the author entertains a special regard. It may surprise readers to know that the Scots, despite their traditional addiction to whisky, are among the best customers of the Abbey, a considerable quantity of Tonic Wine being consumed on Clydeside in particular.

The striking east window of the new Chapel of the Blessed Sacrament at the east end of the Abbey church, which was inaugurated by the Roman Catholic Bishop of Plymouth in 1966, is an example of the work of Dom Charles Norris; a mosaic window, it consists of about 5,000 individual pieces of coloured glass an inch thick, held together by a newly developed cement adhesive. Dom Charles's glass has been supplied to numerous English churches far away from Buckfast, including that of Harlow in Essex. The exterior of the chapel is seen to advantage from the river's opposite bank, where in spring daffodils grow even in flood-sand deposited by the river. The Dart is spanned here by a strongly built wooden suspension bridge and I was delighted on one visit to find four small girls, whom I had seen gathering daffodils in the wood, marching across the bridge and, by the monks' grace they told me, cutting across the Abbey lawns to their homes in the village. It was a charming scene, somehow a vignette of medieval England.

The technique and practice of bee-keeping in many lands has been expertly advanced by the internationally recognised work of a Buckfast Benedictine, Brother Adam Kerhle OSB, CBE. He began his work at the Abbey in 1915, his apiary then occupying the site since chosen for the monks' cemetery. In 1930 Brother Adam moved his hives and equipment to the new apiary; he has 320 hives on Dartmoor for heather honey production and about 100 at Sherberton (Swincombe valley, central basin) for breeding. Flower honey is harvested at the end of July; white honey, from white clover, in late June and heather honey in early September. The honey is sold at the Abbey shop as well as being sent by post to a growing number of customers. Brother Adam, who received the CBE for his outstanding contribution to the science of bee-keeping and has recently published an English version of his book, first published in German, entitled *In Search of the Best Strain of Bees* (obtainable at the Abbey shop) attends conventual Mass each day before starting out to his hives: this is important to him, for he is often not back in time for the evening office of Vespers, which at Buckfast is at 1800 hours.

The sound of the magnificent peal of fifteen bells floats through the great church before High Mass as black-habited, professed Benedictines enter their stalls in the choir to offer praise to God. Buckfast is a community with a purpose, richly fulfilled.

Outside the Abbey wall bordering the Holne road, which passes beneath it, is the ancient North Gate; through this, it is recorded, King Edward I passed on 1 April 1297 on his way from Exeter to Plympton Priory. Near the gate is the Abbey tithe barn, or rather, what remains of it. For long years an incomplete shell, its interior space is now occupied by small modern dwellings; the north wall retains much of its original appearance and the adjoining cottage, known as the Tythe Maisonette, is built upon the original walls of a small, rectangular wing which is sometimes referred to as the Abbot's Lodge. The great barn was, in its heyday, the third longest monastic tithe barn in England: 113ft long, 42ft wide and 46ft high, its walls are 4ft 9in wide at the base diminishing to 3ft at the top, the length exceeded only by the barns at Beaulieu Abbey (Hampshire) and Torre Abbey (Torbay). Behind the barn was the Abbey farm, a substantial remnant of the medieval shippen wall still standing. Miss E. J. Mitchell, tenant of the Tythe Maisonette, showed me interesting artefacts, including medieval iron nails, found some years ago during the digging of a sewer trench near the roadside hedge of her garden. In the angle of barn wall and east wall of Miss Mitchell's garden is the site of the round house, where oxen rotated a cereal-grinding mill. Miss Mitchell remembers the foundation stones of the round house and the base stone of the mill being well defined before she reluctantly decided (for her garden space is even now extremely small) to overlay the site with turf. The stone chute through which grain was fed to the mill is still visible. The house known as the Grange, south of the barn, is a Victorian edifice erected before the rebuilding of the Abbey, and has no monastic significance.

Some two hundred yards east of the Tithe Barn, a flowing leat passes beneath the road. Channelling water from Holy Brook, its destination is Higher Buckfast Mill, a former woollen mill, now the property and works of the Buckfast Plating Company Ltd, where it supplies rinsing water for processes at the works (*see plate 6*). The firm was established in 1953 and now specialises in plating metals in chrome, nickel, tin, gold, silver, copper and brass. Organisations with which the company is under contract include the Civil Aviation Authority, Ministry of Defence, Naval Ordnance, Vickers, BAC and Rolls Royce. The fact that the former woollen mill was built on a site once occupied by the ancient Abbey grist mill suggests that the leat might be a deepened nineteenth-century adaptation of a medieval leat from Holy Brook. Such a supply would certainly have been necessary for the operation of a grist mill.

In the Abbey grounds Dart passes through a deep, narrow, slate trough like that above Holne Bridge, its volume markedly reduced in low-water conditions by the leat to the neighbouring spinning mills. These features, together with the mill and former house of the mill owner, appear on a large, framed plan of the Abbey property hanging in a visitor's parlour at the monastery. Bearing the title 'Plan of the Manor House and lands of Buckfast Devon 1852', it was drawn by Peter Joseph Dalton, Land Surveyor of Cannon Row, Westminster, and is inscribed, 'Total Tiths Award 15A 2R 34P' (acres, rods, perches), with an inset picture of the Abbey ruins. Landowners whose property bounded the Abbey grounds are marked as Samuel Pinner, Solomon Tozer and John Maye.

The spinning mill next to the Abbey was opened earlier this century by John Berry & Company, who made blankets, serge and travelling rugs, the author himself possessing and still using one of the Company's 'West of England' rugs. In 1950 the mill was acquired by the Buckfast Spinning Company, a subsidiary of the Axminster Carpets Company, where pile is spun for use in carpet manufacture (*see plate 7*). Mainly local wool is used, blended with wools from Ireland and New Zealand. The leat from Buckfast Weir now powers the factory's turbines, by which means sufficient electricity can be generated to maintain operations in the event of a grid power failure.

Beyond the mill is the large car park, above which the west valley-side becomes a precipitous limestone cliff. Almost two centuries ago the potential value of this stone was realised and work started at Baker's Pit and Higher Kiln Quarry at the foot of Church Hill, Buckfastleigh. This was quarrying with a difference, however, for on exposing the rock face the workmen were astonished to find a series of beautiful subterranean chambers containing stalactite and stalagmite formations, and, though this impressed them but little, heaps of 'old bones'. The quarries have long since closed, but the caverns at their heart have exercised the attention of paleontologists for over a century and archaeologists and speleologists since 1939. In *A Report on Excavation carried out during 1939–41 by the late A. H. Ogilvie* (Transactions of Torquay Natural History Society Vol 13), Dr Antony Sutcliffe writes of what since has been named the Joint Mitnor Cave:

> During Easter 1939, digging was commenced at the furthest point of the cave and, on 6th May, an extension of large size and exceptional beauty was entered by Mr. and Mrs. J. H. D. Hooper, Mr. W. Joint and (with much difficulty and great discomfort) by Mr. E. Reed, after whom the cave was named. No animal remains have yet been discovered there, but the formations are the finest in Devon.
>
> In June 1939, attention was directed to the openings at the southern end of Higher Kiln Quarry and this led to the final recognition of the Joint Mitnor bone deposit. Like Reed's Cave,

Joint Mitnor had also once extended some distance in front of its present mouth as is shown by a large stalagmite still standing in the quarry floor. Bones were found almost within sight of daylight by Mr. E. Reed and Messrs. W. Joint, W. Mitchell and F. R. Northey, after whom the cave was then named.

On 4th July Mitchell sent the best finds to the British Museum (Natural History) for identification. There they were examined by Dr. A. T. Hopwood, who recognised remains of *Rhinoceros leptorhinus* (Owen), hippopotamus and a large bovoid, probably bison. He replied: "This is a very interesting assemblage which does not agree either with that known from Kent's Cavern or with that from the Brixham Cave ... Please accept my congratulations on your most interesting discovery.' He recommended that Mitchell should refer the discovery to Mr. A. H. Ogilvie at the Torquay Museum.

Ogilvie's subsequent discoveries totalled 4000 mammalian teeth and bones; all, with the exception of a few specimens sent to the Geological Survey Museum in London, were deposited in Torquay Museum.

The fascinating conclusion reached by palaeontologists and geologists on the origin of the Buckfastleigh caves is that they were formed in the limestone below the water-table, that is, *beneath the river bed*. Flowing at about 280ft above sea level, the river lost water by percolation through a honeycomb of cavities in the porous limestone below, which consequently became greatly enlarged. As the river cut down, the lower drainage points of such water were exposed as springs in the valley-side and the limestone cavities, one by one, thoroughly drained. Alternating glacials and interglacials—Ice Ages and warm phases—saw the enlargement of the cavities and cutting-down by the river, and by the time of the interglacial preceding our own (the Eemian, before the last Ice Age), part of the roof of the Joint Mitnor Cave had collapsed and created a gaping shaft. The climate at this time was tropical and the great beasts wandering the plain above fell foul of this trap newly evolved by Nature, its mouth concealed by lush vegetation, and tumbled to their deaths, so depositing their remains for the thrill of discovery by modern man. The shaft is now filled by fallen boulders. Again, I quote from Dr Sutcliffe:

During recent years, a second bone cave has been recognised in the Buckfastleigh district. In 1943 mammalian bones, (since identified as deer and ox or bison), which are probably of Pleistocene age, were discovered by Mrs. J. H. D. Hooper in the "Whitsun Chamber" of the "Glorious Devon Series"—a newly discovered part of Baker's Pit Cave, which was unknown to Pengelly. This part of the cave is situated beneath the graveyard of Buckfastleigh Church and the bones occur in a vast talus of earth and stones, which entered through a fissure in the roof (this has since become blocked and is no longer visible at the surface).

The mammalian remains found in Joint Mitnor Cave include those of wolf, fox, wild cat, cave lion, cave Hyena, badger, bear, straight-tusked elephant, rhinoceros, pig, hippopotamus, fallow deer, giant deer, red deer, bison and horse, several of which appear in the imaginative drawing by Margaret Lambert (*see plate 8*). Although not a cave enthusiast as such, I have visited several caverns containing striking formations. Attending school at Wells, within 5 miles of Wookey in Somerset, I was accustomed as a boy to school excursions to the remarkable Wookey Hole Cave, and knew Gough's and Cox's Caves at Cheddar almost as well. Yet, excepting the Wookey Hole underground river, nothing subterranean has so vividly impressed me as the great cone of rocks and earth fallen from the roof of the Buckfastleigh Joint Mitnor Cave, with which is interlaid the extraordinary deposit of prehistoric animal bones with even the vertebrae of a giant bison in situ and the tooth of a baby straight-tusked elephant. All round the viewer, as he regards the result of this 100,000-year-old land-slip, are the strata or layers of river mud, still retaining moisture and of a putty-like consistency, showing the shifting and cutting-down by Dart to its present level at Dart Bridge. All in all, the Joint Mitnor Cave provides a pre-history book unique in Britain: one that every child should see. The whole subject of bone caves is to have special treatment, for which Dr Antony and Mrs Una Sutcliffe are responsible, in the new extension of the Natural History Museum in Cromwell Road, South Kensington, and have kindly allowed me to reproduce (*see Appendix*) their paper entitled *A Section of an Imaginary Bone Cave*.

Mr Edgar Reed of Buckfastleigh, a speleologist figuring

prominently in the exploration history of the caves, has been of great assistance by putting me in touch with specialists such as Dr Sutcliffe, Mr John Hooper and Mrs Avril Longman, without whose help these remarkable caves would have received scant mention in this book. (Edgar Reed, whose father John used to enter the caves as a boy with a candle and a ball of string—the end of the string secured at the cave-mouth to provide a guide for his return—has had a cave named after him: *see plate 9*.) Finally, it should not be thought that *Homo sapiens* alone now penetrates the caves, for flocks of greater horseshoe bats have colonised them. An encouraging development arising from the interest generated by these caves was the purchase in 1961 of a site for the establishment of the Pengelly Cave Research Centre, the first of its kind in Britain, in Russetts Lane, Buckfastleigh, where information is available and visits to the Reed and Joint Mitnor Caves are arranged. A skilful and tasteful conversion of two farm buildings, the Centre includes a museum with exhibitions tracing the formation of the caves and the arrival of the mammals. Our guide to the Joint Mitnor Cave and Museum was Mrs Avril Longman, whose knowledge of her subject is impressive. The centre may be reached by car by turning up Russetts Lane on the north side of the A38 road near the Dart Garage.

Buckfastleigh Parish Church of the Holy Trinity, although of thirteenth-century origin (there is a record of thirty-six vicars reaching back to 1263) has stood on its high hill that once formed the Dart valley floor for less than a second in geological time. Six of its bells (it now has eight) once rang out across the borderland hills from the tower of the pre-Reformation Buckfast Abbey, a fact brought home to me recently when, from the top of a nearby hill, I realised the sound of the bells to be unusually mellow. Although most traces of the ancient Abbey have vanished, here is a *living* remnant of old Catholic days, a sound heard by tinners in the valley and, lifted to the Moor's escarpment by an east wind, by wool jobbers on the Jobbers' Path and monks and moormen travelling the Abbot's Way. Holy Trinity Church, already uncommon among churches of the Dartmoor country in having a spire, contains also the box pews of an earlier day which completely fill the nave of the church. White's *Directory of Devonshire* for 1869–70 informs us that Holy Trinity Church:

> ... stands on an eminence, ascended by 197 steps, and is a large antique structure, which, after being long in a shamefully neglected state, has been restored and beautified since June 1844, at a cost of more than £1400.

Beyond the east end of the church stands the ruined shell of a medieval chantry chapel containing the vault of the Fleming family of Bigadon, and near the south porch the tomb of Richard Cabell, who died in 1627, a man of such ill-repute that a penthouse was built to enclose his tomb. Only thus, it was thought, could his repeated *post mortem* appearances on Dartmoor, accompanied by rapacious black hounds, be dispelled. Over 300 years were to pass before the discovery that little more than a thin crust of earth separated the bones of this disquieted man from those of the great mammals, in the Joint Mitnor Cave below.

On a narrow spit of land between the brink of two quarries north of the church, William Turner made the sketch previously mentioned. The grey limestone from the larger, Bullycleaves Quarry was used by the eleventh-century Cistercian monks to build their abbey, and by Benedictines for theirs in the twentieth century. It is part of a series of outcrops occurring between Dartmoor and Torbay. Further towards the east, beyond the river, is the outcrop at Linhay Hill Quarry, now worked by the Glendenning Group. Mr Ian Glendenning, a director of the firm, here showed me features which, if considered together with observations on page 53, certainly stir the imagination. First, at the highest point of the working in the north-east corner, is a great rift in the limestone caused, probably, by a continuous flow of water, many of the boulders having a water-worn appearance; and second, in facing north-east from here, I found myself looking along the 450ft contour on the north side of the Ashburton dry valley to a point near Bickington where it is cleft by the approaching valley of the River Lemon. It would therefore seem possible that in standing there, I was on the bed of a tributary of the ancient Pliocene Dart. Circumstantial evidence includes an alluvial deposit 30ft in depth, which Ian Glendenning told me was removed by bulldozers in order to reach the limestone in the rift, which included a large amount of granite debris.

The whole limestone story at Linhay Hill is rich in interest. Limestone, of course, originates as submarine sediment and in places contains the fossilised remains of the creatures, vertebrate and crustaceous, that inhabited the waters. A fossiliferous boulder, exposed by quarry working, has been placed beside a track near the company offices, where permission may be obtained to examine it.

The massive diagonal beds of grey limestone at Linhay Hill were laid down under the warm carboniferous seas that once covered Devon. Here, over an area of almost 20 acres, intensely pressurised folding of these beds during earth movements caused re-crystallisation, producing coloured veins in the joints. This rock, highly compact, will take a hard polish, resulting in the attractive stone known as Ashburton Marble. Although first quarried on a commercial scale during the eighteenth century, it is of interest to note that the marble was used for fireplaces in the west wing at Dartington Hall, between c1390 and the earliest years of the following century. The stone, the only one of its kind produced in great Britain, is still in demand and is sent by Glendenning's to the Jenkins marble works in Torquay for polishing; it appears in London's Hilton Hotel and the GPO Tower as well as in numerous places overseas, including the USA. Also, and not surprisingly, it has been used in the rebuilt Buckfast Abbey, where it is laid in the flooring of the chapels behind the high altar and in the mosaic pavements. The marble is not obtained by blasting—such a method would be too destructive—but cut from the bed with wire saws.

The waterwheels of the former grist and cloth mills of Buckfastleigh town were powered, not by Dart but by the swift and clear tributary River Mardle from south-east Dartmoor, which passes through the town centre to reach the mother stream below Dart Bridge. White's *Directory of Devonshire* for 1878–9 lists Willcocks & Son of Diall Foundry as iron and brass founders, millwrights and engineers, their foundry being beside the River

Mardle. A good deal of iron ore from local mines was smelted and used by the firm, including that from Bulkamore in the lowland Dart country.

Although a busy market town threaded by the old Exeter-Plymouth road, Buckfastleigh's streets are nevertheless unhurried and unhurrying, for both the old and new A38 highways by-pass the town. Why, visitors wonder, was the church built so far from the town? But it was not. The present town grew up beside the River Mardle for the ready use of its waters, and long post-dated the church, which was built to serve a medieval village of labourers, cottage wool spinners and weavers, many of them employed in the service of the great Abbey down by the river. In other words, their homes stood on the hilltop clearing or 'leigh' of Buckfast. As waterwheels and looms supplanted the treadles and wheels of cottage industries, the old village was abandoned and Buckfastleigh had necessarily to 'move' to where we see it today at the foot of the limestone hills. At the present time the last of its mills, worked recently by the Co-operative Wholesale Society, is being demolished to make way for government-sponsored factories for light industry.

Above the south bank of Mardle on the western fringe of the town rises an outcrop of basalt rock, known in Devon as 'blue elvan'; this very hard stone was long ago used in road-making, and large-scale quarrying commenced on the site in 1922. The stone-works beside the A38 are now owned by Kingston Minerals Ltd, and rising clouds of steam indicate the processing machinery that produces the finished material needed by the road-makers. There are two precipitous quarry faces visible from the A38 highway respectively 62ft and 45ft in height. The basalt faces are drilled and blasted with gelignite, and the loosened material crushed, sifted and mixed with bitumen to produce the solution over which our tyres spin at 70 miles per hour.

Returning to the main valley 400yd downstream from the Buckfast spinning mill, the river has here excavated what appears to be a one-sided gorge; in actual fact, however, the more receding but gradually rising east valley-side attains a greater height than the limestone cliffs above the west bank. Standing beside the road (from Dart Bridge to Buckfast) between river and cliff is a tall white house marked 'Black Rock Guest House', a century ago the residence of the Symington family (see page 132). Black Rock, a limestone crag predominantly dark in colour, overhangs the river, and at its base is the low, cavernous opening of Black Rock Cave. Mr J. H. Woodward, who lives adjacent to the guest house, once underwent a memorable experience here. Entering the cave to explore it on a day of stormy weather, he remained inside for some time. In due course retracing his steps, he became aware of a new sound entering the cave, which he soon realised to be the roar of the river and water lapping against rock. It was accompanied by a rapidly increasing depth of water inside the cave—through which, of course, he had to wade. He was not to know that during his stay in the cave a great storm had exploded over central Dartmoor, effecting a sudden rise in river level—always a frightening and dangerous trend of the moorland streams during persistent, heavy rainfall. At the mouth of the cave, Mr Woodward found the water up to his armpits and, emerging into daylight, he had to exercise great care in gaining the steep path from cave to roadside. Not surprisingly, he declares he will never forget it!

Some 150yd downstream from Black Rock, Dart passes from its borderland reach under the medieval Dart Bridge, its four pointed arches poised upon massive, pointed piers. The attributing of this bridge to the early fifteenth century would seem to be open to question, for Dom Stéphan writes in the *Buckfast Abbey Guide* that in 1374, Abbot Symons:

> ... obtained from the Bishop of Exeter a special indulgence for those who would take part in the 'building or repairing' of the Buckfast Bridge, near the village of Buckfastleigh, just as a predecessor of his had granted (1310) a 'participation in Masses and good works of the Community of Buckfast for all contributors to the building of Exeter Cathedral'.

From this it is reasonable to assume that Dart Bridge 'near the village of Buckfastleigh' was built at least two decades before the close of the fourteenth century. It is constructed not of granite, but of local metamorphic slate. A previous structure, perhaps of timber, received the first known documentary mention as 'Dertebrygge' in the Assize Rolls of 1356. In 1406 a bequest was made of 12d for its maintenance. In the Ashburton parish accounts for the year 1546–7 appears an entry of 'Xs. for repairing the brygge called Dert brygge', and in 1564–5 further repairs were apparently necessary, a payment being made of 'XXVIs. to William Whiteway for making [repairing] the Dert Bridge'. The Sessions of 1599 authorised £21 for repairs, and in 1607 it was again in decay. But there it still stands, bearing, until the new road was opened in 1974, the full weight of twentieth-century commercial and holiday traffic.

Receiving the River Ashburn at an artificially 'adjusted' confluence below Dart Bridge, the river passes below the A38 highway bridge into the prolific fertility of lowland Dart country.

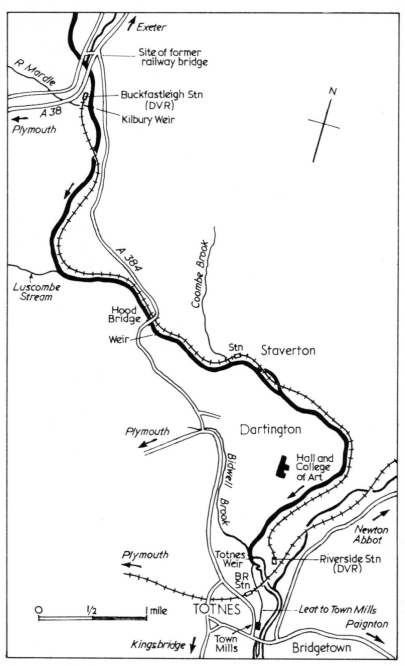

The Lowland Dart

3
THE LOWLAND DART

'Lowland' it may be, but Dart is still amidst the hills. Hills of shale, slate, limestone, tuff and sandstone. Hills bald and hills tree-crowned. Hills patched with fields of grass grazed and ungrazed, mown and unmown; with wheat, barley, turnips, mangle-wurzles, potatoes, cider-apple orchards, cattle and sheep. With little copses and great woods. With deciduous softness and coniferous regimentation. Dotted with barns and buildings, water-troughs and pens. Striped with cattle-paths converging on troughs and with tracks and lanes, like extended fingers, reaching steeply upward from grey-roofed farms beside the valley roads. Echoing through the valley from Easter to October are the nostalgic whistle-blasts of the DVR steam trains, which penetrate the Music School windows at Dartington College of Arts, to raise frowns on the concentrating faces of students intent upon mastering the problems bequeathed to them by Bach and Stravinsky. The valley floor is sometimes enlivened by a 'medieval' fair, as are the roads by the cars of visitors to Dartington Hall, river and railway.

Dart, at this third major stage of its existence, has left behind infancy and exuberance of uninhibited youth on Dartmoor; majesty and wild intractability in Holne Chase. Tamed by the demands made upon it in the region of Buckfast, it now enters upon middle age in its lowland course, and prepares for the tranquil maturity of its estuary.

Lower Valley-side and Floor: Kilbury Weir to Hood

The South Devon Railway Company opened the Totnes-Ashburton line in May 1872, the Royal Assent to its construction

77

being obtained in 1867. In 1890 five woollen mills were still at work in Buckfastleigh, and goods despatched from the little station exceeded the quantity from Newton Abbot and Torquay. After the turn of the century the motor car presented increasing competition and passenger receipts declined correspondingly. Traffic in wool and coal for the mills helped to balance the books for a time, but on 10 September 1962, ninety years after its opening, all traffic ceased. During the penultimate period of its working the line had been operated by the Great Western Railway Company (*see plate 10*), and finally by the newly nationalised British Railways. It was bought by the Dart Valley Railway Association and re-opened in 1969, for the operation of steam-hauled trains between Buckfastleigh and Totnes, and the line provides one of England's most scenic riverside trips. The opening ceremony, ironically, was performed by Dr Beeching, who remarked in his speech that had he not previously closed the line he would not then have been able to re-open it! Overhaul and use of the upper end of the line to Ashburton had been envisaged, but before the scheme could be realised the new A38 highway was planned, necessitating a huge new bridge replacing that carrying the railway; thus the old line was beheaded and the link with Ashburton left high and dry east of the river. Another severed link was that with Totnes Junction, and a temporary platform had to be erected, some way short of the previous junction, since called Totnes Riverside. The Association is endeavouring to raise sufficient funds to enable this link to be forged, at least for passengers, by throwing a footbridge across the river, a costly project still in need of further funding. Opposite Buckfastleigh station water-tower are the weir and salmon ladder constructed to head the leat taking water to the former Kilbury paper mill.

East of the river, and properly in the tributary valley of Ashburn and so not described in detail here, is the ancient settlement of Pridhamsleigh—manor, barton farm and cottages—several buildings retaining medieval features. Pridhamsleigh was for a brief period the home of a branch of the Gould family. William Drake Gould took up residence there in 1736 and his son Edward was born in 1740. In 1760 Edward received a commission in the

15th Dragoon Regiment, which he retained for only five years. His besetting sin, gambling, led to an incident in which a creditor of his was killed and he found himself arraigned on the murder charge (*see Appendix*). Sabine Baring-Gould writes in his *Further Reminiscences*:

> Captain Edward owed to Dunning a large sum for getting him off at the Exeter assizes ... Edward's mother and his relative, Miss Joan Gould of Rock, in Buckfastleigh, paid off a good many of his debts, but as fast as he was relieved, he managed to overload himself with fresh debts, and at length there ensued a final crash, 1777; when, by indenture dated May 14, Pridhamsleigh and many other holdings passed to John Dunning.
> There still remained some lands in Widecombe and Holne, not yet alienated, but these also were made over to Dunning on October 20 1779, after which Edward had not an acre of land left on which to plant his foot, not a house of his own to cover his head ... He lived at Shaldon and died there on June 29 1788.

Gordon Hamlyn-White now farms at the fine old barton, himself a descendant of the Whites of Babeny, an Ancient Tenement of Dartmoor. The dovecote so noticeable a feature seen from the A38 road just below, stands in the farm orchard where ruins of ancient buildings are in evidence. At the orchard gate is this notice:

Pridhamsleigh Dovecote
Listed in the 16th century records of 9th
century manor of Pridhamsleigh
Restored in 1976–7 by Ashburton and
Totnes Amenity Societies.
For admission apply to farm opposite.

A lane ascends the hillside east of the barton (it is bound by the orchard) and leads past a limestone outcrop of some size. In this is the opening to Pridhamsleigh Cave, through which a stream flows into a very deep pool known as Pridhamsleigh Lake. On 2 March 1952 it was explored and sounded by John Graham and James Hodges (then respectively Lieut Cdr, RN and Lieut, RN), who found it to be 80ft in depth and to contain underwater stalagtites. I should mention that the lane leading to the cave is, like the orchard, private, and permission must be obtained to follow it.

At Buckfastleigh Weir the River Mardle enters Dart. *Billing's Directory and Gazetteer of Devon* for 1857 tells us that 'a rivulet [Mardle] joins the Dart, and at this point serves to drive a small paper mill, which contributes a picturesque object to the scenery of that river'. The Totnes road runs along the east bank of Dart and the railway along the west. Austin's Bridge spans the river a short way downstream, carrying the narrow lane from Buckfastleigh Lower Town into the Totnes road. This beautiful old bridge of five arches must be seen from the riverside to be appreciated—but perhaps not from the west bank, where the all-pervading obnoxiousness of Buckfastleigh sewage works tends to prejudice one's architectural appreciation. The bridge is mentioned in Lay Subsidy Rolls of 1330 and gained its name from the former Dart valley family of Austyn, the head of which at that time, William, was probably prime mover in getting the bridge built.

At a bend in the lane is the Buckfast Blue Pottery, the works being housed in the original paper mill for which the leat was taken in at Buckfastleigh, or Kilbury Weir, and after which the railway bridge carrying the Lower Town lane is named, Paper Mill Bridge. Kilbury paper mill, equipped with a large waterwheel and the most up-to-date machinery of the time, was opened in 1785. A peak year in the mill's production was 1820, by which time the country had begun to recover from the effects of the Napoleonic wars. The mill continued, with vicissitudes, to work until 1940. Two years later the machinery was removed and sold and the building taken over by an engineering firm. In 1960 it again became empty and in 1961 was bought by Buckfastleigh Potteries Ltd. Mr R. J. Wilson purchased the factory in 1972 and has successfully run it as a family business under the name Buckfast Blue Ltd. The simple but attractive ware produced at the works, exhibited in a showroom, is now sent all over the United Kingdom. The clay used originates from Dartmoor and is supplied to the firm from the immense deposits in the Bovey basin controlled by Watts, Blake & Bearne Ltd, 11 miles to the north-east. The process employed in manufacture is a commercial one: the clay, stiff and fairly dry on delivery, is moistened before being placed in moulds of plaster of

Paris, each with a firmly closing lid, which are placed in the electric kilns for firing. The factory is heated by electricity produced from a turbo-generator housed where once the paper mill water wheel turned, the energy source still being the leat from the river (*see plate 11*).

Branching eastward from the Totnes road below Austin's Bridge is Green Lane, leading to the remote village of Landscove, with its attractive little Victorian church built a century ago to serve the families dependent for their living upon Penn Recca Slate Mine.

The railway, meanwhile, passing under Paper Mill Bridge, crosses to the river's east bank downstream at Nursery Pool Bridge, remaining on this side until it reaches its terminus at Totnes (Riverside). The valley in this reach has much rural beauty, its sides rising to rounded hills and knolls, with and without woods, where ancient farms and attractive houses face each other across its width. While several on the east and north sides are relatively remote from the river, their opposite numbers on the west and south cling to the hillside just above the shining stream, linked by one of south Devon's prettiest lanes, the Colston Road, its high banks rich with wild flowers in early summer: stitchwort, wild garlic, dandelions, bluebells, campion and ferns nod in the wind-rush of passing cars. Approached at its upper end either from Lower Town or Austin's Bridge, it meanders above the west bank and leads to such scenic gems as Rill, Colston and Luscombe, the river meanwhile passing from Nursery Pool over Caddaford Stickles to Quarry Pool below Luscombe.

It is doubtful whether Rill takes its name from water or hill. Robert atte Hille was there in 1333; in 1382 the settlement was recorded as Hille, in 1590 as Rylle and in 1763 as it is spelt today. Certainly a field spring gives rise to a rill that waters the deep, steep-sided combe above which the farm is perched: the 'goyle' of the rill, as it is called. Above the goyle is the spring in Creeper's Orchard, while below it are placid water meadows studded with sheep and fringing the river bank. Mr Stewart Kington, the farmer, pointed out to me the mixture of architectural styles of which the farmhouse is composed, one of the most unusual being the stern, uncompromising, early-nineteenth-century facade looking on to the court. In the early twentieth century the Warren family was at the farm, where Donald Warren, now living at Landscove, was born in 1900. *The Dartington Rural Archive* contains a picture of farmer John Chaffe Warren and his wife Alice in 1907, their faces as long as can be imagined, whilst their children, William, Mary and Donald—Donald in later life became master of High Beara, Landscove—are mounted in Uncle Tom Cobley fashion on a patient mare, all smiling happily. In Donald's own contribution to the *Rural Archive*, he writes:

> Quite often, my father would tell me that I had to be out and ready to leave at 7 o'clock in the morning to take a cow, sometimes with its calf, to the market. This meant walking the seven miles to Totnes, tying the animal up in the market and getting myself to school by 9 o'clock. I was back at 12.30 to see if it was sold and if it wasn't, the damned thing had to be walked home after school at half past four, in the winter, this meant carrying a lantern to see the way.

Donald Warren has lived his life within earshot of the train whistles—his grandfather rode on the first South Devon Railway train to travel the line from Totnes to Ashburton in 1872 and himself on the last GWR train, in the same direction, in 1962.

The picturesque hamlet of Colston lies next along the Colston Road, consisting of Colston Farm, Colston House and Cottage and Beara Farm. The charming, small mansion known as Colston House was built in 1730 and given a new wing in 1965. The owner, Mr John Walbeoffe Wilson, is a geologist who not unnaturally has developed a keen interest in the physiography of his locality. Panning for tin—and even, in minute quantities, gold—in the River Dart at the foot of his garden, he has, together with colleague R. C. Scrivener, composed a paper entitled *Alluvial Tin at Colston, Buckfastleigh*. John Wilson, in the course of investigating alluvial tin deposit in the catchments of Teign and Dart some years ago, discovered a buried channel in the midst of an alluvial tract up to 6ft *below* present river level. He writes in his paper:

> The tin-bearing sediment is composed of a range of particle sizes from small boulders to silt and clay. It is completely unsorted and

shows no evidence of bedding. In a typical sample, the silt and clay fraction accounts for 30–35 per cent of the whole, it is yellow-brown or, more commonly, blue-grey in colour. Angular and subangular grains of quartz and country rock, with abundant light brown mica flakes, form the bulk of the sand fraction; the remainder consists of rounded grains of quartz with iron ores, tourmaline, cassiterite and other heavy minerals . . . Cassiterite-bearing veins in the Hexworthy and Birch Tor areas have contributed to the deposit . . .

Gold occurs rarely as unrolled flakes up to 5mm across. Its derivation is problematic; detrital gold was known from the alluvial stream tin works in Cornwall (Dines, 1956) and has been recorded from streams in the Sheepstor area of Dartmoor . . .

The non-stratified nature of the Dart valley alluvial deposit is quite striking—'completely unsorted' and with 'no evidence of bedding'—and points to transport of the constituents perhaps 8–10,000 years ago by a flood of almost cataclysmic proportions.

As the Colston Road, from here onwards called Long Lane, continues to Cum(m)ing Farm, it bends to cross the swift stream flowing in a hidden hollow from Luscombe and is joined by an old lane from Bulkamore on the western ridge-crest. It also receives a steep lane descending from Luscombe Farm, a place of romantic appearance and situation. The beautiful combe in which the farm stands has given its name to many families in the district, past and present: to give only two examples, Philip Luscombe was the Receiver of Mail at Rattery Post Office in 1883, and, at the same time, a Mr Luscombe was the Steward at Dartington Hall. The name Luscombe, 'Loscumma' in the Domesday Book, is singularly *un*romantic, for it means the Pigsty Combe; it was held by Jurdan Barnage in 1242 and was still known as Loscombe Barnage in 1326. Nearer our own day, Richard Coulton was at Luscombe in 1839 (*T. Appt.*), Jeffery White in 1850 and his son David White in 1878.

Although no medieval buildings now remain, parts of the Elizabethan house may be seen, including a porch with a room above, at what is now the rear of the house. In the seventeenth century the farmhouse was given the dignity of a small manor house, two ground floor rooms having finely moulded ceilings of that period. Gate pillars were built at the entrance drive and at the approach path to the front door, A new wing was added and a formal garden laid out at the head of a branch combe north of the house. The garden, now containing a circular granite trough and a fluted stone set vertically in the ground, is completely grassed over, but the enclosing walls stand firm, including that at the further end of the garden, so constructed as to afford clear views of the beautiful countryside beyond—in which is set that jewel, the valley of Dart. There is a coach house dating from Luscombe's days of pride, the apices of the two entrance arches surviving in the walls of what is now a stable, this separated by a cobbled yard from another building which was the original stabling, with groom's quarters above. Near the coach house an apple tree was blown down in a gale some years ago; gripped by the roots of the fallen trees was found a large water-smoothed granite stone bearing the inscription 'iiiv', that is, a Roman figure eight in reverse. I have seen the stone but cannot explain the symbol.

The pound house of the farm is ruined, and near it is a giant granite trough which was formerly used in the pound house, though whether as an apple or cider receptacle is not certain. A small, square building, with a raised floor is still known as the Granary, indicating its original purpose. The lower step to the house is a fluted stone similar to the one in the formal garden. It is highly unlikely that these stones were worked in this manner for the farmhouse, or for any secular building; and, as it is known that whole cartloads of stone were collected by the Dart valley farmers from the ruins of Buckfast Abbey during the years, even the centuries, following its dissolution in 1539, there seems little doubt that the Abbey was the source of these stones.

It is interesting that during the eighteenth century the occupants of Luscombe were the Luscombe family, and on a map of 1765 (untitled, but marked at the foot, 'Entered in the Hall Book of the Company of Stationers January 1st 1765') in the possession of the present owner, is the marking—'LUSCOMB (Luscomb Esqr.)'. Mr Julian David has been at Luscombe now for eighteen years and takes much interest in the fine old place. Its decline since the days of 'Luscomb Esqr' obviously set in early in the nineteenth century and a small fortune would be needed to restore it to its country-seat condition of earlier times.

8 The Dart valley 100,000 years ago (above Dart Bridge), an imaginative drawing by Margaret Lambert. The fauna, from left to right, is: two cave hyenas, a straight-tusked elephant, hippopotamuses, a bison calf and cow, and eagles overhead

9 Reed's Cave, Buckfast-leigh. Edgar Reed pictured shortly after his discovery of the chamber in 1939. The tip of the large stalactite curtain on the right has since broken away. (*Photo D. Hooper*)

10 A GWR train with a single coach, hauled by a tank engine, approaching Buckfastleigh from Ashburton in 1962. The piers of Dart Bridge are visible upstream (beneath the engine). The elevation of the valley floor is 100ft. (*Photo John Adams, courtesy of the Dart Valley Railway Association*)

Luscombe Lane, the ancient way from the farm to Rattery, is enclosed by hedges of remarkable height. It climbs the west valley-side, passes a large granite horse-trough that receives a streamlet and, in an overgrown condition, reaches the ridgeway road due east of Dean Prior. On the opposite side of the road is an old slate quarry, from which it is likely slates were taken for roofing the new wing at Luscombe in the seventeenth century. Raking aside a deposit of loam and twigs in the lane, Julian David showed me ruts made in the slate bed by wagon wheels. Certainly the roofing slates would have been brought down this lane, though by packhorses in pre-wagon days. Below Luscombe, the valley road (Long Lane) continues south-eastward with a quite extraordinary number, even for Devon, of serpentine bends. These bring it to a junction with another packhorse lane, this time from Brownston, and a similar crossing of the stream descending from that settlement, past Lower Velwell, Water Lane End and meeting the Buckfastleigh–Totnes road at Hood Barton. Long Lane leaves the valley floor only at Lower Velwell, where Hood Ball rises to the north. A small, slatey outcrop of rock breaks the 341ft, rounded, ball-like summit which affords a detailed view of the lowland Dart. The superior height of the western valley tops is very evident from here, the eastern side reaching nothing of note south of Hole Hill.

Upper Valley-side: West

The western hills make a fine chain from Brim Down to Hood Ball, between which pour the swift, steep tributaries that have undergone constant rejuvenation in order to reach Dart, so active in cutting-down over the ages. It is this formation of the west valley-side that renders it so striking a piece of lowland scenery.

The steep, narrow Loverscombe Lane climbs from Buckfast-leigh Lower Town and crests the valley-side at Bigadon Stables, where views are far-reaching. The stables were built about 120 years ago by the Fleming family, then at Bigadon House, to supersede the inadequate stabling there. The summit of Brim Down rises to 616ft west of the road, which from here is a private way dropping south-east to Bigadon House. The picturesque ruin of the house stands at the head of a combe known as Elberry Cove, which forms the first in the series characterising the west valley-side. It is a sequestered spot, with peacocks strutting about, their raucous screams ringing through the surrounding woodlands. The clock tower of the old house, the clock still workable and the bell hung, rises against a horizon far beyond Luscombe and the Dart valley.

Bigadon appears as 'Byketon' in the Lay Subsidy Rolls of 1333. In the Feoffe of Fines in 1636 it is 'Bigadon', but Benjamin Donn shows it on his map of 1760 as 'Bickington'. It was given as 'Bigadon' on the first edition of the OS map of 1809, since which the name has remained unchanged.

In 1791 John Palk farmed at Bigadon, when the landowner was named in the *LTA* as Grace King. Early in the next century, the King family built the first mansion here, and the old stables surmounted by the clock tower (*see plate 12*) in 1816. Of outstanding interest is the clock—it still works when the huge pendulum is replaced—bearing the name of legendary Dartmoor clockmaker Richard Hillson of Plympton. He was said to have made clocks in his remote workshop, Hillson's House, built in the centre of a Bronze Age cairn on the 1,300ft summit of Staldon Barrow. Here, then, in working order, is an existing Hillson clock *in situ*, which could very well have been made within those four wind-swept walls on far-off Staldon.

That the mansion of the Kings was built upon the foundations of an earlier house is clear from its enclosing an ancient well: this is situated in the 'well' of the mansion staircase, where decorated banisters exhibit the craft of a local wood-turner. In White's *Directory of Devonshire* for 1850, R. J. King is named as the owner of Bigadon; its description runs: 'recently much improved, and contains a fine collection of pictures and some ancient armour'. By 1857 the Bigadon estate had been sold by the King family to Sir John Hunter Littler, KCB, Bart. But Sir John's death soon afterwards left his widow with a responsibility she did not relish, and Lady Littler decided in 1862 to auction the 240-acre estate. On the reverse side of the announcement of sale (reproduced here) appears this recommendation:

SOUTH DEVON.

TO BE SOLD BY PUBLIC AUCTION,

BY Messrs. HEATH & SON,

At the SEVEN STARS HOTEL, in TOTNES, on TUESDAY the 15th day of JULY 1862, at TWO o'Clock in the Afternoon,

THE

FREEHOLD MANSION AND ESTATE,

CALLED

"BIGADON,"

TOGETHER WITH THE

FARM HOUSE AND LANDS,

CALLED

COLSTON & SCOBLES,

SITUATE

IN THE PARISH OF BUCKFASTLEIGH

In the SOUTH of the

COUNTY OF DEVON,

About Six Miles from the Town and Railway Station of Totnes, Five Miles from the Station at Brent, Three Miles from Ashburton, and in the picturesque and romantic neighbourhood of Dean Woods, Buckfastleigh, Buckfast-abbey, Buckland, and Holne-chase,

WITH THE BEAUTIFUL WOODED VALLEY OF THE DART

WHICH SKIRTS A PORTION OF THE PROPERTY.

IT CONSISTS OF

AN ELEGANT MANSION,

AND ABOUT

TWO HUNDRED AND FORTY ACRES

OF

PRODUCTIVE ORCHARD, WATERED MEADOW, EXCELLENT PASTURE & ARABLE LAND,

One hundred and eighty-four Acres of which are let for a Term of Fourteen Years, from Lady-day 1857, for £250 per Annum (which Lease becomes void, if required, by notice from Lessors in case of sale), of the remaining portion, about 20 acres are let to the same Tenant on similar terms, at a rental of £35 : 10 : 0 per annum, and the Mansion and remainder of the Land are in the possession of the Trustees of the late Sir JOHN HUNTER LITTLER, G. C. B.

The Lease will be produced at the time of Sale.

An announcement of the sale of the Bigadon estate. The printer has used eighteen different types of lettering. Elegance was the keynote, the time expended by the type-setter being of less account in 1862 than today

To a Gentleman requiring a Residence, as well as an investment for Capital, it offers peculiar advantages, being in an excellent district for hunting and shooting. The Plantations forming an excellent cover for Game, and the River Dart, famed for its Fishery, skirts a portion of the Estate.

The purchaser of Bigadon was John Fleming, in whose family it was to remain until 1958. Fishing rights extended from Austin's Bridge to Croft's Cottage and John Fleming built a fisherman's bungalow beside the river at Colston. The estate was inherited from John by his elder son Robert Alexander, who built Bigadon Home Farm in 1895. Of Robert's five children—two sons and three daughters—his namesake, the eldest, was killed in the Normandy landings of the last war, the estate then passing to the younger brother John.

At the coronation of Queen Elizabeth II in 1952, John Fleming JP of Bigadon, owner of Buckfastleigh Manor and extensive grazing rights on Dartmoor, presented every child in Buckfastleigh parish with a Bible and Book of Common Prayer. Growing old and more lonely during the early post-war years, John decided in 1958 to sell the estate and move to Scotland, where a branch of his family lived. The purchaser this time, who had for long lived and worked on the estate as tenant of Bigadon Home Farm, was W. F. Vallance. It was the strange wish of John Fleming, who died in 1973, that no one else should live in the house after him and that 'it was to be stripped' as Mr Vallance puts it. Stripped it was—but who rejoices to see a beautiful home made uninhabitable? Fred Vallance thus found himself the owner of a picturesque ruin and a great deal of valuable land. He now lives at Bigadon Bungalow and his son Franklin works the Home Farm.

Bigadon is beautifully situated and should be seen. Drive from Buckfastleigh up Loverscombe Lane, crest the hill, leaving Bigadon Stables on the left; descend a short way and turn sharp right into the entrance to Bigadon Bundalow: it is essential to obtain permission from Mr or Mrs Vallance *before approaching any of the buildings*, which are their private property.

The private road continues from Bigadon to join the Lower Dean–Rattery road at a point where there are fine views of the

Moor beyond the Dean Burn valley. Immediately east of the road are the wooded combes, second and third in the series after Elberry Cove—where never-failing springs initiate forked sources of the streams falling to Colston and Cuming. Raythorn Wood cradles the Colston stream and Luscombe Wood the Luscombe stream. Between the two, and making a gradual descent of a spur, is the overgrown Luscombe Lane and, to the right, the old slate quarry overlooking Buckfastleigh race course.

Above the southern prong of the trident source of the Luscombe stream—curiously, there is no local name for the stream—in a deep hollow beside Long Lane, a still-usable lane running from Bulkamore Farm on the ridgeway road to Cuming provides a rewarding walk. A little over ½ mile below Bulkamore are signs of a disused track branching right from the lane. Gateways have been especially constructed in the hedges to accommodate this track, which climbs to the upper edge of a wood. All this, well over a century ago, was a part of one of south Devon's most interesting and productive iron mines, Bulkamore or Rattery Mine. The wood is Mine Copse ('Iron Mine Coppice' in T. Appt. 1839), where an open shaft, a gunnis, a huge adit on the east side of the copse containing tramroad rails still in situ, and three adits on the north side show scenes of intensive labour. M. J. Messenger and P. H. G. Richardson have carried out documentary and field research on the mine and kindly made available to me their papers contributed in 1977 to Industrial Railway Record and The Devon Historian. Intending explorers are warned, both here and by a notice board at the mine, of the real dangers of the exceedingly overgrown site—particularly during the summer months when lush vegetation conceals many hazards. One adit was re-opened either just before or after World War II but there is no evidence of ore being raised; in fact, the only record of production, given in The Metalliferous Mining Region of the South West, is the substantial one of 4,400 tons of iron ore in the years 1874–5. Evidence of earlier working of the mine consists, first, of the T. Appt. entry of 1839; second, the recorded shipment of Bulkamore iron from Plymouth, and, third, the local knowledge of the transportation of the ore by packhorses along the branch track described, into the

Bulkamore–Cuming lane, through the actual farm court of Bulkamore, across more fields where, again, special gateways were built and so through Rattery, over Mill Cross and down to Rattery Siding (*see below*). Horse-drawn carts were used in the mid-1800s. Ore went to Totnes for shipment in the 'packhorse era'; in the following, 'horse-and-cart era' it went to Rattery Siding, built when the South Devon Railway was extented to Plymouth in 1850, for transfer to main-line trucks. The 'tramroad era' followed in 1874, when a line was laid from the mine to Dartside below Cuming; it crossed the Lower Velwell road near Cuming and the river on a wooden bridge (since disappeared), reaching the specially constructed 'Bulkamore Siding' opposite the foot of the Luscombe stream. The tramroad trucks were cable controlled, the track gradient near the mine being $1:2\frac{1}{4}$—moderating to $1:10$ near the river. The cost of building and maintaining tramroad and bridge over-burdened the company's financial resources, the brief boom period was over by 1876 and Bulkamore was removed from the Register of Companies in 1883.

Not all the ore found its way to Plymouth or Totnes; some went direct to the Buckfastleigh iron foundary of Willcocks & Son, where, after smelting, it was used for local engineering projects (such as at Totnes Weir; *see plate 20*). It is by no means uncommon to find the nameplate of the firm on surviving iron-framed waterwheels in south Devon, the iron of which came from Bulkamore.

The sounds of mining have long since ceased, and the only sounds to be heard now in summer are of soaring, mewing buzzards which have adopted Mine Copse, in its contemporary peace, as their breeding site, the chugging of Bulkamore tractors busy in hay-turning, and the shriek of a DVR train whistle rising from the valley far below. An Ordnance Survey triangulation stone stands at 659ft on the hedge crossing this lofty lowland summit, giving a splendid prospect of the combe-indented nature of lowland Dart country and, beyond, of high Dartmoor reaching across 20 miles to where Cut Hill rises above the infant waters of West and East Dart.

Bulkamore Farm was 'Bolkemore' in 1260—the moor of the

bullocks—and 'Bulkamoor' on the map of 1765 belonging to Mr David of Luscombe and already mentioned. It is now owned by the Dartington Hall Trust and worked by one of their farm managers, Mr H. Jonas. A magnificent old barn and a round house are two interesting features, and the Cuming track turns to pass through the court, so that Mr and Mrs J. Coulton Gidley, who farmed at Bulkamore a century ago, would have been able to see from their kitchen window the ore-laden carts passing on their way to Rattery Siding. Their name, Coulton Gidley, obviously resulted from the union through marriage of the Coulton and Gidley families, farmer William Coulton paying tithes for Bulkamore in 1839 (when Richard Coulton was at Luscombe), and the Gidleys having for several centuries held land on the fringe of Dartmoor.

A few fields west of Bulkamore is the ancient farm of Yelland, also now the property of the Dartington Hall Trust. High Dartmoor has its Yelland, Yolland and Yalland, similarly meaning 'old land', the forming of the first vowel in vernacular speech producing an initial 'y'. A field next the house is called Church Close, though no evidence exists to account for this. The front door of the house is fine fifteenth- or sixteenth-century work, with massive iron studs and hinges. Richard Coaker appears in the *T. Appt.* and Samuel Peeke in Billing's *Directory of Devonshire* as farmers at Yelland in 1839 and 1857 respectively.

East of Yelland and Bulkamore is the lane to Brownston Farm, where the Coaker family have farmed for several generations, preceded in 1839 by John Maddick (*T. Appt.*) and John Hannaford in 1857 (Billing's *Directory*). The farm appears in 1330 as Bruns Tun, that is, Brown's 'Town' or farming settlement. Mr A. Coaker, the present tenant, can remember his father using the round house that still stands at the farm. Brownston—there were once a Higher and a Lower Brownston, Mr Coaker's being Higher—nestles snugly at the head of a combe where an icy spring still provides the occupants of the farm with water; on the further side of the spring is Twin (now rendered Torne), also worked by Maddick in 1839. The stream born of the spring passes beneath the valley road at Lower Velwell, along the south-east foot of Hood Ball and into Dart below Hood Bridge.

Guide-stones once marked nearly every junction on the ridgeway, but most are no longer visible, having been moved, cast down, broken, overgrown or otherwise obliterated. One remaining stone is at the junction near Brownston and Torne, the west face bearing 'R' for Rattery, the north 'N' and the east a mark rendered indecipherable by weathering. From this point the ridgeway lane has only 1½ miles to run before reaching Huxham's Cross above Staverton Bridge, a stretch of lane presenting at gate after gate breath-taking views across lower Dart country.

Valley Floor: Stretchford to Staverton

Returning to the winding valley floor between Beara Down and Rill, where river, railway and road enter in company, the last is seen to diverge from its companions at the head of a flood-plain terminating at the west foot of Hole Hill, where they reconverge. Stretchford Farm lies here under the hill, so steep that the Stretchford people refer to it as 'the mountain'. The farmhouse was built early in the twentieth century on the site of old Higher Stretchford; the ancient house of Lower Stretchford is just along the road southward, where it is known as the Old Pound House—the situation, in other words, of the Stretchford cider-apple pounding house. 'Higher' and 'Lower' farmers in 1846 (*T. Appt.*) were respectively William and John Whiteway.

The large farm of Riverford on the left bank is worked (together with Hole and Caddaford Farms under the east flank of Hole Hill) by Mr John Watson. Of seventeenth-century origin, the house has an added front of two centuries later. The farmer in 1846 (*T. Appt.*) was Thomas Edwards, and John Hoare was at Caddaford. The name of this farm is identical to that of a well-known beauty spot on south-west Dartmoor, Caddaford or Cadover Bridge, and probably of the same name origin—*Caed* (Old English)—'the place of a battle'. (Important river crossings were often contested by warring factions.)

No evidence exists of any bridge at Riverford before the present one, and the name derives from the custom of fording the river on the solid bedrock that here stretches from bank to bank. The practical difficulties of fording when the river was 'up' are obvious enough, and the bridge was built not long after Riverford Farm itself, the name of its builder probably preserved in the first of two local names—Emmet's Bridge and Hood Bridge. Emmet(t) is a name attached to numerous features in the district, including Emmett Wood on land belonging to Riverford Farm.

As the valley-sides beyond Riverford decline to the billowing little hills of Dartington and Staverton, a wide flood-plain known as Long Meadow opens on the right bank opposite Hood Barton. The Luscombe map of 1765 gives the farm as 'Wood Barton', probably its correct name. An initial aspirate, produced by pursing the lips and expelling air by flicking the tongue of the roof of the mouth, is a common substitute in Devon speech for the 'w' in 'wood'. Here, during most summers, a 'medieval' fair is presented. Known as Hood Faire, it is a celebration of Midsummer held during the week-end nearest to that time. Administered by a committee, its profits are distributed among worthy causes in the neighbourhood. Each department—Music, Theatre, Site, Publicity—has its director, and professional groups are engaged by the first two (*see plate 13*). Another popular feature is a pitched battle before the façade of a mock castle.

On the south side of the road opposite Long Meadow is Hood Barton, so named because it is the principal farm on the estate of Hood Manor, where Mr Jack Connabeer farms with his sons. Jack is a master of country crafts—hedging, walling and thatching (*see plate 14*). He has a lifelong association with the river, having been born at Millcombe Farm at the head of Fleet Mill Creek on the estuary, and knows well the habits of the river fish. Lamenting the depletion of the legendary Dart Salmon, he declares the prime causes to have been the salmon disease of the early 1970s and continued over-fishing of the breeding grounds. Like brown trout, salmon travel far up-river to spawn, to the middle or even upper reach of the moorland Dart, and commence their 'running' in February. Brown trout penetrate quite small tributaries, while sea trout hollow out sandy pits in the river bed beneath calm, clear pools, in which to lay their eggs. Jack can recall being told, many years ago, by old people of the locality that following the great blizzard of March 1891, the snow-waters of Dart were found to have caught up live sheep in the riverside orchard and deposited them in the forked branches of apple trees. This reminiscence indicates that the *normal* water-line only a century ago must have been appreciably higher than today.

The completely overgrown, ruined walls of a farmstead lie on the right bank some way above Hood Bridge; this was North Hood, where in 1839 the tenant farmer bore the name of Christopher Pike-Drew. The land, a part of Hood Manor, is now worked by Jack Connabeer of Hood Barton, who says that when the vegetation is down a part of the ruin can still be identified as a twin-seater privy! An old track comes down to North Hood from Lower Velwell over the north foot of Hood Ball, and another follows the riverbank from Hood Bridge. As I walked this early one summer morning I flushed grouse and partridges skulking in Mr Connabeer's golden wheat.

Downstream from Riverford/Emmet's/Hood Bridge is Staverton Station Weir, heading the leat that once supplied the waterwheel of the large Staverton Bridge corn mills. There follows an island and, shortly after the confluence of Coombe Brook with the river, is another, known as Hood Island. This is approachable, with permission obtained at the farm, from Long Meadow. The foot of the island is linked with the right bank by a modern timber bridge built in medieval fashion, the logs lashed together and only the less important slats nailed. On the bank nearby are two thatched structures, the thatching Jack Connabeer's work; used for Hood Faire, they are a circular timber building containing an open fireplace with an immense iron grid, and, much smaller, a stall with a service counter.

At Staverton Bridge are several items of interest: the DVR station, the joinery works belonging to the Dartington Hall Trust, the mill and the bridge itself. To start with the last, as first in structural seniority, it is one of southern England's finest surviving medieval bridges, thought by many writers, including Hoskins, to have been built in 1413 — the same year as Holne and New Bridges. It seems, however, that the present stone structure is less old than is supposed, for in the Register of Bishop Lacy of Exeter, II, folio

653, the episode recounted below is specifically stated to have taken place on 'a *narrow wooden structure* called in common speech Staverton Brygge which spans the swift-flowing Dart stream' (my italics). There is a tradition in Staverton that at the ancient village ford near Town Mill the passage of the Buckfast monks was so often contested that the abbots saw the need for a more convenient crossing place. This tradition could account for the presence of a wooden bridge, built probably in the fourteenth century.

The odd thing is that contributions were sought in 1413, both in labour and cash, towards the building of a bridge, indulgences being granted by Bishop Stafford of Exeter in return for offerings towards its construction. The Bishop instructed the Archdeacon of Totnes to collect alms for the purpose from the deaneries of Moretonhampstead, Ipplepen and Totnes. It seems surprising that this all-out effort should have been made for a wooden bridge, at a time when stone structures had become common; yet no alternative reading is possible of the relevant passage in Bishop Lacy's Register. This has been checked for me by Mrs Audrey Erskine, Archivist of the Cathedral Library, who writes: 'it is certainly a wooden bridge which is referred to in 1436:

super quodam stricto ligeno ponte Staverton Brygge vulgariter nuncupato ultra rapidum flumen de Derte publice noninatum extendente.

Mrs Erskine comments on the indulgences granted in 1413 to the effect that 'often these appeals by the bishops did not actually result in immediate building' and that the precise date of the bridge must remain an open question. The existing stone structure has seven arches of obtusely pointed shape with refuge bays over the piers, or cut-waters. Its length is 69yds and the width of the roadway 10ft, but the parapets are unusually low for a bridge of this type. A bequest recorded in 1418 of 3s 4d towards its maintenance was probably a result of Bishop Stafford's appeal. There were reports of its decay in the seventeenth century, and two entries occur in the Dean Prior parish accounts, one for 1687 showing a payment of 8s 4d to Constable Maddock for 'repairing Staverton Bridge', and the other, '1716 paid for sand the same 1s', but other than the facts given here little is known of its history.

Public brawls seemed to be a normal part of daily life in old England and one is recorded as having occurred on Staverton Bridge. In *TDA* 50 of 1918, the Reverand Oswald Reichard relates this story, which he translated from the register of Bishop Lacy (II, folio 653, AD 1436), a part of of which is quoted above:

> Sir John Laa otherwise Lage then vicar of Staverton had been attacked by one of his parishioners John Gayne with opprobrious and vituperative language, and that Gayne in an outburst of frenzied anger was threatening to kill him with a great club which he carried when Gayne's wife interposed and seizing hold of Sir John by the sleeve from behind was holding him firmly, preventing him from defending himself or from escape as they were on a narrow wooden structure called in common speech *Staverton Brygge* which spans the swift-flowing Dart stream. Gayne then made a lurch at Sir John who being in a corner and shut in in front and behind in a state of extreme fear such as might befall a brave man and unable to escape without attack and to avoid death by meeting force with force or to put up in defence against attack, wounded his aforesaid assailant in the very act of attack with a certain knife called a *Baselard*.

John Gayne was carried dying to his home, where he confessed it had been his own fault. It was also stated at the trial that the priest could not have fled because Isabella Gayne had held on to him by his sleeve. He was acquitted by Bishop Lacy, who judged that Sir John:

> ... not being otherwise able as is aforesaid to escape death by meeting force with force was lawfully acting in self-defence up to the death of his assailant.

It is worth mentioning, in the interests of accuracy, that Father John Laa was not the Vicar of Staverton, but a chaplain performing curate's duties.

The road from bridge to village passes between the railway station (above the bridge) and the mill (below). The former, of course, dates from the building of the line in 1872, and provides a useful 'period piece' for film producers, most recently having served that purpose in the BBC television series 'A Horseman Riding By'. Car-parking facilities near the bridge are limited and the proper way, beyond compare, to explore this piece of country is to travel by DVR from Buckfastleigh, alight at Staverton Bridge station, wander about on foot and catch a later return train to the town.

Below the level crossing is Staverton Bridge Mill. Corn-milling took place on this site for many centuries until the 1920s, and a reference to the Bridge Mill leat weir is implied in records of Abbot Robert Symons, longest ruling medieval abbot of Buckfast (1358–95), who took steps to ensure that 'the weirs of Staverton were not turned into a barrier against the salmon's way to Buckfast!' (Stéphan, *Guide*). The mill leat had to be diverted in 1872 when the railway line was laid, and the mill, where the wheel shaft still remains, was enlarged during the 1880s. When the Dartington Hall Trust was formed half a century ago, the trustees purchased the mill as a suitable base for a building and contracting venture subsequently named Staverton Builders Ltd. Since then, the firm's scope and reputation has won them an independent existence under the title Staverton Contracting Group, or, as they are known where they operate, simply Staverton. From a purely local venture, they had become an organisation versatile enough to construct the Ocean Terminal at Southampton, Hams Hall Power Station in the West Midlands, the Plymouth Church of Christ the King, the South Devon Technical College in Torquay, the Divisional Police Headquarters in Plymouth, the Police Training College in Exeter, the vast new County Hall in that city, and various industrial, hotel and residential developments and schools throughout the West Country. It is greatly to the credit of the management that the old building, its interior skilfully converted to suit its modern role, appears to the onlooker still as the riverside mill, with its approach beside the bridge entirely unspoilt.

Downstream, between the river and the road to the village, is another very successful venture of the Dartington Hall Trust, Staverton Joinery Ltd. Originally a branch of the former Staverton Builders, and occupying the buildings here since 1946, it was given independent status under its present title in 1977. The joinery carries out much contract work in the Middle East for the supply and fitting of timber interiors and furnishings; materials were shipped in 1979 to Dubai for the new municipal headquarters there and Prince Faisal of Riyadh, Saudi Arabia, has been a client for some years. The fitting out of the extension to the Natural History Museum, South Kensington, is the work of Staverton Joinery—including 52,000 drawers for the storage of specimens in the care of Dr Antony Sutcliffe, which will include those from the bone cave at Buckfastleigh. The board room for the new European Weather Centre in Reading, the executive offices of Saudi Airlines in Jeddah, the dignified City Council offices and the large extensions to the Airport, both for Exeter, and furnishings for the executive offices of the Department of the Environment in London, are a few of the recent contracts that take general manager Percy Haywood jet-hopping over a large area of the globe.

South of Staverton Bridge and sited on a former river terrace, is a group of mostly new buildings known as Apple Green Court, belonging to the Dartington Solar Quest. This unusual title is best explained in the words of the Quest's brochure:

> The beautiful headquarters of the world-wide Dartington Solar Quest movement are set in a 65-acre riverside estate by the soft-flowing Dart, near Totnes in South Devon, England.
>
> The Dartington Solar Quest is concerned with the love and purposes of God. It is a teaching centre, not a religious sect. The lessons there all boil down to the same thing—the rediscovery of 'God Force' and with its indispensable assistance, the long, hard work towards re-establishing the purity of Man and his world. The goal is the reattainment of pre-Fall perfection for all things on earth.
>
> The Solar Quest is particularly strong in Nigeria where the Elmhirsts and fellow Quest trustees visited in 1974. In Lagos there were quickly ten study groups of 12 people each, working from instructions and guidance sent them from Dartington . . .

Certainly Apple Green Court is a place of peace. Mrs Sheilagh Shore, Manager of Solar Quest in England, is the step-daughter of Mr W. K. Elmhirst—son of the late Leonard and Dorothy Elmhirst, co-founders of the whole great Dartington enterprise—tells me that her mother, whose idea the Solar Quest was, and step-father are frequently at Apple Green Court. The headquarters of the Quest was opened in 1975 by the Rt Revd Wilfred Westall, then Bishop of Crediton. One of the buildings is an adaptation of a former farm building. This was a part of Dartington Barton, where in 1839 (*T. Appt.*) Thomas Skinner occupied the farmhouse and used the court, garden and orchard. His fields on the river bank below Staverton Bridge were called Lower Orchard, Little Meadow and Miller's Marsh—the last obviously having some association with a former miller at the Bridge Mill.

As the road from the bridge nears the village, a narrow lane leaves it and leads to Staverton Vicarage; beyond some cottages in the lane is a high-banked footpath to the river. The path crosses the railway beside an old GWR trespass warning before reaching the riverbank at the second of 'the weirs of Staverton', that properly known as Staverton Weir. Here begins the large-capacity leat channel that once fed the water wheel of Staverton Town Mill, a busy corn mill until business ceased in 1925. In the early 1930s the Dartington Trust purchased the mill and installed water turbines and generators to supply electricity to the estate. In these days of grid electricity such self-supporting enterprises have unfortunately become redundant, and the mill has since been tastefully converted into a dwelling for a staff lecturer at Dartington College of Arts and is still known as Town Mill. Town Mill is entered in the *T. Appt.* of 1846 not as such, but as The Lee; also marked clearly on the Tithes map were orchard, building and mills, and The Lee, being the long meadow south of the mill. Miller and occupant of the 'Building' in 1846 was William Matthews.

In the village is the Sea Trout Inn, so called because its fishing rights include a stretch of river favourable to fishermen when the sea trout come up to spawn. That the fruits of Dart waters were ever abundant was officially recognised as long ago as 1086, when entries in the Devonshire Domesday Book show a somewhat discriminatory tax levied on Dartington fishermen:

2 fishermen at Dartington paid 80 salmon
A fishery at Dartington paid 30 salmon.

Above the inn, until the early years of this century, was another named The Ring of Bells now a private house. This stood on the right of a lane north from the cross-roads near the Sea Trout Inn and tethering rings for horses are still to be seen attached to the walls of the house. Its inn-keeper in 1846 (*T. Appt.*) was Thomas Barrett. Yet another inn, named Church Inn (innkeeper, Harry Skinner) stood beside a lane forking right from the crossroads. There can be little doubt that Staverton cider was thoroughly appreciated in its homeland, for considerable patronage would have been required to support three licensed houses, even if their landlords had supplementary occupations, as was usually the case.

The lane from the Village to Town Mill crosses the railway at Knapper's Crossing (named after a former crossing-keeper) and the mill leat, before bending to approach the mill. In ancient days, it led from this point across a flood-plain meadow to the river, where a stony ford between two deep pools formed the direct route from Staverton to Totnes: hence the *staen-a-ford tun* (vernacular: Stanaverton) or settlement on the stony ford.

Beside the lane stands the early-fourteenth-century parish church which has, writes Professor Hoskins in *Devon*, 'a plain, battered W. tower from the 13th-cent. church'. It should perhaps be pointed out that Hoskins gives the dediction of the church as to 'St Paul', which normally implies the Apostle Paul, whereas the patron saint is actually St Paul de Léon of Brittany, who is said to have sailed up the river from Dartmouth until, arriving at the *staen-a-ford tun*, he decided there to preach the Gospel and establish his *ecclesia*, or congregation of converts to the Faith. The Revd C. A. Cardale, Vicar of Staverton, writes in his *A Short Guide to Saint Paul de Léon Parish Church of Staverton*:

> Saint Paul's dates are in the 5th century, and there are factual reasons for the existence of an Anglo-Saxon building on this site, 40 feet above the river.

The nave and chancel were enlarged to their present spaciousness at the direction of Bishop Stapledon after his visitation of 1314. The statue of St Paul de Léon over the door of the south porch is a Victorian replacement of a medieval figure, a victim of Cromwellian vandalism. (See Note 1 on page 109.) The porch, 'battlemented with string-course and billet moulding', contains a

11 (*right*) 'Buckfast Blue' ware in an electric kiln, glazed and ready for firing. Note the tramlines, making the kiln mobile

12 (*below*) The dial and bell tower of the Hillson clock at Bigadon Stables. On top is the weather vane. The arch shows that there was originally an entrance wider than the existing doorway

13 Hood Faire (1978). The instruments (left to right) are: a hurdy-gurdy, two shawms, a tenor drum and a tabor

14 Jack Connabeer of Hood, a Dart valley farmer and craftsman, thatching an outbuilding

porch chamber in which, in times when priests lived sometimes at a great distance from their parishes, the vicar visiting his parish would lodge on a Saturday evening in readiness for the Sunday services. If, as sometimes happened, the living was vacant (see Note 2 on page 109), a visiting locum tenens would occupy the chamber. Father Cardale refers to this chamber as a 'parvise', but G. H. Cook, in *The English Medieval Parish Church* writes:

> The name parvise, commonly applied to the room over a porch, is an inaccurate designation, the term being derived from *parvisus* ... an enclosed area west of the church.

The broad, light interior houses a beautiful rood-screen, a Georgian pulpit and chained copies of *Foxe's Book of Martyrs* and E. D. Drake-Bockman's *Staverton on the Dart*. Also on display is a document titled 'Muster and View of Arms 1569 for the Parish of Staverton ... certified by John Scintlager, Arthur Champernowne, John Moor Knight, Pyers Edgecombe Esq and William Strode Sheriff of the Countie of Devon'. Strode was a descendent of that Richard Strode, Member of Parliament for Plympton, who fell foul of the stannary authority in 1516 (see p 19). At the west end of the nave above the font hangs a small but beautiful brass chandelier, presented to the church by the West Country author, the Revd Sabine Baring-Gould, whose forbears were from Combe in Staverton. (See Note 3 on page 109). The numerous burials of Goulds beneath the floor of the church include John, March 1562; Edward, March 1607; Elizabeth, 1633; Edward, 1661; Joan, his first wife, 1655; Margaret, his second wife, 1662; Julian (a female), 1672 and Zachary, 1643. Baring-Gould was allowed to remove the ledger-stones and brasses commemorating these burials to his church at Lew Trenchard, west Devon, in 1877. (See Note 4 on page 109).

On 24 March 1148 Robert, Bishop of Exeter, granted to the Cathedral Chapter the churches of seven manors 'of which Staverton is one' (Cathedral Archives), a gift confirmed on 14 March 1152 by Pope Eugenius III. A century later, on 14 March 1269, Bishop Walter Bronescombe appointed Walter de

Teignmuth *quod cum Vicarie de Stavertone*. As the canons of Exeter appear to have been remiss in discharging their duties towards certain parishes, the Bishop intervened and on 14 September 1269 constituted it a vicarage (Bronescombe, *Reg*, 262):

> To all who may view these letters, Walter by divine mercy bishop of Exeter everlasting greeting in the Lord. Be it known to you all by these presents that whereas the vicarage of Staverton has been so long vacant that according to the Statutes of the Lateran Council the collation has developed upon us, we have granted and conferred it out of good feeling upon our beloved son the presbyter Walter de Tenegemue and have appointed him canonically perpetual vicar in the same church, assigning to him and his successors after him by name of vicarage all the altar-dues of the said church, and corpse presents, together with tithes of apples, hay and mills as also the whole glebe and the buildings belonging to the said vicarage, including those lands which belong to the dean and chapter.

In 1288 the vicarage was valued at £4 and the chapter's revenue from it at £7 6s 8d (*Bronescombe*, 465). The inclusion of apples as tithes is an interesting indication of Staverton's importance as a cider-producing parish 700 years ago. The present vicarage was built late in the eighteenth century, a writer in *Devon & Cornwall Notes & Queries* (Vol 33, 1974) giving the relevant excerpt from the diary of the Revd Thomas Kitson of Shiphay for 30 November 1784:

> Mr. Taylor, Mr. Edwards and I visited the spot for Doctor Baker's new vicarage at Staverton.

Thomas Baker MA had been instituted to the living on 19 December 1759. He died in 1803 and John Lane Kitson MA was instituted in his place on 17 May of the same year.

Richard Doty, Vicar in 1403, was licensed by Bishop Stapledon to celebrate Mass 'within his vicarage house' and in 1435, when John Parker was Vicar, Sir John Laa was named as Chaplain and Penitentiary for the Deanery of Ipplepen. In 1540, 'Richard Makyn and Henry Drowse, lately monks of the suppressed monastery of Buckfast', became chaplains 'employed by the parishioners'. John Horsham held the living from 1630–63 and experienced difficulty with certain parishioners over tithes, meeting with much hostility in the matter. Not only tithe crops but animals had apparently been left in the chancel of the church for the Vicar to remove, resulting in this instruction by the churchwardens:

> Yearly after St Mark's Day (25 April) the tenth lambe is to be left bound or tyed in the parish of the saide Churche neare the place where a ewe tree there now groweth right over against the Church porch there.

The yew tree that 'there now groweth' is said in Staverton to be 1,000 years old. And so it might be. Branches of that very tree are still seen reaching 'right over against the Church porch'. One of the troublesome farmers was a George Rowe, who with others 'sell apples now, and have given up pounding so as to avoid (tithe) payment on each hogshead'. Also in the churchyard is an ancient cross set upon a modern Pedestal and socket stone and with an incised cross on each face between the arms.

At the south-south-east end of the church the *Patronous Ecclesia* has his own field—'Paul's Meadow' says the 1846 *T. Appt.* It is interesting to note that the church lies south-south-east to north-north-west rather than the normal east to west; the reason for this is not at all clear, but could have been caused by the position of earlier foundations. Later Vicars of Staverton include William Martin (incumbent from 1825–50) who, true to the theme of more than one Victorian novel, married into the local squire's family when he took Jane Champernowne (1807–92) as his wife.

Father Cardale is responsible for another booklet, *The Madonna of Saint Paul de Léon Staverton*, which tells of a figure created by wood-carver Douglas Rowse, who in the summer of 1970 'came and set up a one man camp on the island below the Vicarage in the River Dart'. Here he began work on a driftwood log 'and carved a very fine Madonna and Child' (*see plate 15*). This he set up on the island and its fame spread. Then, whether by vandals or flood is not known, it was dislodged and swept downstream. The carving was rescued from the river by a Bridgetown (Totnes) man who returned it to Staverton parish and was rewarded. The Madonna was then set up on the south wall of the churchyard, where it is now easily seen from the lane to Knapper's Crossing.

Staverton is cider country—famed as such. It is usual in most lowland parishes of England to find each farm with its one or two orchards; in Staverton, to take only two farms as examples, a minimum of six orchards is not uncommon. Kingston Barton has seven and Barkingdon Manor—where the Victorian farmhouse is built upon the site of an old manorial farm—six, named in the *T. Appt.*: Lower, Moor, Great, Little, Water-spout and Washwell. John Maye was farmer and cidermaker in 1846; today it is Mr Raymond Hill and his father Edwin whose own father expanded the farm's cider business to a minor commercial scale after World War I.

At Barkingdon, the air is heavy with the scent of apples and sound of machinery. I was able to watch the cider-making process from the arrival of apples in tractor-drawn trailers from Berry Pomeroy and Dartington to the brew that is popular at our own kitchen table. The fruit is tipped into a large hopper, from where it drops on to a belt conveyor which delivers it into an apple mill. After milling, it is spread upon thin nylon nets known as 'cloths', which take the place of straw in the old farmhouse method. The cloths, each bearing a layer of milled apples, are laid in the great press; the juice from the crushed fruit is then piped into a reservoir, and from there pumped into a 10,000 gal vat. It is next pumped to vats in the fermenting house, immense vessels of traditional oak, iron-banded, holding 20,000gal. Here the juice lies for six months or more, under-going a natural fermentation unassisted by the addition of yeast such as many commercial cider-makers use. The vats are flushed out with clear water every year after use and treated externally with linseed oil. Eventually the juice, which by now forms a very dry, or 'rough' cider ('scrumpy' in Devon), is pumped into small storage vats where syrup is added. The syrup is needed to smoothen and sweeten the brew—to whatever extent is demanded by taste. Raymond Hill says that tastes are less dry than they used to be, the old, untreated, rough cider now being in less demand than in the days of manual haymaking, when raging thirsts demanded vast quantities of liquid.

Raymond Hill's cellarman, Stephen Dyer, showed me the

1. The Revd John Bickley Hughes, instituted Vicar of Staverton on 25 November 1874, contributed an informative article on the church to the *Exeter Diocesan Gazette* in which he wrote that: 'This defect has been made good by the kindness of a visitor and the Saint now surmounts the entrance of the Porch.'
2. 1560/1, 7 January, Master John Smythe Doctor of Laws instituted Vicar, the benefice being *de jure vacantem*.
   1564/5, 24 February, institution of Richard Gammone, Doctor of Laws and Theology, later deprived of the living.
   1629/30, 20 March, institution of John Horsham, Master of Arts, deprived of the living on 30 October 1662. Succeeded by Roger Specott, the benefice being *legitime vacantem*.
3. Sabine Baring-Gould (1834–1924) was an interesting and unusual man, well-travelled, priest, Dartmoor enthusiast, amateur musician, folk-song collector, novelist. During a visit he made in 1880 to the church of St Jacques, Malines, Belgium, gas lighting was being installed in place of chandeliers. Baring-Gould bought two of these chandeliers and presented one to the church of his ancestors at Staverton and the other to his own church at Lew Trenchard.
4. The circumstances surrounding this action were apparently unknown to John Betjeman, who wrote critically of Baring-Gould in his foreword to William Purcell's biography, *Onward Christian Soldier*, in these words:

What vicar and Diocesan Advisory Committee would [today] allow a Squarson [a parson-squire] to remove tablets from other churches and put them in his own, as Baring-Gould did at Lew?

As the record has previously been put straight only within the comparatively small reader-circle of a booklet sold in remote Lew Trenchard Church, I am glad, on behalf of Sabine, to have opportunity of amplifying a protest made in that booklet by a former Rector, the Revd Bickford H. C. Dickinson. Quoting Betjeman's comment, the Rector writes:

This gives an entirely false impression of what took place, for it was on the advice of the Vicar of Staverton that Sabine acted. In 1877, while he was living in Mersea [he was Vicar of East Mersea in Essex], he received, to quote his Reminiscences, 'an appalling letter from the Vicar of Staverton. The Architect of the Dean and Chapter, Ewan Christian, had undertaken the 'restoration' of the church. The Ledger-stones had been torn up and thrown out into the graveyard and our family vault was being filled with concrete. All that remained to me of the Staverton estate were the bones and memorials of my ancestors. If I desired to save either or both, the Vicar wrote, I must go at once.'
To one of Sabine's temperament there could only be one answer to such a challenge. He hastened down to Devonshire and on arrival found that the only possible way of saving the Gould ledger stones from complete destruction was to remove them to Lew Trenchard and preserve them there.

process at the works, afterwards returning to his task of filling jars (nowadays strong plastic containers) holding 4–9gal and oaken casks 10–20gal. The Hills have used exclusively English apples for seven years now, 200 tons being purchased from Dart valley farmers in 1980. Distribution of Hill's Devon Cider is by road to distant Scotland, as well as to nearby Buckfast Abbey, where the monks are connoisseurs. The works are electrically powered, the romantic days of the old pound house having quite gone—at least where the operations of the commercial cider-maker are concerned. A picture to be seen in Anthony Kingdom's book, *The Ashburton Branch*, shows barrels of cider standing on the platform at Staverton Bridge station in 1921. Most of these barrels are likely to have come from Barkingdon and they are awaiting carriage to the port of Totnes.

The wooded indentation in the land—a feature so richly displayed in lowland Dart country and exemplified at Coombe— ends just above Staverton Bridge, the brook entering Dart at Bridge Island; its course through the combe takes it below the pretty farming hamlet of Wash. The name originates in the existence of a communal sheep-wash beside the brook there. Barkingdon is situated near Wash, its orchards lying on the slopes of the tumbling little hills of Staverton parish. Many farmers from the surrounding district take their cider apples to Barkingdon to be 'pounded'.

Upper Valley-side: East

To survey the east-to-north valley-side it is best to start on the hilltops near Baddaford. A stream already mentioned, Coombe Brook, running below Baddaford Farm has flowed from Halsworthy near Ashburton and, between the farms of Higher Penn and Higher Beara, it passes into a combe, or valley of considerable depth known simply as Coombe. At its head is Lower Coombe Farm, where a modern house supersedes an ancient long-house of uncommon length, formerly known as Coombe. Some original window mullions and bars remain in the decaying building and a cobbled court lies before it. A huge granite trough opposite the longhouse is likely to have been a farm trendle, or ham-salting trough.

Coombe was, through several generations, the home of the senior branch of the Gould family, a tenure transferred to William Sawdye, who appears as occupant in the *T. Appt.* of 1846. Margaret, second wife of Edward Gould of Coombe, was the subject of a brass removed to Lew Trenchard Church, and is described thereon as the 'Pearl set in Goold'. She was the daughter of Wilmot Dunning of Gnatham in Walkhampton, and the relationship between the two families doubtless led Captain Edward Gould of Pridhamsleigh to engage John Dunning, first Lord Ashburton, as his defence counsel at Exeter in 1786 (*see Appendix E*).

Looming above the old house are spoil-heaps of the great Penn Recca Slate Mine and, opening into the hillside, the dangerous, cavernous drivage known as Coombe Tunnel. A document in Exeter Cathedral Library shows that the agreement of Sawdye had to be sought before an access road to the tunnel mouth could be made:

MANOR OF STAVERTON

Memo that William Sawdye the Copyhold Tenant of a Tenement called Coombe, by Copy of Court for his life has with the leave and license of the Lord of the Manor permitted John Bursleigh White of Millbank Street Westminster who under a grant for the Lords is working the Slate Quarries at Penn in the said Manor to make a Roadway over the said Copyhold Tenement ... for the purpose of the said Quarry.

A track climbs the hillside from Lower Coombe, from which a bridle path branches left to reach the level of the slate spoil-heap. Upon the very edge of this mountainous, scree-like pile. overlooking most of lowland Dart country, a wooden sculpture was erected a few years ago. The work of wood-carver Douglas Rowse, creator of the Staverton Madonna, it is a figure of Christ with Arms Out-stretched and forms a dramatic addition to the scenery here. During recent years it fell, and to have come upon it lying prostrate in this lonely place would have given a shattering surprise to any uninformed visitor (*see plate 16*). The figure is over

10ft high and its arms, with clenched fists, measure 4ft 3in and 3ft 7in, the right arm being extended further from the shoulder. It is pleasing to be able to record that following a discussion between Father Cardale and myself, the figure has been re-erected by some of his parishioners.

Penn Recca Mine proper is situated between Higher Penn and Ruggadon and is an appalling place, several hundred feet in depth, made the more so by the great spread of foliage lining its bowl and thinly veiling the void below. There were formerly two distinct and separate quarries, Penn and Recca, run by William Searell & Partners, and J. B. White & Partners respectively (*T. Appt.* 1846). An inconsistency is noticeable in the spelling of the former surname. As early as 1781 the *LTA* showed Richard Searle as paying dues for Penn, yet the *T. Appt.* (above) gives 'Searell'. A letter dated 30 April 1829 to the lessee from the landowners, the Dean and Chapter of Exeter Cathedral, was addressed to Mr Allen Searle; signed on behalf of Ralph Barnes, Clerk to the Chapter, it warns Searle that action would be taken unless the account of quarry dues for the previous year was settled. The lessee himself, however, uses the second version, for in 1827 his rendered account of monies due to the Dean and Chapter ran as follows:

Ist May 1827 Account of Slate sold from Penn Quarry. This is to Certify that there hath been sold from Penn Quarry in the Parish of Staverton 754,900 Slate from Michaelmas 1825 to Michaelmas 1826.

By the Lords dues on 754,900 Slate at sixpence per thousand

377,450 . . . . £18.17.6

By the like on 12,000 feet of Rag Slate at two shillings per thousand

. . . . 1.4.0

£20.1.6

Signed— ALLEN SEARELL

At the foot of the document appear these notes:

October 1827 Mr Allen Searell will call at the office this day week.
Ton Slates, or Rags are sold by the ton of 21 cwt.

Concerning the two versions of the surname it may be noted that
Jacob Searell was a church-warden of Staverton in 1690.

On 5 June 1834 the lessee of one of the quarries was a Mr
William Williams of 15 Hooe Street, Stonehouse, who wrote to the
Dean and Chapter asking for financial aid in draining water from
the working, which he estimated would cost upwards of £500.
This letter includes the curious statement that 'Penn Quarry near
Ashburton has not been worked for the last 20 years, when they
were worked by Mr Dickson who bankrupted them.' There was
also a 'William Mugford age 32' who applied in 1823 to lease Penn
Quarry for fourteen years. As a twenty-year period prior to 1834
encompasses the busy productive years of Allen Searell and Son at
Penn Quarry, I think that in both cases 'Penn' properly indicates
Recca.

Another account for the period rendered from Penn to Exeter
appears thus:

ACCOUNT

There has been sold from Penn Quarry from Mich⁵1830 to
Mich⁵1831   490,625 Slate and 13,516 feet of Rag.
Duty Paid to Dean and Chapter £13.12.3
Allen SEARELL JUNR.
November 2nd 1831.

Searell's son was then in charge, though the accounts do not show
any subsequent year to compare with the bumper one (above) of
1825–6.

By 1845 the Dean and Chapter of Exeter felt the time had come
for a full and proper survey of the slate mine, and on 10 June of that
year appointed 'Richard Taylor of Pinner near Falmouth
Gentleman' to 'Survey the said quarry or quarries and make such
Report Map Plan Statement Valuation ... as shall be deemed
necessary'. This professional approach was obviously the planned
prelude to expansion at the works, for the then huge sum of
£35,000 was spent between the date of the Survey and 1857, which

included a considerable outlay on the construction of a tramroad of 20in gauge to the working faces. In 1850 another plan was needed; it was commissioned by the Dean and Chapter from an Exeter architect named W. Dawson and is reproduced here.

The quarries were combined about a century ago under the name Penn Recca and are described in White's 1870 issue of their *Directory of Devonshire* as having been 'worked for several centuries'. Anthony Emery states in his *Dartington Hall* that the Earl of Huntingdon is known to have obtained slate 'from an existing quarry at Staverton' in the 1390s for the roofing of his new house, Dartington Hall. This is an unmistakeable reference to Penn slates. In the reign of Charles I, Ashburton Parish Church was re-roofed with Penn slates, which remained in place until *c* 1840, when another reroofing was undertaken. In 1870 the works were in the hands of a joint stock company who installed improved equipment and employed, at that time, over 100 hands, by which time underground mining of the slate was well advanced and the great Coombe Tunnel had been driven. A fine chimney stack was

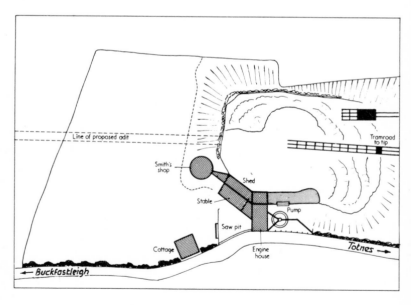

Extract (redrawn) from the 1850 plan of Penn Recca

built which still stands now partially ivy-covered. St Matthew's Church at Landscove, chapel-of-ease to St Paul's, Staverton, 'was consecrated in 1851 to serve the growing population of the village due to the working of the Penn Slate Quarries' (Cardale, *Guide*).

White's 1878–9 issue of their directory states that:

> Great quantities of the slate are sent to many parts of the kingdom, and many local farmhouses are roofed with it. The slate is found in immense blocks and is of a beautiful sage-green colour.

According to Donald Warren, formerly of Rill Farm, his uncle Andrew Warren built Rock Cottage at Buckfastleigh some years before World War I, and 'this was roofed with the last slates to come out of Penn Recca'. Not far from Landscove, where Donald now lives, is a building, now altered out of recognition, that once was a barn containing sleeping cubicles above stabling, where the men in charge of the Penn Recca horses slept during their working week. They worked in shifts, for the all-important horse-power needed after-work care and very early morning preparation in order to be ready at the mine when the slate-miners arrived.

At Penn Cottage in March 1891, the year and month of the Great Blizzard and in the midst of that phenonemon, Richard Lee was born. His father had care of the smith's shop, engine house and stable, the remains of which are still visible today. The challenge occasioned by Richard's arrival to the doctor and midwife, who had to travel from Ashburton to attend him and his mother, may be imagined—a circumstance since absorbed into local lore! The cottage doorway is now in a dangerous condition, a sagging wooden lintel barely supporting the crumbling masonry above. A decade or so after Richard Lee's birth the quarries closed down.

In January 1949 the Coombe Tunnel was explored by Edgar Reed and W. Joint (pioneers of the exploration of the Buckfastleigh caves). Reed, in his report, refers always to Penn Recca as a mine rather than a quarry, because access to and egress from the slate chambers was effected by tunnels. In the late spring of that year the mine was surveyed by P. Cahill, using a prismatic compass and metallic tape. He discovered that the resonance of the slate was such as to set up long-lasting echoes capable of sounding three-note chords.

The main east valley-side hills between Coombe Brook and Dart form an unbroken north-west to south-east chain from Higher Beara to Riverford, the highest and most striking being Beara Down (459ft) and Hole Hill (approx 425ft). A view across Coombe, Lower Coombe Farm and the Penn Recca spoil-heap may be seen from the east slope of Beara Down, whilst the summit of Hole Hill affords a panorama of southern Dartmoor from Butterdon Hill to Black Hill beyond Hey Tor, including Brent Hill, Three Burrows, Eastern and Western Whitaburrow, Sharp, Mil and Corndon Tors, Hameldon, Buckland Beacon and Rippen Tor.

South of Staverton Bridge rises the hill covered by North Wood. A lane, branching north-east from the road near Huxham's Cross leads to a wide drive through the wood to the summit of the hill. This, a portion of the Dartington Hall Farm Trail, passes a stand of giant California redwoods, a notice beneath them stating that the oldest stand of conifers in North Wood was planted in 1900—over two decades before the Dartington Hall project was born. The remainder were planted by Dartington Woodlands during World War II and the wood has become the haunt of woodpeckers and, in all their diminutive beauty, goldcrests. The redwoods, though not reaching the dimensions of those in their native land are still impressive, and are equipped by Nature with bark that helps them resist the devastating effect of forest fires.

At the summit of North Wood are four early British enclosures; three form a row the fourth being unaligned, nearby. The group is enclosed by a low, outer earthwork. Pottery sherds found when the site was excavated in 1965–6 suggested its period as AD200–400, that is, during the Roman occupation of the land. The earthwork would have surrounded a village of wooden huts. Other detached rings may be older and date from the pre-Roman Occupation Iron Age. The fertile soil of the flat hilltop would certainly have facilitated the growing of cereal crops. The extensive view over the River Dart which would have been obtainable from the village is now exchanged for one of tree-tops,

the entire site having been densely overplanted and rhodo-
dendrons embellish even the earthworks.

According to the *Totnes Times* for 13 June 1868, the decomposed
body of a young man discovered in North Wood was removed to
Mr Beer's Champernowne Arms to await a Coroner's inquest, and
the verdict was one of suicide. Apparently the boy was a leather-
worker's apprentice and from time to time had suffered unkind
treatment both from the saddler and his wife. The Champernowne
Arms no longer exists.

Valley Floor: Dartington to Totnes Bridge

Across the river from North Wood is Staverton village, and south-
east is situated Dartington Litho Ltd, founded in 1973 to
undertake printing for offices and departments of the Dartington
Hall Trust, and now taken over by the Devon Print Group of
Exeter.

Formerly adjoining the Litho works was the head office of
Dartington Woodlands Ltd, another venture now operated
commercially by an Exeter firm, Fountain Forestry Ltd. A booklet
describing the work of the Trust states that during its early years:

> There were innovations in forestry, 2000 acres of woodland on the
> estate and on Dartmoor were developed along progressive and
> economic lines by Wilfred Hiley. Much of the work in farming and
> forestry had far-reaching repercussions outside Devon, but, in more
> recent years, the emphasis has been less on research than on the
> commercial running of a predominantly dairying unit ... The Trust
> has now set up an experiment in 'low-input' farming on a third of the
> farms' acreage. A programme of courses in organic husbandry is
> being offered by the Yarner Trust, a new venture designed to answer
> the needs of an increasing number of smallholders who have been
> drawn back to the land. The woodland plantations remain a model
> of great interest to the outside world and will soon have matured
> into a 'normal' forest, in which annual plantings equal fellings.

In addition, Mark Kidel of the Trust informs me, cheese is made on
the Trust farms from their own milk and sold locally and in
London. Dartington village lies due south of North Wood, two

notable buildings on the outskirts being the parish church and the Old Parsonage, now known as the Old Postern. Christianity probably came to *Derte tun*, the farming settlement by Dart, not later than in Saxon times. It is recorded in Domesday Book (1086) as 'Dertintona' and in 1176 as 'Derdington'. The name High Cross Hill, the eminence north-east of North Wood, may signify the site of a preaching cross, a place where the Gospel was perhaps first preached at Dartington. There are indications that the lords of the manor during the Dark Ages had their hall where the celebrated Dartington Hall now stands, and that a Christianised noble erected the first church, perhaps a wooden one, close by. Records of parish priests start in 1152 and excavations of 100 years ago revealed the foundations of a thirteenth-century stone church. The site of the later medieval church, of which the tower alone remains, was inconvenient for the villagers and, as the Revd John Bishop's leaflet *The Parish Church of St Mary the Virgin, Dartington* explains:

> In 1878 the foundation stone of a new church was laid in a more central position, on glebe land near the Parsonage (now the Old Postern) and not far from the main centre of population, Week. The new church of St. Mary the Virgin was consecrated on April 27 1880 by Frederick Temple, Bishop of Exeter, and subsequently, Archbishop of Canterbury.

The architect, John Loughborough Pearson also designed Truro Cathedral, and at the time of his completion of the Dartington plans he was already in the midst of designs for Truro. To quote again from Father Bishop:

> The roofs follow the same plan as in the old church. The Beer Stone arcades from the old church were re-erected on Portland Stone bases to make them loftier. The mouldings of the Chancel window were used again . . .
> The Tower is completely new work. Its rich decorations were the work of Harry Hems. The Porch has a fine star-vault of fifteenth century workmanship which comes from the old church . . . Each year swallows nest in a vaulting of the roof of the porch. Keble-Martin, the clergyman-naturalist who grew up at Dartington, remembered their annual visits from his schooldays. The main door

is of great antiquity. The oldest part of the present church is the Font. The octagonal bowl of rough moorstone granite dates far into the Middle Ages.

Members of the Champernowne family of Dartington Hall who were Rectors of the parish were Francis (1737) and, for twenty years (1859–79) Richard, a Master of Arts and father of that Arthur commemorated in the tablet at the west end of the church; the Champernowne coat of arms appears there and the memorial reads:

> Arthur Melville Champernowne Born 16 August 1871 Died December 1966. He was the last of his family to occupy Dartington Hall where his ancestors, always pious benefactors of the parish, had lived since the year 1554. This church which they moved from Dartington Hall in 1880 and the Churches at Brooking and Landscove are their memorial.

Both J. H. Newman (later Cardinal Archbishop of Westminster) and John Keble, eminent Victorian divines, preached at old Dartington in the pulpit since transferred to the new church. The high altar was:

> ... brought from the old church, where it had been installed in 1836 by Archdeacon Froude ... The design is based on that of the High Altar at Cologne Cathedral, and ... oak came from the roof of the Great Hall of Dartington Hall, which had just been taken down.

The church, standing on a pleasant, pastoral plain overlooked by North Wood and beside Parsonage Cross, a road junction busy in summer, is a beautiful building, its conception a lasting credit to architect Pearson. Mention appears elsewhere of a picture presented to Dartington old church by Totnes artist William Brockeden, but which never reached the new building.

Running westward from Parsonage Cross is the lane to Week, a very ancient part of Dartington parish. In 1403, Agatha Maioun, wife of Walter Ferlecombe of Totnes, gave her house and garden to the parish for use as a church house at Week.

The document concerned (detailed by Elaine Bishop in *TDA* 107 of 1975), contains the following:

> All my cottage with garden adjacent at le Wike ... with all that empty plot of land between the aforesaid cottage and the watercourse on the south side of the said cottage.

A larger church house was subsequently needed and built upon land given by the Rector as a portion of his glebe, the new house being mentioned in a deed of 8 January 1518 (9 Henry VIII):

> All that house called the Church House, *alias* the parishioners' house ... which John Huxham shared equally with William Allerton *et aliis* ... of the gift of Edward Trobrigge, clerk, late Rector of Dartington ... as a parcel of his Centuary land.

The Church House even had a tennis court, first mentioned in 1566:

> mendynge of the tenes courte ...
> redynge of the tenyse court ...

Mrs Elaine Bishop writes:

> Frequent repairs during the great period of the church ales and on into the 17th century would seem to testify to vigorous use ... Its resident tenant often had to be host, too, to unwelcome lodgers, for local felons when apprehended were kept there overnight under guard. Vagrants, too, enjoyed a brief stay, as did pressed men on their way to Dartmouth.

Following World War II the house was sold by the parish and is now the property of Miss B. M. Jewell, who kindly showed me the interior. In each of the two principal ground-floor rooms is a fine fireplace with oak lintel. It is apparent that ale was bought, heated and consumed in these rooms, for the lintels bear numberless burn marks, the result of drinkers testing the heat of the poker they had thrust into the fire before plunging it into their ale. I am indebted to Miss Alison Rose, who has undertaken a study of the house's history, for the following entries concerning it from the Dartington parish records:

> 1593   Rcd: of Thomas beard and Thomas hawkyne ffor the encrease of the ale at Whitsentide
>
> vij—vjd (£7.0.6d)

1611   Receywed of Thomas Hawkinge and Own martyn the ale wardens

ix li lxs iiijd

1615   Receywed of John Tocker and nycholas houses the ale wardens for the increase of the corne at Whitsondae

xj le viiijs vjd

1602   Rcd. of George Ascott and Thomas Shinner for the corne belonginge to the churche with the encrease of the ale and sich monye these yere

vij le

Miss Rose remarks on an interesting entry of 1589, one year after the Spanish Armada:

Itm pd: to the wachinge and wardddyng of the Speannerdes   vijs
Itm pd: for a peare of showes a sharte and a peare of stockens for the Spannard   iiijs ixd

An entry in the *T. Appt.* of 1839 showing an unnamed 'Public House at Week' with Josias Whiteway as innkeeper, is likely to refer to the Church House, where cider and ale were sold a century and more ago.

The Dartington Hall Trust has several times received mention as the parent of ventures, some unusual, all successful, situated on the estate lands. As we are now closing in, as it were upon the remainder and upon the heart-beat of them all, the Hall itself and the Trust's headquarters, this might be a fitting place to explain to the reader what it is all about. Under the interrogative heading 'What is Dartington?', the Trust's brochure opens with these words:

Dartington's name in the outside world has most often been associated with progressive education, music and more recently with glass. All these connections exist, but they are only individual parts of a uniquely broad range of activities that have grown out of an experiment in rural regeneration launched by Leonard and Dorothy Elmhirst over fifty years ago ...
Today, the Dartington Hall Trust, a charitable body, controls or assists a wide number of ventures in business, farming, education,

research and the arts ... the Elmhirsts and the Trust they set up, attempted to create a working community in which people could find scope for personal development and a sense of fulfilment, as well as earning a living ... Dartington is a place in which human values are given, as much as is possible in the context of hard realities, a high priority.

The rolling, multi-coloured landscape of the Dartington farmlands, the rounded hills crested by woodlands, is of striking rural beauty. A long track, very satisfying to walk, runs from the Hall entrance, follows the Deer Park wall and curves between High Cross Hill and Chacegrove Hill before descending to Old Parsonage Farm. 'Chacegrove' is a corruption of Chase Grove, which version appears as late as 1839 in parish *T. Appt.*, when Henry Champernowne was at the Hall. Situated as it is, at a high point within the Deer Park, the wood obviously was the grove of the chase in earlier times before the park was enclosed. Indeed, between wood and river is the site of an ancient hunting lodge. Seen from the highest point of the track, Dartington Church tower stands boldly against the background of Yarner Beacon.

Dartington is mentioned in a royal charter of 833, as well as in Domesday Book. Excavations at the Hall have revealed evidence of a house of thirteenth-century date at which time the manor of Dartington was held by the Martin family, eight generations in succession having been lords of the manor from the early twelfth to the mid-fourteenth century. The Martins were for a short time succeeded by the family of Audley, until the end of the fourteenth century, when the present buildings were erected of Beer stone by John Holand, Earl of Huntingdon. Anthony Emery (author of *Dartington Hall*) writes in a Trust booklet entitled *Dartington Hall and its Work*:

He (Holand) was the half-brother of Richard II, but their relationship was not an easy one owing to Holand's impetuous temper which involved him in two murders during the early years of Richard's reign (1377–99). To the relief of many people, Holand joined an expedition to Spain in 1386 led by his father-in-law, John of Gaunt, and when he returned two years later he retired from active participation in politics. Dartington was situated in what was then considered an extremely remote part of the country and far from the centre of government at Westminster. Nevertheless, Holand chose it as the site of his new residence and built the majority of the present structure between 1388 and 1400.

The Holand family emblem, a wheatear, is to be seen on the groining of the entrance porch.

Sir Arthur Champernowne, Queen Elizabeth I's Vice-Admiral of the West, bought the Hall and estate in 1559. Second son of Sir Philip Champernowne whose family had been established at Modbury since the time of Edward II, Sir Arthur was the owner of three ships lying at Dartmouth: *Chudleigh* (140 tons), *Mary* (25 tons) and *Greyhound* (60 tons). Sir Arthur, according to Emery in *Dartington Hall*:

> ... was related by marriage to some of the well-known seafaring families of the sixteenth century—Gilbert, Raleigh, Grenville, Seymour, and Carew ... He was particularly concerned with the activities of pirate and enemy shipping off the western coast. On several occasions he was enjoined by the Privy Council to take piratical shipping, as in the case of the thirteen ships from Flushing which were blockading Torbay in July 1576. French shipping received particularly short shrift at Sir Arthur's hands and he frequently forced the sale of their cargoes on the grounds that they would otherwise perish before reaching their destination.

Gawen Champernowne, one of Sir Arthur's five sons, had command of cavalry troopers in 1586 as part of defensive preparations against the expected invasion by the Armada-borne troops of Philip of Spain. A descendant of Gawen's, Captain Francis Champernowne, emigrated to Kittery, Massachusetts, in 1637, whilst an ancestor from the family's pre-Dartington days, Sir Richard de Chambernown, had been Member of Parliament for Devon in 1324 and 1331. A later Sir Arthur Champernowne, Member of Parliament for Totnes from 1714–17, paid £28 in Land Tax (*LTA*) in 1747 for the Dartington estate, but in 1751, due to a revision of assessments, only £21. Emery remarks that the Champernownes:

> ... were not a wealthy family and the great agricultural depression which extended from the late 1870s until the present century

reduced the estate and the family's ability to maintain it. The Hall is important architecturally because the extensive remains were built to a plan of national rather than local importance. Several medieval houses survive in other parts of Devon, but Dartington is a mansion whose completeness and extent can be matched by few other residences in this country. The Hall is not unlike the educational foundations at New College, Oxford, and Winchester College, but as a private house it is the only major residence to survive from the reign of Richard II in either England or Wales.

(See plate 17.) Arthur seems to have been a traditional family forename for the Champernowne males, and White's *Directory* of 1878–9 names Arthur and Charlotte Champernowne as the Dartington Hall gentry. It also names, not inappropriately, John Beer as victualler at the Champernowne Arms, a beer or cider house of those times near Shinner's Bridge.

In 1925 Leonard and Dorothy Elmhirst bought the estate, which included Hood Manor, from Arthur Melville Champernowne, set up the Trust and initiated the unparalleled pattern of activities that have justifiably become world-famous. The decayed roof of the great hall had been demolished as unsafe in 1813 and was rebuilt by Staverton Builders in 1931.

A medieval homestead such as Dartington Hall cannot be supposed to be without its hauntings, and Miss Theo Brown, Recorder of Folklore for the Devonshire Association, contributed the following to *TDA* 92 of 1960:

> There was a tradition (at Dartington Hall) that a lady in white appeared before one of the family was going to die, and the only instance my sister (writes Miss Elizabeth Champernowne) can remember was when the front part of the house was let to friends, the James family. When the maids were shutting the front door they ran screaming with terror because, they said, a lady in white had walked across the lawn. That was exactly three weeks before my great-uncle Richard Champernowne, then Rector of Dartington, died in 1890, and my sister can remember Mrs. James telling my mother about it.

Of the two next, the first would seem to be a harbinger of musical days ahead:

Once [writes Miss Champernowne] my sister heard exquisite piano playing, so clear. She ran to the drawing room, thinking it was my mother, who was a fine pianist, but found the door locked on the outside and the room all dark, and my mother was in quite another part of the house. On another occasion my sister and I were going into the room below the drawing room, right under the piano, when we heard deep chords on the piano. When we told my mother about it, she said "What an extraordinary thing", for *her* mother used to hear the piano playing like that.

My sister says she does remember our old Steward telling of a headless horseman coming through the lowest gate in the drive, close to the river.

The road running eastward from Parsonage Cross leads to the Hall; branching from it is the drive to the Old Postern, a splendid Tudor building, once the parsonage, now used as a dormitory for Foxhole School. A minstrels' gallery overlooking the great hall, and a beam-supported, L-shaped gallery, are interesting features of the house.

Very near to the Old Postern, the Old Parsonage Farm was built in 1931–2 which, declares the Trust booklet:

... was of a totally new design, including continuous roofing and concrete flooring. Research and experiments at Dartington led to the establishment of the International Conference of Agricultural Economics and Oxford's Institute of Agrarian Affairs.

At the main cross-roads near the village centre the Ashburton road is carried over Bidwell Brook, a tributary of Dart rising near the medieval manor of Venton, by Shinner's Bridge. Although this name appears to have been Skinner as recently as the early years of the present century—as well as on maps of the previous century— each version justifiably has its adherents. Both names occur among villagers and farmers in the parish over the last three centuries—to give but one example of each, Thomas Shinner was a cottager and Thomas Skinner the farmer at Dartington Barton in 1839—so that it is not possible to decide precisely which was the original name. Most of the buildings here belong to the Dartington Hall Trust; the older part of the village, Cott, lying off the south street where the Cott Inn is situated, is very popular with tourists. This wonderful old building, as the Inn brochure says, has:

... been satisfying clients for 650 years. It served its first customer in 1320, during Edward II's reign, but whether he drank wine, ale, perry, mead or beer the Cott Inn has served a good many people since.

It is reputed to have been built by Johannes Cott, its first landlord, and is sited beside the ancient road from Totnes to Ashburton. The inn, the second oldest in England, celebrated its 650th birthday in 1970. Caught up in the internecine strife of Commonwealth times, it is likely to have been favoured by the presence of the ill-fated King Charles I. Later, the landing at Brixham of William of Orange heralded a period of enduring peace, and the inn was visited by such celebrities as Daniel Defoe in 1724, rich with the profits of publication of his *Robinson Crusoe*. The inn's name, according to the Totnes town guide-book, derives from that of a fourteenth-century merchant of the locality, who shared in the prosperity of Totnes with its boat-building and export trade in cloths, hides and Dartmoor tin. In the nineteenth century the Cott was conjoined with adjacent cottages, and still retains its 3ft thick walls, the original window openings and panelling taken from the ancient Dartington Church at the time of its demolition. In *T. Appt.* of 1839, Edward Parnell is shown as tenant of the Cott, with its adjoining plots, garden, orchards and vineyard.

Along Plymouth Road are the looms of Dartington Tweeds Ltd, where visitors may watch almost all the processes involved in producing cloth from lambswool fleeces to the finished rolls of tweed. Fine yarn is produced on a ring spinning frame where loose fibres are drawn out from the 'roving' to reduce its thickness and give the yarn its essential strength by twisting it so that the fibres adhere together, a process achieved by a 'traveller' rotating on a spindle at 8,000rpm. Dartington Tweeds was first established at Shinner's Bridge Mill, where the launder from Bidwell Brook and the waterwheel are still seen beside the Totnes road. The wheel, occasionally allowed to revolve, serves now only as an advertisement for the Tweeds, as the manufactory, except for some finishing processes, moved to Plymouth Road in January 1956. Here, a shed then housing a Milk Marketing Board grass-drying plant was taken over. The cording process began at once, followed soon by spinning, and in 1959 the looms were moved from the old textile Mill. The waterwheel at the latter had been bought from a Welsh mill for installation as part of a pre-war experiment.

West of Dartington Tweeds is the lowly eminence, between Plymouth Road and Bidwell Brook, known as Yarner Beacon. Its earliest mention, in 1333, as 'Yorneres' is referred to in *Place Names of Devon* where the authors suggest that the name means 'eagle slope' or 'eagle bank'. In the Dartington Churchwardens' Accounts for 1586 is the entry: 'making of the beacon and the house to the beacon'. This was in accordance with the direction to Head Constables that they should:

> ... cause in every place of arrival within the Hundred a small beacon a-low by the waterside to be made, and one greater upon the highest hill next adjoining as has been accustomed. The said beacons to be watched night and day by fit men of good discretion three by night and one by day.

There were also instructions that horses should be in readiness to inform the 'Lieutenants' and the Justices. (*TDA* 109 of 1977). The approach to the beacon would seem to have been by a track once branching right from the narrow lane between Dun Cross and Week, its lower portion vanished through centuries of disuse and its higher part remaining as a short grass track, with gateposts at each end, dividing the upper and lower parts of Beacon Copse. In the trees directly above this grassy way is a single prehistoric rampart, breached by a path leading upwards from the grassy way to a hollow on the wooded hillside. An old wall in the hollow is without doubt the remains of 'the house to the beacon' in which 'fit men of good discretion' could shelter and prepare hot food when off duty.

The hill summit, which once would have been kept clear, is now overgrown, and remains exist of a minor earthwork—the inner rampart, in fact, protected by the lower one already mentioned and consisting of earth and small stones—in the centre of which the beacon was built. Its wooded knoll is a conspicuous landmark in the Dartington locality, of which it provides a detailed view. The beacon was one in a local chain built to warn of the threatened invasion in the reign of Elizabeth I. Yarner is not visible from the Dartmoor beacons and its watchers would have received the fire signal from Dittisham's Fire Beacon Hill. The signal chain was well planned. An invasion at Plymouth would be 'broadcast' via Pen and Western Beacons and transmitted by Dittisham Beacon. Thus the secluded country of the lower Dart and the Admiral of the West at Dartington Hall would be informed by Yarner's reaction to the Dittisham signal, and the town and harbourside of Dartmouth by those of the (former) Dartmouth beacon at Beacon Parks, which again was visible from Dittisham. Conversely, should Dartmouth be the port selected for attack by the enemy, Plymouth would be informed by the sequence in reverse.

Parts of Yarner farmhouse, below the beacon, are of great age; an original oaken porch door-frame remains, and the keystone of the porch, since incorporated in a later entrance, bears symbols that may well denote a reconstruction:

$$E$$
$$E \quad (?) \quad E$$
$$1517$$

East of the crossroads at Shinner's Bridge is the Cider Press Centre, built by Staverton Contracting Group, where a restaurant and retail shop sell products made on the estate. The attractive display of Dartington glass here was not made locally, but at the Trust's glassworks, established in 1967 at Torrington in North Devon. The potter's wheel, however, turns at the Pottery Training Workshop situated in the Cider Press Centre—where cider-making ceased in 1952 due to a sharp decline in demand. A founder-member of the Pottery Workshop, Michael Casson, well known as presenter of 'The Craft of the Potter' on BBC television, gave an exhibition of his work at the Centre in 1979.

And what of the great Hall of Dartington, largest and most important medieval house to be built in the West of England? It is indeed the heart-beat of the whole huge venture. Leonard Elmhirst, who with his wife Dorothy created the venture, had worked with the Indian poet and philosopher Rabindranath Tagore from 1920–4, married Dorothy Whitney Straight, daughter of American millionaire William C. Whitney, in 1925, and together with his wife sought 'to launch an ambitious experiment in discovering ways to bring economic and social vitality back to the countryside'. The Elmhirsts' qualifications for creating the Dartington enterprise were based upon the experience they had gained in collaborating with Tagore in West Bengal where they founded an Institute for Rural Reconstruction. The Trust's brochure says:

> In 1924 Leonard was able to hand over this Institute to an all-Indian staff, and was invited by Tagore to join him on a cultural mission to China. Later in 1924, Leonard accompanied him on a visit to Latin America and Italy. They discussed plans for launching an enterprise in England not unlike the one on which they had worked in partnership in India. In April 1925 Leonard and Dorothy were married.

Searching for a country house and estate suitable as a basis for such an idea, they found, in semi-derelict condition (*see plate 18*), the great house of the Champernownes beside Dart. They completed the purchase by June 1926 and in September, with immense faith, moved in and opened a school. Education, agriculture and forestry, industry, and the arts were fields in which experimental work started almost at once, and famous names associated with the achievements of Leonard and Dorothy Elmhirst at Dartington include composer Alan Rawsthorne, choreographer Kurt Joos, potter Bernard Leach, headmaster W. B. Curry, flower arranger Constance Spry and artist Mark Tobey. Meanwhile, as a concern in its infancy, Staverton Builders (then including Staverton Joinery) moved in upon the practical scene, renovated and reroofed the Great Hall and commenced a programme of building to house the activities initiated by the Dartington Hall Trust which continued to be chaired by co-founder Leonard Elmhirst until his death in 1974. His devoted wife Dorothy had predeceased him in 1968.

Situated around and integrated with the Great Hall are the offices, kitchen, buttery, courtyard, barn theatre and staff rooms. The beautiful gardens are open to the public without charge, and contain a figure by the great British sculptor Henry Moore. Entitled *The Reclining Woman*, it is inscribed:

> For Christopher Martin
> First Administrator of the Arts Centre at Dartington Hall
> 1934–1944
> HENRY MOORE   Sculptor

and was sited by Moore himself in 1947. He has written:

> I wanted the figure to have a quiet stillness and a sense of permanence ... as though it has come to terms with the world and could get over the largest cares and losses.

The remarkable grass terraces, forming with the level area of the dell below a striking open-air theatre, known as Tournament Ground, provide a fine view of the Hall and of the remains of John Holand's extensive suite of apartments built in the late fourteenth century. The row of Irish yew trees, named the Twelve Apostles, was planted by the Champernowne family about 300 years ago. It is thought that they were intended to screen a bear-baiting pit that formerly existed at the lower end of the Tournament Ground. Emery, in *Dartington Hall* writes of the Dartington garden that it:

> ... supports a small department for the training of horticulturists. Therefore it is not a stultified creation, but one which still practises the fine art of gardening and forms an integral part of the educational and artistic activities at Dartington ... The result is one of the outstanding examples of garden design created in the 20th century.

Nearby are Dartington Hall School of which Foxhole is the senior school and Aller Park the middle and junior; and the Dartington College of Arts, where full-time courses are provided in art, music (*see plate 19*), dance and drama. Life at Dartington is free and untrammelled. It is also very demanding. It is, indeed, true to say that 'you get out of it what you put in'. Today, Dartington Hall and its enterprises, brain children of the Elmhirsts, are world-famous.

As the wide, now placid river flows through the grounds it is overlooked by Chacegrove and North Woods. With the character of a squire's country-seat parkland it is peaceful, yet never deserted. Students, staff, friends, visitors, tourists; there are always people about. From the Hall, the long drive descends to the Totnes lodge, bringing into view the roofs and church tower of the old town beyond the broad river.

In approaching the lodge, the drive crosses a wide flood-plain where, 400 years ago, the tidal waters of Dart lapped in a creek — one of several sea creeks silted up by the Dartmoor tinners' wastes. One rather special boat on this creek, according to oral tradition, carried Queen Elizabeth I to Dartington to be entertained at the Hall by Sir Arthur Champernowne (this before the building of the first Totnes Weir). The plain between river and drive is to this day called Queen's Meadow, and the lodge gates, now never closed, are those mentioned in the ghostly tradition on page 124.

Immediately outside the grounds a signposted footpath leaves the roadside and leads to Totnes Weir, a structure well documented in Totnes records, and one that creates a major problem for competitors in the annual Dart Raft Race from Buckfastleigh to Totnes. The course measures ten challenging miles and anything home-made that floats is eligible to enter. On 5 October 1980 the race attracted 340 entries crewed by 2,000 people, all cheerfully prepared for a chilly wetting. Most of them got it. The winner covered the course in 1hr 31 min.

Totnes Weir dates back to 1581, when a weir of timber and furze was built by Geoffrey Babb below Bidwell Brook Foot, under the direction of Gawen Champernowne of Dartington Hall, to divert water to Totnes Town Mill, where Babb was miller. This was replaced by one of stone in 1585 — since rebuilt and repaired several times. While the footpath continues to the town, the opposite bank of the river is enlivened by the arrival and departure of DVR trains at Riverside Halt, the passengers, insulated from Totnes by the lack of a footbridge, stretching their legs on the platform. It stands within the parish of Littlehempston and in 1629 the lord of that manor, the Marquis of Worcester, complained that the new weir was constantly causing the flooding of his meadows. The Marquis took the then miller, Thomas Priestwood, to court over the matter, and although Priestwood agreed to lower the weir, he had to bear the heavy expenses in the case. River floods caused frequent breaches in the weir, 1684 being a particularly burdensome year for Totnes Corporation, by then owners of Town Mill and Babb's Weir. Edward Langworth carried out repairs in 1702, and a year later the Duchess of Bolton contributed the very large sum of £1,000 towards rebuilding the weir. The new structure was badly damaged in 1707; in 1751 £250 had to be spent on repairs, and £350 in 1784. Repairs to the weir for six years ending 1871 cost no less than £2,770, imposing a large drain on milling profits at Town Mill, by this time the property of the Charity Commissioners.

It seems that no adequate means had ever been provided, since Geoffrey Babb built the first weir, of ensuring the up-river passage of fish in general and salmon in particular, a matter of some surprise when one considers the several generations of Champernownes at the Hall who, it might be imagined, would have wished to catch the aristocrat of river fish within their own parkland. The fishing rights of a lengthy stretch of river, reaching from Totnes Weir almost to Kilbury Weir, were by the mid-nineteenth century owned by three manors—Dartington, Hood and Bigadon, the first two under one ownership. In March 1880, therefore, Arthur Champernowne of Dartington Hall and John Fleming of Bigadon House jointly addressed a letter to the *Western Morning News* proposing the construction of a 'fish pass' at Totnes Weir. The project was in principle supported, in a letter to the newspaper dated 6 March, by Thomas Roe of the Committee of the Dart Fishing Association, but the means proposed were criticised. Another appeared from Arthur Champernowne on 9 March saying that 'Mr J. Rossiter the Miller promised his cordial co-operation'. Also supporting the scheme was 'William Weldon Sympington Esqr. of Black Rock, Buckfastleigh' (now the Black Rock Guest House). It was hoped, rather optimistically, that the public would subscribe towards the cost of the fish pass, but here the promoters were disappointed. They therefore decided to make a bid for the purchase of Town Mill, leat and weir; the Charity Commissioners asked £2,700; the promoters, in the person of Arthur Champernowne, offered £2,500, which was declined. Ultimately, the

Commissioners' price was agreed and the property passed to the promoters. The whole transaction, occasioning a considerable exchange of correspondence between Champernowne and Fleming, who invariably wrote from his London address at 8 Billiter Square, was undertaken specifically for the insertion of the fish pass now seen at the weir, and completed by 1881.

Totnes Town

Below the weir, the now-wide river reaches Town Marsh, is crossed by the Exeter–Plymouth railway line, receives the River Hems and bends due south, between the industrial estate and Newton Abbot Road, to approach Totnes Bridge and the heart of ancient Totnes town. Situated on its right bank above the bridge is the Harris Bacon factory, a part of which—the large, old stone building beside Coronation Road—is the historic Town Mill. The leat continues to bring water from Totnes Weir—where the great iron sluice gate bears the name of Willcocks & Son, Buckfastleigh (*see plate 20*)—now used for washing and cleansing purposes at the factory; bricked-up apertures of former conduits, and the mill race itself, may be seen from the pavement in Coronation Road.

Records show that corn was milled on this site in 1133, when there was a series of three tidal mills. Their wheels were powered at high tide by a short leat from a tidal marsh, where the industrial estate now stands on land long since reclaimed. In 1549, Barnard Smyth occupied Town Mills—two 'sea mills', one flour and one fulling, whilst another tidal mill, for malt, stood nearer Dartington, at a point where the turnpike gate was to stand in later days. This is without doubt the former sea creek through which Queen Elizabeth I sailed to reach Dartington Hall. When Harris brothers Charles and Thomas, butchers in a small Wiltshire country town, combined in the early nineteenth century to found the firm now known as C. & T. Harris (Calne) Ltd, they had to solve the major problem of temperature control for their wares. This they did by producing bacon principally during the winter months and collecting ice from local sources—ponds and canals—for use in storage; when a mild winter placed ice in short supply, block ice was imported from Norway and delivered to Calne by canal.

Harris's had sought to establish a bacon factory in Totnes before World War I, and in 1912 purchased Town Mills where they operated the corn mill in addition to the factory. Milling finally ceased after World War II and the firm converted the mill into a store and offices; the leat from Totnes Weir was included in the property, and now supplies water for the steam boiler as well as for passing through cooling equipment, an economic alternative to the use of mains water.

Pigs reared locally are slaughtered under humane and clinical conditions, and bacon is cured according to Harris's original Calne method, which explains why their bacon, wherever produced, is known as Wiltshire bacon and is branded with a crown and 'Harris'. Supplies of bacon, sausages and pies go out from the Totnes factory to all parts of the West Country.

In 1792 a scheme was prepared for a canal between Totnes and Ashburton, for which F. King was surveyor. It was to be taken in from the River Dart just above Totnes Bridge and would terminate on the plain, south of Ashburton town, where the A38 road now runs between Bowden Hill and Linhay Hill. The canal would rise 202½ft by means of no fewer than twenty-four locks and would cost £15,000, the equivalent sum in 1981 being £447,186. No wonder the proposals were abandoned, for Ashburton had already passed its peak as a stannary town and wool market, and the profitable days of the large copper mines, such as Brookwood and Wheal Emma, yet lay half a century ahead.

It is clear from the comments of Leland early in the sixteenth century that there was general concern over the silting up of creeks and harbours by tinners' wastes:

> The river of Darte by tinne workes carrieth much sand to Totnes Bridge, and chokith the depth of the ryver (all) downward, and doth much hurt to Dartmouth Haven.

Geoffrey Babb, builder of the timber weir, Mayor of Totnes in 1581 and 1596, rented Town Mills from the Corporation for £5 a year. Obviously an energetic man, it was he who replaced his own original weir of wood and furze by a stone structure in 1585, at the same time enlarging and extending the old tidal leat.

Richard Cole was Mayor of Totnes a century or so later, and in 1713 ordered that any alehouse keeper not grinding his corn at Town Mills should be deprived of his licence. In the twentieth century, the one remaining, principal grist mill ceased to function in 1946, by which time it had been in Messrs Harris's ownership for thirty-four years; grist mill and factory, indeed, worked entirely on Dart water power until 1940. Grindstones in the old watermills of south Devon were either of granite or French burr-stone; according to a notice in the *Exeter Flying Post* for 4 October 1787, this stone was imported from Rouen and landed at Exmouth Quay.

Totnes appears as Totenais in the *Devonshire Domesday*. The Normans built the castle, a stone church and stone town walls early in the twelfth century. Leland wrote in his *The Itinerary of John Leland In or About the Years 1535–1543* (Ed Lucy Smith 1907) following a visit to Totnes:

> The castelle of Totenes stondith on the hille north west of the towne. The castelle waul and the stronge dungeon be maintained. The loggings of the castelle be clene in ruine. Many gentilmen hold their landes by gard and service to this castelle.
>
> This toun hath beene waulled: but the waulles be now clene down. A man may see wher the foundation was of them. Ther be yet 3 gates by west, est and . . . north.

It is likely that a settlement had existed by the river since Celtic times. A brief account of the history of various Totnes institutions, given under relevant headings, appears in Elizabeth Gunnell's *Totnes*. Here we are concerned chiefly with the town's 1000-year-old dependence upon the river—its lifeline for 900 of those years, from the reign of King Edgar (959–75) until the railway was built in 1847. Edgar's royal Saxon borough, like the first two of its sister boroughs—Exeter, Barnstaple and Lydford—stood at the head of a navigable estuary and had its own mint (as also had Lydford), producing coins between the reigns of Edgar and William Rufus.

Like most medieval towns and villages, Totnes had a bull-baiting pit, and on 6 April 1900 a bull ring was found on the Plains just west of the Wills monument. Affixed to the top of the post, which was 2ft 4in below ground, was an iron rail on which a D-ring had free movement. The bull to be baited was tethered, by means of a collar and four yards of rope, to the D-ring. Entries in town records concerning the bull ring occur from time to time, including one of 'one shilling for the making and fixing of a new ring'. An account of bull-baiting was written in 1694 by one John Houghton, who spoke of the collar and rope, by which means 'the bull circulated to watch his enemy, which is a mastiff dog ...'. I admit to being surprised by the mention of 'a mastiff dog', having always believed bull-baiting dogs to have been much smaller—bulldogs, in fact. The custom among the womenfolk present was to wear large aprons for the express purpose of catching the dogs when tossed by the bull; a bulldog is a fair weight, but if Houghton was right, the ladies were in for a real trial of strength when a mastiff came hurtling through the air towards them. This barbarous sport did not become illegal until 1835, when Richard Soper was Mayor of Totnes.

The town's cloth trade early assumed importance, Totnes taking second place only to Exeter at the dawn of the sixteenth century. The parish church of St Mary, a fine fifteenth-century building in red sandstone, is also described in Leland's *Itinerary*:

> There is but one paroch chirche in Totenes, and that is set in the midle of the toun. Ther is a greate steple tour, and the greatest belles in al those quarters.

In 1675 the Vicar of St Mary's was John Prince, author of the historically important *The Worthies of Devon*. An upper chamber above the south porch is reached by a partly projecting newel stair, and the stone chancel screen, once surmounted by rood and rood-loft, is altogether remarkable. Prior to the construction of the magnificent tower in 1449, which is described by the Revd J. E. Morris in *The Parish and Priory Church of St Mary, Totnes* as 'unquestionably the noblest in the county', 'six supervisors were appointed, with Roger Growdon as master-mason, and an overseer, and instructed to visit the belfry towers at Kelington (Callington in Cornwall), Bokelond, Tavistock and Asshberton'.

15 (*right*) The Staverton Madonna, a driftwood sculpture by Douglas Rowse (1970)

16 (*below*) 'Christ with Arms Outstretched', another driftwood sculpture by Douglas Rowse (1970). It was erected on a spoil-heap at Penn Recca Slate Mine, but fell in 1978. It was re-erected in 1980

17 Dartington Hall in 1797 (from a painting by T. Bonner). The Great Hall and the north court were intact at that time, but the south court was in ruins. The picture is drawn from beneath the gatehouse arch

18 The Great Hall at Dartington. The broken roof, demolished in 1813, left the interior open to the weather for over a century before its rebuilding in 1931. Readers who have attended concerts here will know that artists now enter through the doorway (far corner) and perform in front of the great fireplace

'Bokelond' would have been Buckland Monachorum parish church near Tavistock. All able-bodied parishioners were urged to assist in the work and those taking part were issued with 'shovelys, matokky, pekesyes, seseguys and crawes'—shovels, mattocks, pickaxes, an unidentifiable tool and crowbars. The red sandstone was in all probability cut from the medieval quarry at Roundham Head near Goodrington and transported to Waddeton or Galmpton Quay, where it was loaded on barges and taken up-river to Totnes. Here a special quay was built at the riverside, the roadway near the bridge being widened, and obstructions were removed from the Fore and High Streets so that the stones could be dragged on sleds to the church. St Mary's at this time also had its Church House, now Nos 11 and 13 in the High Street.

At the approach to Totnes Bridge a cross-roads is formed by Fore Street, Coronation Road (built only in 1937), the bridge approach and the wide way know as the Plains. In the centre of the way here is a granite obelisk bearing on its east side a sculpted profile of the Totnesian it commemorates, his identity and achievement set out below on a marble plaque:

In Honour of William John Wills Native of Totnes: the first with Burke to cross the Australian Continent. He perished in returning 28th June 1861.
Erected by public subscription 1864.

According to the town's official guidebook, *Historic Totnes and District*, Totnes has been selected 'by the British Council of Archaeology as one of the top forty "Gem" towns of Britain and the central area has been designated as a Conservation Area to aid the preservation of its historic character'.

A clock formerly in the tower of St Mary's Church was removed in 1887 and re-installed at Tuckenhay Paper Mill. It had been commissioned by the church authorities from an interesting and talented Totnesian of whom few people today seem to have heard—William Brockedon (1787–1854). The son of a Totnes clockmaker, William inherited his father's craftsmanship and, for good measure, was himself gifted as a painter and inventor. When only fifteen, William completed the making and installing of the town clock in the East Gate which had been commissioned from his father, then fatally ill. Archdeacon Froude, Vicar of Dartington and the Champernownes at the Hall patronised and supported him, in token of which he presented his *Scene in the Life of St Peter* to (old) Dartington Church. The painting is not in the new church and is possibly amongst a collection owned by a member of the Champernowne family; at all events I have not yet been able to trace it. Brockedon, also in acknowledgement of patronage, presented his *The Raising of the Widow's Son at Nain* to St Saviour's Church, Dartmouth. This immense canvas gained him a prize of 100 guineas from the British Institution for a painting by a British artist.

Brockeden the inventor patented a process for vulcanising rubber—so paving the way for cycle- and car-tyre manufacture—and in 1819 devised a method of drawing fine gold and silver wires through holes pierced in glass. Indeed, his skill in mechanics was outstanding and won for him a Fellowship of the Royal Society. His son Philip became a civil engineer and one of Isambard Brunel's most favoured pupil-assistants. There are still to be found in the Totnes area some eight-day clocks bearing on the face 'Brockeden, Totnes'. The pronunciation of his name is 'Bruckton', like that of the farming hamlet in Dittisham parish where his family originated.

Totnes castle sited on its 'motte' (mound) to command a view of the river crossing, is well worth visiting, and provides a rewarding prospect of the town and surrounding countryside. Mr S. E. Rigold MA, FSA, an Inspector of Ancient Monuments, writes in the official leaflet of the Department of the Environment:

> One of the leaders in the Norman campaign in the West was Judhael ... son of Alured ... He settled here and became known as 'Judhael de Totnes', where he founded a Benedictine priory and almost certainly raised the earthworks of the castle which subsist to this day ... Totnes was granted to Roger do Nonant, who continued to hold it even after Judhael returned to favour under Henry I.

There can have been no lack of Dart salmon on Judhael's domestic board, for records show his Salmon Fishery dues to have been:

Loddiswell 30 salmon per year
Cornworthy 30
Dartington 80

Rigold writes also of a later period, that:

> Totnes had been granted to a faithful, if somewhat filibustering,
> Lancastrian, Sir Richard Edgecombe of Cothele, whose family
> continued to appoint constables. When Leland, the travelling
> antiquary, visited Totnes about 1535, he recorded a state of affairs
> that had probably obtained for two centuries past.
> About 1559 Sir Piers Edgecombe sold the castle to Sir Edward
> Seymour of Berry Pomeroy, an ancestor of the present Duke of
> Somerset.

The previous Duke, seventeenth of his line, placed the castle in the
guardianship of the Ministry of Works (now Department of the
Environment) in 1947.

Hoskins states in *Devon*:

> There is no documentary reference to Totnes before the coins begin.
> The name means "Totta's *ness*," Totta being an Old English
> personal name, and the *ness* the ridge of hard ground that runs down
> from the castle site almost to the banks of the river. Such a site, just
> where the Dart begins to broaden out into an unfordable estuary,
> was almost certainly occupied before the 10th century.

Percy Russell, however, in *The Good Town of Totnes* disagrees with
this derivation, remarking that the double 'tt' in Totta, found on
only one Saxon coin, was an error and that *tot* means a look-out.
Hence 'Totanais', appearing on the earliest known minting, means
the look-out, or castle, on the ness.

In 1088 a Benedictine Priory was founded by Judhael on a site
near the castle; it was dedicated to St Catherine and given by its
founder to the Abbey of St Sergius at Angiers in Brittany. The
former Saxon church of St Mary was used by the monks until a new
conventual priory church was built early in the thirteenth century.
Strife occured in 1445 between Prior Richard, and the Corporation
and town church. (The new St Mary's, in building at that time, was
intended expressly for town and civic use.) From the town's official
Guide we learn that:

By the eleventh century it was a Borough town, and was granted a charter of privileges by King John, including the right to a Merchant Guild, at the beginning of the thirteenth century.

A river ford would have been in use by Celtic travellers long before the first bridge was built, but usable only at low tide, a situation which the Romans would never have tolerated. A wooden bridge is likely to have been built when the settlement was elevated to borough status, at which time merchandise for the town was brought up the estuary by ship. The town wall of Norman Totnes had three gates, of which two survive, the East and North Gates, the latter having been enlarged in 1837 and is the meeting point of the Fore and High Streets. The gate formerly had three arches, one, controlled by iron gates, for carriages, one for horsemen and a 'needle's eye' for pedestrians.

In 1130 Guy de Nonant obtained the grant of a fair for Totnes, to be held on 15 August, the Feast of the Assumption of the Blessed Virgin. The borough was represented by two Members of Parliament from 1295 until 1868, one of which was Nicholas Ball, a Member in 1584; his fine town house, still to be seen at No 16 (now Barclays Bank) High Street. Totnes suffered an above-average share of plague deaths towards the end of the sixteenth century, when ninety-seven burials were recorded at St Mary's Church in 1589, and in the following year the frightening number of 269: (*cf* numbers for Dartmouth p 196). In 1596 Queen Elizabeth I granted a charter entitling the town to a Guildhall, for the medieval Merchant Guild of Totnes had always met at No 8 High Street; the new hall, however, with its ornamental council chamber, was not completed until 1624. Today, three and a half centuries later, it still houses the Town Council, as well as the Magistrates' Court.

In the fifteenth century, when Totnes had become an important West Country port, the town ranked tenth among the twenty-five richest in England. A hundred years later Totnes cloth was exported to many centres on the Continent and Totnes fine hose had become well known. The cloth was of a narrow, rough type, white and undyed, sold in 12yd lengths 1yd wide. These lengths became known as 'Devon dozens', a description appearing frequently in Totnes Port records.

Town records show that early in the thirteenth century a stone bridge was built across the river with a chapel dedicated to St Edmund at its west end. Chantry Certificates of 1546 state that this chantry was:

> ... founded by William de Kantelupe, for the maintenance of a pryste to say masse and pray for his sowle in a chapel at the west end of ye bridge of Totness.

Five monetary bequests were made during the first quarter of the fifteenth century for the maintenance of the chantry and indulgences offered for its upkeep in 1434 and 1441. There are no records of further endowments and it was undoubtedly during the second half of the fifteenth century that the bridge was replaced by the magnificent structure that continued to serve the town until 1826. This was a packhorse bridge with seven arches and six cut-waters, illustrated in a print of *c* 1820 which is reproduced in Gunnell's *Totnes*. The bridge bore a distinct resemblance to Staverton Bridge, to which, indeed, it was next in position downstream. The resemblance is clear also from a print dating from the early sixteenth century. The bridge was described by Leland as:

> Totenes Bridge on Darte of 7. archis.
> Little Totenes a flite shot byneth Totenes Bridge.

It was demolished only six years after the print of 1820 was made, and replaced by the fine one now carrying the immense weight of late-twentieth-century traffic. This bridge was designed by Devon-born Charles Fowler, who had come to prominence after designing Covent Garden Market, as well as the Higher and Lower Markets in the City of Exeter. The foundation stone of the bridge was laid in 1826 by Mr R. W. Newman, Member of Parliament for Mamhead; Shepherd & Olding of Plymouth were the contractors. The bridge (*see plate 21*), which was opened on 25 March 1828 (Patronal Festival of Totnes Parish Church), cost £12,000 and had toll gates until 31 October 1881, when they were removed and burnt on Town Marsh.

Prince Charles, under the orders of his father King Charles I, was in Totnes on 30 December 1645 to rally the Royalist armies. On 5 January 1646 he rode to Dartmouth in the cause, and was attended by Lieutenant-General Wentworth. It was a cause, nevertheless, already lost.

The flourishing commerce of the town in the seventeenth century justified a large new hostelry, and in 1680 the Royal Seven Stars Inn (now Hotel) was built by George Rooke, with a coach entrance where the porch now stands. Over a century later the much travelled J. B. Swete stayed at the inn and remarked on it as 'a very pleasant house, managed by extremely civil people and affording very good accommodation'. George Rooke became Mayor of Totnes in 1686.

In 1553 King Edward granted a charter of foundation for a grammar school in Totnes. The school flourished, later being housed in a small stately mansion in Fore Street. Here, for a short time, the author served on the staff as the school's Music Master. The Mansion, as it is now called, at present houses the Sixth Form of Totnes Comprehensive School. Among the pupils of King Edward VI's Grammar School was numbered Charles Babbage, inventor of the mechanical calculator, forerunner of the modern computer. A Dr Richard Pococke wrote in 1750:

> ... this town is a great thorow fare from Exeter to Plymouth, tho' not the post road; it abounds in good shops to supply the country, and has a cheap and plentiful market. The people are polite and generous.

On the east bank of the river is the suburb of Bridgetown, once a separate borough and called by Leland Berry Pomeroy Town:

> Byri Pomerey Town lyith hard on the est ende of Totenes Bridge. Byri Pomerey chirch almost a mile of: and Byri Pomerey castelle aboute half a mile from the chirch.

Restoration work has recently been completed on the Church of St John the Evangelist, built in 1820 by the Duke of Somerset as a chapel-of-ease to Berry Pomeroy Church, and gutted by fire on 9

July 1976 (*see plate 21*). Arson was proved but the arsonist never discovered, and damage was caused to the extent of £100,000. Several fire brigades attended the blaze and pumped water direct from the river below the Seymour Hotel; the only valuables saved were a chalice, patten and cross. The church's first minister, the Revd James Shore, 'went to prison in 1848 for his beliefs' (*Totnes Times*): they must have been radical, but I have never discovered what they were. On the former organ of St John's in 1958, as part of my duties I accompanied the grammar school Carol Service.

Striking views of town and port may be seen from the top of Bridgetown Hill, and from Totnes Down Hill on the old road to Ashprington, where one is in close proximity to the river. Lower Totnes and Bridgetown are divided by the waterway and backed by Berry Pomeroy Church and Castle. Sounds of hammering, shifting timber, machinery, men's voices, seagulls and traffic crossing the bridge, rise from the river front, while a flotilla of small boats moored off the Island await their sailing orders. New craft of Honnor Marine lie in orderly ranks in the firm's yard. The narrow, twisting lane descending Totnes Down Hill turns into Moat Hill, passes the approach to St Peter's Quay and becomes Kelmore Street; running behind the old houses fronting the Plains it emerges into that broad way near the Wills monument. On Moat Hill, near the foot of the descent, is the restored Cherry Cross, a medieval relic of granite thought to be connected with an early church on the site. Edward Masson Phillips writes in *TDA* 69 of 1937:

> A large circular base, probably ancient as it has been broken and repaired, supports a modern square socket-stone, the vertical edges of which are chamfered.
>
> The shaft, the lower portion of which is modern, is of rectangular section with chamfered edges and tapers slightly upwards. The upper portion is ancient, and one face of the cross-head has a wide recessed cross cut upon it, the limbs extending on to the head and arms a short distance down the shaft.

Although Dart is tidal for some way above Totnes Bridge, the bridge marks a clear dividing line, as may be seen by a glance from its parapets, between the river of the town and the river of the port. The wide, marshy tract through which it approaches the bridge, and the busy Newton Abbot road ascending its east bank, form a marked contrast to the downstream scene. Thus the tidal Broad Marsh spells the end of the lowland reach, so rich in rural crafts and cultures, and forms a short transition to the Maritime Dart, a vital constituent of England's history.

4
THE DART ESTUARY

A fascinating aspect of the study of a river is the series of contrasts between mountain or moorland reach and estuary; especially is this so in the case of Dart. The swift stream at source, no wider than a garden path and just capable of carrying heather stalks torn from the banks—and the placid flow of the, in places, $\frac{1}{2}$-mile-wide navigable stream bearing timber-laden ships from Russia. The total lack of settlements at nearly 2,000ft—and the compact pattern of historic colonisation proximate to sea level. The arrow-like darting of rainbow trout in far off, boulder-strewn, peaty waters—and the more staid progress of bulky sea trout, salmon and bass between the keels of numerous boats. The croak of raven, mew of buzzard and clack of wheatear over rocks and wind-blown rushes—and everywhere the cry of the ubiquitous sea-gull. An exchange of mansions for hut circles, churches for stone circles, ferries for stepping stones, castles for tors, ship-builders for sheep farmers and watermen's taverns for moormen's cider houses.

One thing is certain: to appreciate either—as well as the intermediate reaches—one must experience the contrasts. Literally to walk from Dart Head to Dartmouth would involve the walker in much trespassing—especially in the lower reaches, but careful planning with the map and a sensible blend of motoring and walking will provide a representative experience of the river throughout its entire course.

Of all reaches, the estuary offers most obstacles to straightforward riverside walking, especially the necessary lengthy diversions around the heads of creeks; attacks on the flank, therefore, awheel or on foot, form the best method of approach. An introduction to the essence of the reach would be threefold: first, obtain the

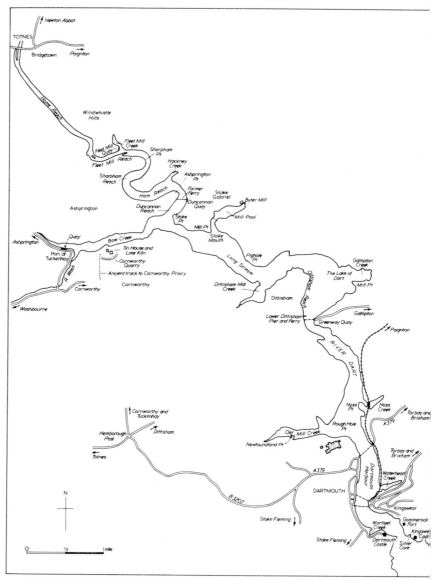

The Dart Estuary

recommended chart (*see Appendix C*); second, simply walk the length of the Island at Totnes; third, take the return trip by river steamer. 'Flank attacks' by car at Stoke Gabriel, Greenway Quay, Tuckenhay and Dittisham, and a steam-train ride from Paignton to Kingswear are educative, but the steamer trip brings one more realistically into contact with the scenery and history of this magnificent reach of Dart. The further planning of riverside walking as outlined in the text would be a natural sequel affording experience at first hand of the physical nature of the valley.

The Port of Totnes

Few car-borne travellers crossing the river at Totnes Bridge, intent upon reaching or returning from the golden sands of Torbay, see anything to suggest that they are passing through a port of historic importance—one where vessels have carried imports and exports on the river for many centuries and where historic ships have been built, for example the galleons *Crescent* and *Harte*, built as a contribution by the townsfolk to Sir Francis Drake's anti-Armada fleet of 1588.

Nothing is known of the quays of the Middle Ages, other than that they certainly existed. It is recorded in the Pipe Rolls of 1180 that 800,000 slates were shipped from Totnes for the building of Winchester Castle and 100,000 for that of Porchester. I am indebted to Percy Russell's *The Good Town of Totnes* for this information, but I question his further statement that 'the quarries were mainly to the south of the town'. I know of no slate quarry south of Totnes that could have supplied slates in such quantities, but if 'north' be substituted for 'south' there remains no difficulty: Penn Recca was likely to have been in production soon after the Norman Conquest.

There is little doubt that St Peter's Quay was first among the port's purpose-built quays and the point of despatch of the slate consignments. It is tempting to regard the quay as that built for the ancient settlement on the nose of Totenais where Cherry Cross and the supposed church nearby were part of the first riverside village, overlooked by the eleventh-century castle of Judhael. The quay of Bridgetown on the east bank of the river must also have originated many centuries ago. The *T. Appt.* of 1841 shows seven quays and storehouses, several 'offices, dwelling houses and gardens', and the Fishery House of Nicholas Mitchell & Co.

The first Totnes quay to be historically verified was that constructed in 1449 for landing the stone used in the new tower of St Mary's Church: this was carried by 20-ton square-rigged barges. By this time regular shipments of Dartmoor tin were sent from the stannary of Ashburton to the Continent, and leather and cloth from Totnes, where the population then numbered over 3,000, were much in demand, the latter in the form of 'Devon dozens'. Eventually the cloth trade suffered a sharp decline; a finer cloth known as 'kersey' was in rising demand, but Totnes failed to respond to this new trend, with inevitable consequences to its cloth exports, which never recovered. During the great trading days of Henry VIII's reign, according to a leaflet produced by Totnes and District Society, the successful merchants built their houses:

> ... crammed together in narrow sites on the main street. So they built backwards as they expanded, and decorated their frontages for prestige. Elizabethan House, now Totnes Museum, preserves some typical features of these houses.

After the dissolution of the monasteries, King Henry granted lands of the former Totnes Priory to Katherine Champernowne—only a few years before the purchase of the Dartington estate in 1559 by Sir Arthur Champernowne.

Extracts (transcribed) from Totnes shipping records are of interest in showing the activity and trade of the port over three centuries commencing in the reign of James I:

> Kayage or Quay dues for 1614. In the *Hopewell* of Dartmouth, Christopher Brookinge of Totnes, merchant, exports 2 packes one end containing 53 Devon dozens... 8s. 10d.
> Also Richard Lee of Totnes, merchant, exports 8 packes containing 187 Devon dozens .... 15s. 00d.

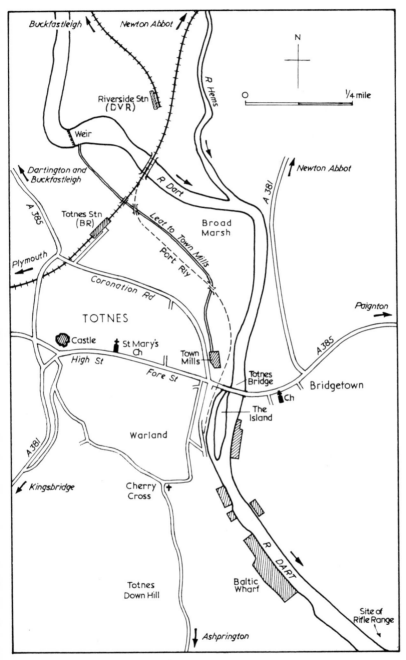

Totnes town and port

John Kelland and Shinnel Wise, Totnes merchants, also export Devon dozens in the *Hopewell*.

[The *Hopewell*, and other ships carrying Totnes cloth to Normandy and Brittany, carried back canvas, paper, playing cards and buckram.]

Schedule of the rate of Kayage of Laces and other Commodities exported in 1711:

ffor every Pack of Woollen cloth	o. 3d.
„ „ End „ „ „	o. 2d.
Chest of Sugar	3d.
Piece of White tinn	1d.
Tunn of Lead	3d.
Hogshead of Wine, Oyl, or the like	1½d.
Barrell of pitch, Tarr, Nayles, Herrings, Butter or the like	1d.
Mill stone	3d.

In 1735, John Souchard of Totnes:

... sent to London by Ship 90 casks of cider (5,418 gallons) & paid excise of £45.7.4 at 10/8 per hogshead. The Ship was lost with all hands. John Souchard claimed the return of his money 'as there was no advantage to anyone for the tax'. The excise authority made a full refund.

(Records, Totnes Museum)

Ships built at Totnes came from the Island yard and were launched downstream on the flood-tide. In 1821, *Resolution* was launched at Totnes, a two-masted schooner of 117 tons. *Hiram*, 134 tons and of similar specification was launched a year later. *Resolution* was Brixham-owned and served until 1872, when she was broken up. *Hiram*, also Brixham-owned, was lost in a storm in 1856. At the time when these vessels began their working life, large sailing ships could not reach Totnes, but had to lie up in deep water at Sharpham Reach, where their cargoes were transferred to small vessels (*see below*) that came out from Fleet Mill Quay, to be taken ashore. One consequence of this time-wasting expedient was the indulging by seamen in a good deal of extra tobacco smoking, using their clay pipes. Many pipes were broken, became clogged or in other ways unusable and were thrown overboard, to be dredged up over a century later from beneath some 8ft of mud in Fleet Mill

sels load at this Wharf for Stockton, Ipswich, Gainsbro', Leeds, Dartmouth, Faversham, Swansea, and Maidstone.

t HAYS WHARF, Southwark,

One of HARRIS & FOLLETT'S Vessels

Clears from the above Wharf on THURSDAY.

FOR

Dartmouth,

TOTNESS,

Brixham, Kingsbridge, &c.

NOW LOADING,

The NIMBLE, William Thornton Master,

TAKES IN GOODS AND PASSENGERS FOR

skerswell	Blackauton	Cockington	Little Hemstone	Paington	Staverton
ongifford	Berrypomeroy	Dartington	MODBURY	Rattery	St. Mary Church
ington	Buckfastleigh	Deane	Morleigh	South Brent	Tuckenhay
irton	Bridge Town	Denbury	Malbrough	Slapton	Torbrieu
ey	Churston Church	Dittesham	Narldon	Stokegabriel	Tor Abbey
head	Chapelstone	KINGSBRIDGE	Newton Bushel	Salcomb	Woodland
hempstone	Cornworty	Kingsware	Newton Abbott	Stokenham	And all places adjacent.

oods received after dark.—The last day of taking in Goods is **THURSDAY.**

Master or Wharfinger to be spoken with at the said Wharf, or on the Irish Walk in 'Change hours.—Not accountable for loss by fire, or leakage.

re particularly desired not to advise your Correspondents till your Goods are shipped.—Please to send particulars of what the packages contain, and money for Wharf Charges.

ods for the above-mentioned and adjacent places are not received at this Wharf but on the conditions following, that the Wharfinger will not be accountable, or engage to forward them by any particular vessel named in ceipt given ; or for loss by fire, high tides, leakage or wastage, vermin, act of God, the Queen's enemies, or loss oned by imperfect directions, marks, or packing; neither will any advice be given of the shipment of Goods may be left out of former vessels.

vill please to observe, the Wharfinger or Owners will not pay any claim for loss or damage, unless application is made within three months from the date of this Receipt.

JOHN HUMPHERY, Wharfinger.

	Wharfage and Sufferance.	£.	s.	d.
{ Twenty three Packages }		1	"	"

June

26/11/44

A wharfage notice for Hays Wharf, Southwark. A great amount of West Country produce was carried to Hays Wharf a century and more ago, from Plymouth, Totnes and Dartmouth, Teignmouth and Exeter (including Dartmoor granite from Teignmouth) and Sharpham Reaches. They form a remarkable collection now in the possession of Mr Arthur Brook of Totnes who, until his retirement in 1969, had held the post of Clerk and Surveyor to the River Dart Navigation Commissioners for forty-seven years.

The inconvenience caused by the limitations of tidal unloading at Totnes Quay became at last intolerable, and in 1834 (4 William IV) an Act was passed in Parliament 'for Deepening, Extending and Improving the Navigation of the River Dart, from Totnes Bridge to Langham Wood Point, in the County of Devon'. The then Duke of Somerset was in the forefront of the agitation that brought about the Act and consequent improvement. At that time a sand quay lay a little downstream from the present Baltic Wharf, the Mill Tail was in constant use by shipping and fords on the river were still in use at Ashford Slip (Mill Tail) and near Folly Stickle. Little Hempston Manor stood beside the ancient trackway to the latter ford and tradition has it that none of its windows overlooked the trackside for fear of unlawful entry by marauders. Prior to the Act the increasing size of cargo vessels meant that few of them were able to sail into the port even at high tide, so aggravating the age-old problem of shipping cargoes to and from Totnes. During the early 1830s as many as forty-seven small vessels, each capable of carrying 20 tons, some based at Totnes, some at Dartmouth, were used for the express purpose of trans-shipping Totnes cargoes.

In carrying out the work authorised by the 1834 Act, the Dart Navigation Authority built a wall linking the Island with the new bridge; behind it they dumped stones and silt, so laying foundations for the broad way used by pedestrians today. The Act certainly boosted trade in the Port of Totnes. As early as 1836—indeed, as soon as the dredging had been completed—a company was formed to establish a steamboat service between Dartmouth and Totnes. Exports from Totnes in 1837 included wool, flour, potatoes, leather, serges, Buckfast worsted blankets, willow rods, boots, shoes, cider, and granite, and Bulkamore iron ore and Penn Recca slates. A glance at the Wharfage Notice reproduced here will show that river passenger traffic had become an important source of revenue to shipmasters by 1844. Imports continued to be very numerous, as might be expected where port and quayside facilities

19 A student group at Dartington College of Arts rehearsing a Beethoven string quartet (1978). The players include the author's daughter Anna (at rear), the others being Elspeth Cowey (violin), Michael Jones (violoncello) and Julia Page (viola). The first three players were, by 1981, students at, respectively, the Royal Academy of Music, the Royal Manchester College of Music and the Royal College of Music

20 Totnes Weir. The trees beyond are within the Dartington Hall estate

21 Totnes Bridge. Behind the Seymour Hotel in Bridgetown is the tower of St John the Evangelist's Church. Note the fire-blackened tower window and clock aperture, pictured shortly before restoration

22 An ancient map of Lower Dart, *c* 1540. Top left is Dartington Hall. Below it (to the right) are Totnes town and bridge. Far left is Ashprington Church and below it is Dartmouth, with St Saviour's Church. Opposite Dartmouth is Kingswear. Across the river below Dartmouth is the great barrier chain, with Dartmouth Castle (left) and Gommerock Fort (right). Bottom right is Kingswear Castle. (*British Library MS Cott, Augustus I, vol 1, art 39*)

had been improved and the railway still lay in the future. In 1844 they included coal, culm, wheat, beans, bacon, soap, starch, soda, drapery, saddlery, earthenware vessels, furniture, skins, dyewood, plaster of Paris and mahogany. Carriers, long-distance wagoners, saddlers, ostlers and Dickensian coaches kept the turnpike roads busy and the little townships alive, and the early years of Queen Victoria's reign were on the whole very prosperous ones for the port of Totnes. The *Totnes Times & Gazette* for 13 June 1868 gives the following shipping news:

TOTNES SHIPPING:
Arrivals—Coal, general cargo, culm, casks
Departures—Cider, timber, ballast, umber, cider (again); several light.

The recently inaugurated paddle-steamer service was noticed by the newspaper: 'The fast steamboat "Newcomin" plies between Totnes and Dartmouth daily.' The departure times followed for one week ahead. At that time, steamers of shallow draught were used which were capable of sailing between Totnes and Dartmouth by a fixed schedule regardless of tides. This service was used by passengers to and from Totnes railway station, though many people found the service to London from Dartmouth via Kingswear to be more satisfactory. Customs dues at Totnes in 1893 are displayed on a board at the museum:

1893 Charges for Cargoes:
For every Boatload of Fish exposed for Sale at the Quays or Wharfs   1s. 6d.
For every Bushel of Wheat and Vegetables   1d.
For every three . . . of Leather   6d.
George Windeatt   Town Clerk

Early in the present century a more extensive programme of dredging and port improvement became necessary and work began in 1932, embracing reaches further downstream than previously. It was carried out under the supervision of Arthur Brook (p. 154), by the River Dart Navigation Commissioners; this body is responsible for the control of navigation on the river, including the maintenance (by dredging) of a channel and clearway for shipping, and the imposition of speed limits. From Langham Wood Point to Dart Head the *fundus*, or river bed and banks up to normal water-line, is the property of the Duchy of Cornwall, a boundary declared in 1333.

A modern chapter in the ship-building history of Totnes belongs to the years 1941–5, when Frank Curtis Ltd of Looe built and fitted out twenty-three acoustic minesweepers at their Mill Tail (Totnes) yard for the Royal Navy (*see plate 23*); the first to be completed accompanying the first convoy to sail to Russia. All were built of wood—Devon oak or larch locally grown.

Fibreglass sailing dinghies and trimarans regularly leave the Dartside building yard of Honnor Marine at Seymour Wharf, downstream from the Steamer Quay, for customers as far away as the Pacific coast of North America. The firm was founded shortly after the last war by Pat Honnor, a retired colonel of the Royal Marines—Honnor the Marine. When the firm's sheds were in building and the road being constructed, a deep and extensive layer of sawdust was discovered beneath the surface weeds, indicating the site of Frank Curtis's wartime sawmills. Transporting the sawn timbers to the Mill Tail yard was simply a matter of floating them across on the tide. The Drascombe Flotilla of Honnor's boats are today designed by John Watkinson and built with teak-trimmed glassfibre hulls. Notable voyages undertaken in these Dartside boats include that of David Pyle, who, in 1969 sailed for Australia from Emsworth (Hampshire) in a 'lugger' of 18ft 9in; part of this formidable journey was accomplished by taking the boat overland, and Pyle safely reached his destination in the spring of 1970.

Before the end of last century Messrs John Symons & Co had established a cider factory on the Plains at Mill Tail (*see plate 24*). Their intake of apples frequently included consignments from France—in large quantities during the inter-war years—as well as wagon-loads brought in from the Dart valley farms. The old factory now serves as a store for metal windows and is part of the complex of Messrs Graham Reeves Ltd, whose timber yards are extensive.

Scandinavian ships bring spruce and fir from the Finnish port of Hamina and from Vastervik in Sweden. Graham Reeves also import soft woods from British Columbia on the west coast of Canada; cargoes travel in ships too large to use the navigable Dart, and are discharged at Cardiff and hauled by road to Totnes. Russian redwood and spruce are loaded at Leningrad and carried by chartered German coasters right up to Baltic Wharf. (*See plates 25 and 26.*)

In 1895, Francis John Reeves, successful merchant and son of a Totnes builder, began to import timber, at first through Fox Eliot & Co of Millbay Dock, Plymouth. Finding this new venture profitable, Francis Reeves started to buy timber direct from Scandinavia. Consignments were carried to Totnes by three-masted schooners from Baltic ports, towed up from Dartmouth by steam tug and discharged at St Peter's Quay and Mill Tail. Supplies to customers went out by rail (distant) and horse and wagon (local). The building of Baltic Wharf and associated buildings began in 1961, and today the timber supplies of the huge Reeves Group are distributed from Totnes by road, throughout the West Country from Somerset to Lands End, using a dozen lorries or more a day.

A branch railway line over 6 furlongs in length was planned and built from Totnes station to the Quay as long ago as November 1863. The necessary Act of Parliament was obtained but it forbade steam traction beyond the level crossing built for the bridge approach. At this point, known as Tram Gate, heavy horses took over and hauled timber and apple wagons to and from the Quay terminus. Exports from Buckfastleigh accounted for much of the merchandise carried on the Totnes Quay line. Interesting statistics covering both the Ashburton and Totnes Quay lines are provided in Anthony Kingdom's *The Ashburton Branch* and reproduced here by kind permission of author and publisher:

GOODS TRAFFIC ON THE BRANCH, TAKEN AT ITS ZENITH.

Incoming Traffic

ASHBURTON
Coal—Domestic and loco coal for the engine shed.
Animal feeding stuffs/Farm seed/Fertilizer.

BUCKFASTLEIGH

Coal—Domestic/Commercial for the mills, electricity and gas depots.

Wool/Sheepskin/Hides—from all over the Westcountry and Oxford area.

Farm machinery/Ironwork/pig iron—for the foundry.

Wood pulp/sulphite/clay/resin—for the paper making industry.

Sand and Timber—from the Quay line.

Whitsuns only—Racehorses.

STAVERTON

Meal/Grain.

Timber—for the joinery works.

In addition to the above there were the usual 'pick-up goods' of a general type at all three stations. All traffic differed during the passing of time and the above represents a good cross section during the lines zenith.

General input of coal was 20–25 wagons per week.

General goods traffic was in the region of 40 wagons per day.

Racehorse traffic was at the rate of 60+ horses per meeting.

Outgoing Traffic

ASHBURTON

Umber—for paint manufacturing.

Malt—from Tuckers maltworks.

Milk/Rabbits (from Huntingdon Warren on Dartmoor).

Cattle—outgoing from the 4 cattle fairs per year.

BUCKFASTLEIGH

Wool/serge—mainly despatched to Bradford area.

Quarrystone—arrived at station in steam lorries.

Pelts/Leather.

Timber.

Paper/Newsprint/Wrapping paper—from paper mills.

Cattle/Milk/Rabbits—market trade.

Apples—to the Quay for cyder.

Seed.

STAVERTON

Cyder—from Hills factory.

Furniture etc.,—from Stavertons mills and joinery works.

As for the incoming traffic, there were the 'station truck' despatches of general goods.

General output of coal empties was 20–25 wagons per week.

General output of goods wagons was 20–25 wagons per day.
Cattle trucks from Ashburton fairs were 70 or more per fair.
Horse box traffic was in the region of 10–20 trucks per meeting.

Note:—During the second world war, the American Army had a massive stores complex at Buckfastleigh catering for approximately a $\frac{1}{4}$ million men. There was also a number of 'buffer depots', the storage of food supplies for an emergency during wartime, set up by the Government at Buckfastleigh. Heavy traffic for both of these items were additional to the branch during this time but of course, details are not available.

QUAY LINE GOODS TRAFFIC, TAKEN AT ITS ZENITH.

Incoming Traffic

Sand—dredged from the river Dart and brought to Totnes by barge.
Trees—for Reeves timber yards.
Grain/seed—Holmans warehouses.
Apples—for Symmonds cyder works. (Old Chapel).
Pigs—for Harris bacon factory.

Outgoing Traffic

Timber—from Reeves timber yards.
Cyder—from Symons' works.
Bacon—from Harris factory.

General goods traffic on branch at its zenith was approx 30 wagons per day. In more recent years there were building supplies and engineering goods to Stavertons Works and animal feeding stuffs, grain etc., to South Devon Farmers.

During the second world war, the old racecourse was used for the building of wooden bottomed boats for the war effort and supplies for this industry were carried on the line.

It is scarcely necessary to remark that a waterway such as the navigable Dart is alive with small craft of every description. Sailing, rowing and canoeing are sports seen in action at Totnes throughout the year, and a notice in the *Times & Gazette* for Wednesday 14 August 1867 shows that the Totnes Regatta was even then a successfully organised event.

River Link, the river passenger-boat service between Dartmouth and Totnes is operated by Dart Pleasure Craft Ltd from April to September each year and is well supported, as it deserves to be. The operators have adopted this name to distinguish their service from those of boat owners running trips up the estuary from outside resorts. Two of the company's vessels were formerly operated by the old River Dart Steamboat Co, and three of their fleet took part in the evacuation of troops from Dunkirk in May 1940. For sheer variety of scenery and historical interest, the return river trip to Totnes is, in my opinion, unsurpassed in England. Modern luxury houses standing on wooded banks, and pleasure-boat jetties—features of, for example, the Windermere shores—here give way to historic mansions, ports, quays and creeks of significance in England's history. It is from the river more than any other viewpoint, perhaps, that the rolling nature of the Dartside hills is noticeable. One also is nearer the tree-top heronry between Greenway and Waddeton boathouses, the movements of the young birds in their nests plainly visible.

The open waterway of Dart certainly attracts a greater number of wildlife species than does an inland lake and myself and my family saw an osprey over Ashprington Point, from the deck of the *Dartmouth Castle* on 22 August 1980. Disturbed by the boat in his gliding sweep of the river, the great fish hawk—white patches and 'points' on wings clear to see—made off into the trees overhanging Hackney Creek. It was a moment of great ornithological satisfaction.

The congested summertime roads of the West Country leave train and river boat as incomparably the best ways of reaching Dartmouth and spending a few hours there.

As, river-borne, one moves downstream from the Steamer Quay into Home Reach under the keen eyes of fishing cormorants perched in riverside trees, the homely roofs of Totnes surmounted by church tower and castle keep slip away into a grey distance—the misty background of the river's birthland. The particular mountainous lump in view is that of Hameldon in the eastern highlands of Dartmoor. It is interesting to reflect that the source,

East Dart Head, lies 100ft higher than Hameldon's lofty crest and 30 river miles upstream from Home Reach.

At this point description divides between west and east banks, each taking in stretches of river as convenient, for so much history lies on both sides of the river that this seems the only practicable step.

West Bank to Dartmouth

From Baltic Wharf a riverside path—until World War II a horse and wagon track and before that a carriage drive—follows the right bank and begins a gradual ascent of the valley-side under Higher and Lower Griddle Plantations. Reaching the Sharpham farmlands it joins the drive from Ashprington village and provides a direct link between Sharpham House and Totnes, at which end of the drive formerly stood twin lodges; in constant use in the days of horse-powered transport, it is still known as Sharpham Drive. During the war years many loads of timber felled in Sharpham Woods were taken along it to the yards of Graham Reeves. The mansion at the end of Sharpham Drive occupies an enviable position above the valley on the Sharpham promontory, which declines from 449ft near Ashprington Cross to river level at Sharpham Point. The river boat crews like to tell passengers it is called Calendar House, from its possessing 365 window panes, 52 rooms, 12 corridors, 7 entrance doors and 4 chimney stacks, though alterations and modifications over the years have now effectively dissolved such statistics.

The first Sharpham House was Elizabethan, the birthplace of Edward Drew, Recorder and Serjeant at Law to Queen Elizabeth I as well as Recorder of the cities of London and Exeter. His son, Sir Thomas Drew, was High Sheriff of Devon in the reign of Charles I, and his grandson also, under James II. Sharpham was, however, sold by Edward Drew to John Giles of Bowden. John Prince, in his *Worthies of Devon* (1701) described the house as a 'pleasant seat' with 'a fair prospect of the river ... whose daily flux and reflux affordeth, in the season, the choicest fish and fowl of various kinds, both for recreation and hospitality'. Philip Cockey was occupant in

1749, when a survey was carried out and a plan drawn showing a formal garden reaching down to the very riverside.

The story of Sharpham later leads to Lieutenant Philemon Pownoll RN Commanding HMS *Favourite* off Cape St Mary (Cadiz) in June 1762 he attacked, in company with HMS *Active*, a Spanish galleon, *Ermiona*, carrying great treasure aboard. The Spaniard surrendered after a broadside from *Favourite* and Pownoll boarded her to seize a prize worth £544,658. Its division between the two British ships and allocation of the captains' shares brought Pownoll £64,963. With this he purchased Sharpham, with the intention of demolishing the old house and building for himself a new mansion on its beautiful site. Robert Taylor was commended to him as the best architect for his purpose and building began *c* 1770.

Marcus Binney, who wrote about the architect's work in *Country Life* in July 1967 refers to Sharpham as 'Taylor's masterpiece', where 'the compactness and unity of (his) designs reach their climax'.

A remarkable feature of Sharpham is the elliptical staircase and landing capped by a glass dome; of this architectural masterstroke Marcus Binney wrote:

> Apart from the niches and plaques, the walls are completely bare, leaving nothing to distract from the dazzling conjury of the cantilevered stair. All who set eyes on it ask the same question: how does it stand up. The first flight beginning from terra firma is comprehensible; it is the long broad landing on the first floor that first awakes uneasy feelings especially as one passes the doors and sees that the massive slabs are set less than two inches into the wall. But it is the second flight, 35 steps without a break, that really arouses anxiety. The visible means of support are nil, and the stairs seem suspended like a rope bridge across a Peruvian gorge, and one secretly longs for the security of a stair rail on both sides. It is impossible to pause on this final flight, one is forced to hold one's breath till the top. But neither is the top landing a place to linger, the yawning mouth of the hall floor summons from below, the dome presses down heavily from above. One leaves it at once, concealing a gasp of relief at being on solid foundations again.

Sadly, Pownoll had only ten years in which to enjoy his mansion, for he was killed in action on 15 June 1780. His wife had predeceased him, so that the estate passed to their only daughter, Jane. She promptly eloped to Gretna Green for a secret marriage with Lieutenant Edmund Pollexfen Bastard of Buckland Court. The couple had a son, John, who, inheriting Sharpham, gambled it all away. So the mansion in its idyllic setting passed subsequently through different hands, including those of Richard Durant in the mid-nineteenth century, until, in 1981, it is the home of Mr and Mrs Maurice Ash—Maurice Ash is Chairman of Dartington Hall Trust—who have converted some of the rooms into flats for Dartington students. A piece of sculpture by Henry Moore consisting of two parts and entitled *Reclining Female* stands near the main entrance. This work, although in similar vein to the Dartington *Reclining Woman*, is more abstract in character, as might be expected, because a period of twelve years separates the two works. Another, smaller piece, *Cora* (otherwise *Persephone*) stands on the west side of the house and is a bronze by the late Barbara Hepworth.

Sharpham, astonishingly, is described by Hoskins as 'plain, almost ugly', but I find its unpretentious yet dignified façade a most pleasing and discreet addition to an unspoilt landscape of noble proportions, possessing as it does a river frontage of $2\frac{3}{4}$ miles.

Estate-farm manager Garth Bromley recalls that, during the last war, German fighter planes, with great skill and daring, used to fly low up-river and machine-gun the landing barges of the invasion troops then in training. Swooping up the valley and over Sharpham Hill, the pilots were trigger-happy enough to fire at any group of people they imagined were engaged in military activity; so it was one day that the nuns and pupils of a convent school evacuated from Southsea to Sharpham House, and in disciplined PE formation in the grounds, found themselves targets for a Nazi pilot and quickly had to dive for cover! The marks of the aircraft's cannon shells can still be seen on the fabric of the house.

From the plateau on which Taylor's masterpiece stands and Moore's *Female* reclines, the land, coloured by woodlands and fields of sheep and Jersey cattle, sweeps down to Sharpham Point.

Sharpham Quay, now grass-covered, was constructed for the landing of the Portland stone specified by Taylor for the house, the steep drag up to the building site being accomplished by a team of shire horses. A limekiln and quarry stand at the rear of the quay where limestone was delivered and from which lime fertilizer and building stone were carried away by barges. Beyond an inlet where Sharpham boathouse is situated (also enlivened by student boarders) the steep declivity is clothed by the trees of Great Wood. Its density near the river bank is threaded by Great Run, the path leading to Ashprington Point; on a spring day here my son and I watched the courtship pursuit of mallards over the mudbanks, swans taking off for fresh feeding grounds, two herons fishing, a winged survey of the waters by a great black-backed gull, a cormorant and several shag and shelduck. Over this scene floated the echoing calls of landlubber pheasants in the wood and the mewing of two great buzzards soaring majestically overhead. As we continued along the path, its bank adorned by maidenhair and hart's tongue ferns, our eyes and noses were regaled by bluebells, wild garlic, primroses and anemones. The experience was a complete delight, unspoiled and virtually unchanged over the ages.

High on the north slope of Sharpham Hill the estate has its own 'tor', a slatey outcrop known as the Old Volcano—a name, of course, not literally meaningful. From the hillside field called River Park one can see below the Sharpham Drive slipping into Totnes, while across the river is the conspicuous expanse of bulrushes at the foot of Fleet Mill Creek, a little valley enfolded in the red sandstone hills of south Devon, there topped by Fleet Mill Hill.

For domestic servants and estate workers Sharpham long depended upon the village of Ashprington (Ashprenton in 1588), of which it really is an aristocratic appendage. Aeschbeorcht the Saxon, like many of his fellows, chose a hillside or hilltop site for his settlement rather than the riverside, for his was not a maritime people, and there grew up a perfect nucleated English village. Nothing is known of early Christian worship on the peninsula between Dart and Harbourne, for the beautiful church takes us back only to the fourteenth century, the tower being dated *c* 1350 and the nave a century later. A chamber once existing above the south porch has disappeared, though staircase and door to it remain. An interesting pointer to earlier worship on the site is the chalice, dated by experts at 1275 and the oldest still in use in any parish church in England. Inn (The Durant Arms—Richard Durant appears in the *T. Appt.* of 1844 as resident at 'Sharpham Mansion'), shop, church, school (provided by Richard Durant in 1847) cottages—all are tight together.

From time to time the villagers would visit the seaside resort of Paignton, a journey made on foot via Stoke Gabriel. This entailed walking the long lane from the village to the ferry at Ashprington Point, Duncannon Lane, where high hedgerows are heavy in autumn with the largest wild blackberries I have ever seen and where the mirror of Duncannon Reach sends shafts of rippling light through the hedge near the lane-end gate. Again, all is completely unspoilt. Reaching the gate and descending the grassy slope to the river, the traveller's custom was to call 'Boat ahoy' when the occupant of Ferry House on the Stoke side 'would have the boat out in a jiffy'. The Duncannon ferry worked until 1939. The last ferryman was named Hammick and his father and grandfather had plied there before him. Jack May of Ashprington, now in his late seventies, often made the journey as a child and remembers how the juveniles, at the end of a happy but tiring day, were coaxed up the homeward drag of Duncannon Lane by promises of a prize on reaching home for the largest number of glowworms counted.

The placid River Harbourne, sole tributary of the navigable Dart to rise on high Dartmoor, approaches its beautiful little estuary at Bow Creek south of the village and reaches the ancient crossing place of the Tuckenhay road at Bow Bridge, where ford, steps, arch bridge, overhanging trees and the Waterman's Arms inn create a charming scene. A typical country incident at the Waterman's Arms of sixty years ago is recorded in the *Dartington Rural Archive*, and concerns a Mrs Andrews of Cornworthy who drove everywhere in a donkey trap. The donkey, Charlie, was always treated at the inn to a dish of ale, but sometimes ungratefully declined to resume his journey afterwards. This state of Charlie's suspended animation and the consequent dismay occasioned to his mistress was on one occasion observed by a Mr 'Scratchy' Skedgell on emerging from the taproom. The *Archive* entry relates Scratchy's intervention:

'What's the matter missus? Can't ee get 'im to go?' 'No' said 'Lady Dora' (as Mrs Andrews was locally known), 'I can't get him to go no how'. 'Get up in the trap there missus, and hang on to the reins. I'll get'n to go fur 'ee.' Picking up her long black skirt, Lady Dora got into the trap, made fast her net with pins and took up the reins. Scratchy cut a blackthorn from the hedge nearby, picked up the donkey's tail, put the blackthorn under it and banged the animal's tail down on it. Caw struth, there was no holding Charlie as he swayed along the road to Cornworthy.

As Harbourne widens into its estuary head, Hill Quay stands on the left bank, highest placed of the several Bow Creek quays and one of several purpose-built for the landing of limestone and despatch of lime. A short way downstream the right bank is breached by the incoming River Wash. Between quay and confluence is the fascinating Tuckenhay Quay, its associated buildings forming the environs of a hamlet with an industrial history unequalled in Devon. It appears as 'Tokenhay' in 1550, 'Toke' being a corruption of 'tucking', and 'hay' meaning 'field', really the field of the tucking mill, a site for such work highly favoured here by the plenitude of flowing water. Tucking and fulling—Ambrose Trift paid a tax of £1 12s in 1747 for 'Tuckney Mill living'—in time gave way to paper manufacture, an operation also needing an abundance of water. In 1850 White's *Directory* lists a paper mill, corn mill, quays and working quarries which were supplying stone for London's streets.

Numerous limekilns in the district testify to the demand by farmers in the South Hams for lime as a field fertilizer, produced commercially here and the *T. Appt.* for Ashprington parish in 1831 shows payments by Joseph Coombe of 4s and J. Perring of 15s for land with operating limekilns. Several large kilns remain near the Waterman's Arms: indeed, there were at one time no fewer than fifteen kilns working in and around Bow Creek. Kenneth Isham, in an article appearing in *The Western Morning News* of 16 December 1966, wrote:

In areas where no local limestone was available a considerable trade was carried on along the coast and into the estuaries where kilns were situated to receive the stone from ships and barges. The country around the valley of the Exe was supplied with stone from the Torbay area while the South Hams and the coastal belt of South-east Cornwall obtained their raw material from the extensive quarries in the Plymouth area.

Principal lime merchant at Tuckenhay 140 years ago was Thomas Mudge. Limestone for the Bow Creek kilns came also from the Torbay quarries by water. The success of the lime-burning trade in this particular area largely arose from the demand from the relatively inaccessible farms west of the river, because of the steepness and appalling condition of the roads, which made portage of lime from further afield too costly; deliveries from the Bow Creek and Dartside kilns were practicable because packhorses were used until the widening of many lanes early in the nineteenth century made the two-wheel horse-drawn cart a better means of transport.

Isham states in his article that records show lime was produced in Dart country in the early fifteenth century, and a purchase item of 50 quarters of lime at 10d per quarter appears in the Dartmouth accounts of 1488–9 for use in building the castle tower. In Dartmouth in 1529 2½ quarters of lime cost 2s 6d and in Ashburton in 1566 '2 sacks of lyme' cost the same. Most of this was for builder's mortar and it was not until the late sixteenth century that lime began to be applied to the land. The practice greatly increased in the eighteenth century and the demand for lime as fertiliser rose to unprecedented heights during the Napoleonic wars when so much extra land was placed under cultivation.

Other uses for lime were: mixing with tallow and linseed oil to make a water-proof wash to apply to cottages, and in woollen mills for cleansing hides and sheepskins. Frank Booker, in *Industrial Archaeology of the Tamar Valley*, states that most of the Tamar kilns are likely to date from 1770–1830, and it appears the Dartside kilns are of the same period. The lime was burnt by stacking alternate layers of coal and limestone in the kiln to produce slow combustion, igniting it and securely fastening the door, sometimes with a clay sealer. The heat generated was intense and many kilns had to be replaced or rebuilt during the peak period of the trade. One ton of Plymouth limestone—it came from the quarries of Stonehouse and Cattedown—produced 11cwt of high-grade lime. Charles Vancouver, in *General View of the Agriculture of the County of Devon* (1808), states that 'lime was the prevailing article of manure in most parts of the county' and that manuring consisted of '80 Winchester bushels of lime per acre, mixed with twice the quantity of hedge-row mould, road scrapings, or other fresh soil convenient to be procured'.

An interesting lime-quay lies on the right bank a little over $\frac{1}{2}$ mile below Tuckenhay at a hidden place known as Tin House. A path from the foot of Corkscrew Hill is approached by a flight of steps and stile, but is unfortunately blocked nearer the river. At the site is a small, rounded, grass-grown quay and a kiln with a massive, rounded outer wall. Adjoining it is the ruin of a small cottage where the lime workers lived, in its latter days roofed with corrugated iron—hence the name Tin House—and occupied by a gamekeeper.

At the approach to Tin House a narrow, grassy lane descends to the riverside through a short combe between Corkscrew Hill and Ware Hill; there is little doubt that the disused quarry beside Tin House supplied the actual stone for the building of Cornworthy Priory, which would have been carried up the lane in countless pannier-basket loads by pack-ponies. Stone was also taken from this quarry in 1481 for the completion of Dartmouth Castle.

There once was a ropeworks in Tuckenhay, some ruined walls of which remained until recently in the garden of a house at Orchard Terrace, and the cobbled stone floor of the old works was found beneath the topsoil in the garden by a previous occupier, Mr Sam Cox. The later use of the leat to the works for field irrigation is clearly remembered by Mr Cox. A local student of Tuckenhay's industrial history, Richard A. Evans, has kindly allowed me to quote from a thesis he has written:

> It is easy to imagine this rope being needed by the sailing ships which used the quays and possibly by the shipwrights of the port of

Dartmouth. Although I have not found any written records of this enterprise, I have had confirmation of it from several of the older members of the hamlet, who remember their fathers talking about the place and how the rope was laid out along Darky Lane prior to coiling.

As hemp was grown locally a century or so ago, it is hardly surprising that a hempen rope manufactory should have sprung up in this busy little port.

There is evidence of a former bustling activity on the quays of Tuckenhay. Transport by water of various commodities to and from the hamlet became an established part of its trading during the late eighteenth century, to which period the quays, warehouses and Maltsters' Arms inn belong, and in the mid 1800s shipments of lime, corn, malt, paper, cider and road stone were despatched. Cider and malt were produced on the quayside, where William Manning and John Earle had their cider works and quay, Thomas Mudge his quay, offices and warehouse, and where Thomas Edmonds' malt house gave contemporary authenticity to the Maltsters' Arms inn above. By 1890 John Symons & Co of Totnes had taken over the latter—Mr Symons building for himself the pleasant Victorian residence known as Tuckenhay House near the quays—Robert Trenchard was maltster, manure and lime merchant and importer of coal for the paper mill, and William Samuel licensee of the Maltsters' Arms.

Tuckenhay Corn Mill, situated near the post office, is architecturally odd man out in the hamlet, being built of red sandstone rather than the local stone used for almost every other building. The stone may have come from Roundham Head quarry and been brought to Tuckenhay by water. Relics of the mill's working days include the crushing mill, large waterwheel (intact but rusting) with rim and buckets of iron on wooden 'arms' (spokes), sluice, launder and leat from the River Wash. The transmission of power-drive from waterwheel axle to millstones is by a large wooden cogwheel engaging an iron-toothed cog; the object of this was to avoid the vibration that is inevitably set up when both cogs are of iron.

William Fowler was miller at the close of the last century,

making flour from the grain of Tuckenhay farmers. Charlie Manning, first of the native Tuckenhay 'big time' industrialists, took over in 1912 and developed a flourishing trade in bran for cattle food, his son, Charlie II, following him in 1936. After World War II the mill was used mostly for grinding rough corn (again as foodstuff) and the crushing of local apples for cider.

The silting up of harbours at the mouths of swift rivers has presented an age-old problem already discussed, and one which Tuckenhay has not escaped. A wall long ago built in midstream in the Harbourne estuary to deflect incoming silt from the deep-water channel at the quays can still be seen at low tide. Richard Evans tells of a noteworthy activity of almost 180 years ago:

> One of the smaller buildings just off the River Wash mooring point ... is the old gas-house, erected about 1806 by a Mr Abraham Tucker. In this house he apparently conducted some experiments with gas lighting believed to be an early attempt to light the hamlet. Remarkable when one considers that gas lighting only came to London in 1810.

Cider exports from the Tuckenhay works of John Symons & Co, and later of the Manning family, were by barge. Loading at Manning's was always popular among the bargees as free cider was distributed. The *Dartington Archive* records that the cider in those days:

> ... was made by handpress. Power to crush the apples came from a waterwheel. The men used to walk round and round, pushing the handle of the press to squeeze out the juice. A cooper was employed to see to the barrels, which had to be washed out and stored.

The *Archive* also reports that:

> A Dutch vessel, carrying a load of 360 tons, once got up on a 6ft tide, but most British vessels need 12ft for the Tuckenhay quays. Many vessels have got stuck on the mud, when an unwise captain decided he was not going to wait for the pilot tug from Dartmouth ... When a vessel was on its way from Dartmouth, it was preceeded by a phone message. This was the signal for the man, jokingly known as the 'harbour master', to collect his crew.

The most considerable influence in the life of Tuckenhay has been paper manufacture. The textile process of tucking at Tucking Hay seems likely to have been supplanted by paper-making in about 1829, and in the following year Stephen Spry of Cornworthy—the boundary between that parish and Ashprington follows the right bank of the River Wash—appears in parish records as a 'Papermaker'. The first paper mill certainly was established here by 1829, and another followed in 1832, the two being on opposite banks of the River Wash; it is the first of these, on the right bank, with which Spry was connected, and which continued to work until recently, the other apparently having only a brief existence. White's *Directory* for both 1857 and 1870 give Richard Turner & Son as owners of the working mill; by 1870 as many as 100 men were employed. By 1890, Henry Symons of cider fame had joined in ownership with Turner (the 'Son' of 1857). In 1889 a considerable extension was built on to the mill, including a clock tower. At that time the Vicar and churchwardens of St Mary's, Totnes, wished to replace their Brockeden clock with a more modern one. Symons bought the Brockedon and engaged Mr Borough of Totnes to install it at Tuckenhay Mill, where it is to be seen working today.

In 1910 new vats were installed, and a boom in the paper trade following World War I led to the addition of three more. Paper was produced both for the home market and export trade, including bank-note paper for Siam, Jamaica, Seychelles, Cyprus, 'Double Cap' paper for the *Cape Times* in Johannesburg, ledger paper for gold-mining companies in Tanganyika, and paper used by King George VI for mounting his stamp collection. By this time, Tuckenhay House was occupied by Arthur Millbourn Esq, whose company, under his name, took over the mills, and one of whose sample books is shown here. The firm, then working to full capacity (*see plate 28*), specialised in:

> Best hand-made writings, drawings and ledger papers, loams, bank-notes, cheque papers, old style hand-made printings, vellum parchment for deeds, deckle-edged note and envelope papers.

These products were exported from secluded little Tuckenhay to

India, Malaysia, Burma, Canada, South America, South Africa and Egypt. In 1950 a document bearing the new watermark 'OYEZ' was produced for the Law Society and in the following year came the new Millbourn Blue Wove Long Ledger paper. A change in ownership followed in July 1951 and three years later new machinery was installed; hand- and machine-made paper were, for the first time in the history of the mill, produced side by side, and the Tuckenhay paper workers were proud to make, in 1953, paper for the Proclamation of the Coronation of Queen Elizabeth II. But the great days were nearly over and 5 January 1962 saw the last hand-made paper leave the vats of Tuckenhay; sadly, the production and export of rag-pulp for paper-making took the place of the traditional craft. Cotton rag was the principal medium used and it was sent out in 7 or 8ft bales; linen shotts were supplied for bank notes and twill for strong, heavy paper. The business continued until 1970. Many men of the hamlet have memories of the mill's great days: Tom Wakenham, for twenty years engineer at the mill, remembers when the 240-ton coaster, *Reedness* (*see plate 29*), bringing coal for the mill, went aground in the harbour in

British Hand Made Drawing

Watermarked "A. MILLBOURN & CO. BRITISH HAND MADE."

Royal	.. .. ..	(19 x 24)	44 lbs.

" Not" and "H.P." Surfaces only

Imperial	.. ..	(22 x 30)	60, 72, 90, 140, 300 & 400 lbs.
Double Elephant	..	(26¾ x 40)	133 lbs.

Last two sizes stocked in "Rough," "Not" (Medium) and "H.P." (Smooth) Surfaces

INSIDES 480 Sheets

Made by
ARTHUR MILLBOURN & Co. Ltd.
TUCKENHAY MILLS, TOTNES, DEVON
ENGLAND

Telephone : Harbertonford 230.   Cables : Unbleached, Totnes.

The cover of a sample book (*c* 1950) from Millbourn's paper mills. The tough, fibrous nature of several of the samples makes them virtually indestructible

1932; also huge quantities of paper being loaded on to ships at the quay. Sam Cox was a paper-maker for nearly half a century; his brother Jack worked at the large limekiln near the Waterman's Arms and their father and grandfather had been beatermen at the mill. Jack Lynn of Orchard Terrace made bank-note paper for Singhalese rupees, Siamese tricols, West Indian dollars, Jamaican notes in three colours—red for labourers, yellow for middle class, white for upper class!—£1 notes for the Seychelles and 10s, £1 and £5 notes for Cyprus. He recalls that old army haversacks from World War I were pulped to make vellum, and wood pulp was used to give parchment its characteristic 'rattle'.

In 1977 a London surveyor bought the great mill building and tastefully converted it into holiday flats and cottages with a communal sports centre and swimming bath. His own flat was once the paper-drying loft of the mill and possibly the original tucking mill and 'hay' of Tuckenhay; a leat and large waterwheel pit were found on the east side of the building during the work of conversion.

Behind the paper mill, Edgecombe Lane climbs steeply from the hamlet along the very edge of the deep Wash valley and leads directly to the Cornworthy road beside Edgecombe Barn, offering a delightful walk through a lush, peaceful countryside.

Arthur Manning's coal and corn business involved constant use of Tuckenhay Quay until the outbreak of World War II, all his merchandise arriving by water. Barges carrying 300 tons of coal were unloaded by three men—one each at the basket, wheelbarrow and derrick—who were paid at the rate of threepence per ton. The last ship of any size to discharge her cargo here was the steamer *Reedness* in 1939. Manning then turned to cider-making, using the premises and press formerly worked by Symons & Co. The works were later taken over by his grandson David, until 1980 licensee of the Maltster's Arms.

A successor to the bygone industries of Tuckenhay is the craft of wine-making. On the exterior of the old brew-house beneath the Maltster's Arms is the signboard, 'Pepe & Son Winemakers'. Sicilian born Giuseppe Cannizzario, war veteran and prisoner-of-war in Tunis in 1943, came to England in 1961. Son of a professional wine-making family, Giuseppe settled in Torquay and he eventually realised a long-held ambition to start a winery in England when David Manning offered to rent him the brew-house on the quay at Tuckenhay. He is there filling bottles with wine made from imported grapes that he has crushed with a hand machine, offering all visitors generous samples of his expertise. 'Pepe' makes beautiful wines, full-bodied and with a distinctly individual flavour. This Sicilian craftsman, seen almost daily hovering between vast casks and vats in his dimly lit winery, has yet one ambition to realise: to possess his own vineyard on the sheltered slope of a south Devon valley near the winery. Pepe's products are listed as mead (highly favoured by customers), marsala, cherry wine, Moscaletto, apple wine, rose, rosso (dry red) and bianco (dry white). He started seven years ago with ten barrels and now has 120 in stock.

Below Tuckenhay Quay, Harbourne River pours her waters into the Lake of Dart, so named because the eye from mid-river cannot see any opening. A narrow lane leaves Tuckenhay Bridge to make a zig-zag ascent, behind a small housing estate, of 'the steep and tortuous' Corkscrew Hill to reach Cornworthy Cross. Evans remarks that he has 'walked it many times and has never ceased to wonder at the endurance of children in the past', for the young of Tuckenhay had formerly to walk each day to Cornworthy school. The motor road to Cornworthy, affording striking views of the Tuckenhay mill complex, remains on the west side of the River Wash to its confluence with the River Arl at Mill Pond, where it crosses both streams and passes Edgecombe Barn to reach Cornworthy Cross and Priory Hill. Whether one arrives by car or on foot at the T-junction of lanes there, it is astonishing to behold an impressive medieval structure towering behind the hedgerow of a field, with no apparent entrance. This was the gatehouse of Cornworthy Priory, a convent founded between 1231 and 1238 by a member of the Braose family, lords of the manor of Totnes, for a prioress and twelve nuns of the Augustinian order, and dedicated to St Mary. The choice of this unusually exposed site could have been influenced by the nearby spring, which would reliably have supplied the water needs of the community. Their small income included a proportion of the ecclesiastical living of Cornworthy. The nuns also provided board and lodging and in 1333 took in, by Bishop Grandisson's written permission, 'a certain respectable female called Alice, wife of John Deaumarle, provided she maintained herself without expense or inconvenience to the Nuns, kept suitable hours and was discreet in receiving secular persons'. In 1470, Thomasyn Dynham, Prioress of Cornworthy, asked 'Laurence Knyghte gentleman' to pay 240 pence each a week for his daughters Elizabeth, aged 7, and Jahne, aged 10, whom the convent had taken in 'to teach them to scole'. Prioress Dynham retired in 1520 after ruling the community for half a century and was succeeded by a relative, Avisia Dynham. In 1535, previous to the suppression of all religious houses, the King ordered a valuation to be made of ecclesiastical properties, findings being recorded in *Valor Ecclesiasticus Henry VIII*. The little house at Cornworthy mustered an income of £62 2s 10d, less than half that of either of the other Devonshire convents (Canonsleigh and Polsloe) and less than one sixth of that of Buckfast Abbey. Following the dissolution of the Priory in 1539, when community strength had declined to seven nuns, the Prioress was granted a yearly pension of 13s and the conventual land and buildings were rented to a Thomas Vowell for £6 13s 6d. Mary Pomeroy, a daughter of the noble family of Berry Pomeroy Castle, was for some years a canoness at the Priory. This little religious community lived humbly and peaceably on the outskirts of Cornworthy for nearly 300 years. An informative booklet by Elizabeth Drew, *Cornworthy Priory*, is available in the parish church.

The gatehouse has withstood the ravages of seven centuries remarkably well. The main arch, for horse-drawn wagons, has barrel vaulting, and the small one beside it, for pedestrians, has fan vaulting; the ceilings of both are in good condition and the bosses are worthy of restoration. The workmanship expended on the gatehouse of this tiny nunnery is typical of the Age of Faith. Within the ruin, now totally neglected, another surprise is provided by the perfect state of the spiral staircase approached through a decorated arch on the south side of the gateway, where twenty-five steps lead to the upper floor. Here is a ruined chamber with three window lights, a fireplace and a perfectly preserved garderobe in the south-west corner. Views over Cornworthy village to the east and the Harbourne valley to the west may be seen from this lofty vantage point. There are two window lights in the staircase, one intact, the other crumbling. I am firmly of the opinion that this venerable ruin deserves preservation by the Department of the Environment and hope that this account of it might come to their notice. Of the conventual church and buildings nothing remains; a hollow in the hillside near the spring could have been the convent fishpond. To visit the gatehouse, drive down to the village and stop at Court Prior Farm, where permission can be obtained to enter the field where the ruin stands. It is reasonable to suppose that Court Prior Farm had direct associations with the priory, such as supplying the community with dairy produce.

Cornworthy (Corneworthye in 1588) was the original *Cornworthig* of the Anglo-Saxons, their clearing for cereal growing; although not a waterside village as such, it had to render a substantial payment in fish to the lord of Totnes in the years following the Norman Conquest, and lies mostly on the hillside facing Court Prior Farm and the gatehouse. The parish church of St Peter, dating mainly from the fifteenth century, rises above the village with an overseeing brief more typical of a St Michael dedication. It contains Georgian box-pews and a pulpit with a sounding-board surmounted by an angel with a trumpet. The clear glass windows giving distant views create the impression of height found also at Buckland-in-the-Moor and Buckfastleigh churches. The mounting block at the church gate is a favourite anvil for thrushes needing to crack snail shells, and scores of fragments litter the top step in spring and early summer.

On the north side of the churchyard are two enormous tombstones made of slate marking the graves of children: one is $4\frac{1}{2}$ft wide and over 4ft high. Beyond the churchyard wall is Cornworthy Court Farm, a comparatively modern house surrounded by farm buildings of some antiquity, once thatched, now slate-roofed, with peacocks providing a sound uncommon in

a farm-yard ensemble. It is probable that the farm, now worked by
Mr Donald Hartnell, is of Saxon origin for, as Hoskins writes in
Devon and its People: 'The Saxon farmers at first had their
farmhouses in the village, probably grouped around an open space,
now the village square.' In this case the buildings are adjacent to
the ancient green, or square, a large piece of which was given over
to the building of the Victorian school. In the farm court is the base
of a large apple crusher.

Cornworthy school stands beneath the shadow of the church
tower and was attended by those children from Tuckenhay. The
east wall bears the emblem of a boar with a dagger in its back and
the initials 'RD'—Richard Durant of Sharpham.

White's *Directory* of 1850 mentions the excellence of cider then
produced in the parish, a trade discontinued many years ago. It also
records that the village was served by 'Foot post daily to Totnes,
the nearest Money Order Office'. Tides, of course, would have
made a predictable river post uncertain, especially as Cornworthy
is nearer Harbourne than Dart. Two steep little combes open
below the high ridge of Furze Hill—where views over the village
are very fine—separated by the gently rising 333ft point of Ware
Hill; beyond the combes come glimpses of the land above Bow
Creek rising steeply to the Sharpham lands, while the East
Cornworthy road, ascending above the priory via Water Lane and
running due east from the ridgeway junctions of Furze Hill Cross,
Butts Cross and Longland Cross reaches a height of 434ft before
plunging down to Dartside, giving breathtaking glimpses from
successive gateways of that beautiful reach of the river known as
Long Stream, with Stoke Gabriel village on the opposite bank.

A lane leaves the ridgeway road at the sign 'Whitestone Farm'
and descends to the riverside settlement of that name, called after
the field name of the enclosure immediately above White Rock. Mr
Edmund Drew (a descendant of that Elizabethan Edward Drew of
old Sharpham House) and Mrs Elizabeth Drew (author of the
Cornworthy Priory booklet) are fruit farmers, growing Bramley
apples for the wholesale market, and occupying a pleasant modern
house beside the ancient North Barn. This barn has a linhay
supported by rounded pillars of slate set in courses, a feature in

general unusual but found elsewhere in Dart estuary country.

The large river frontage of the farmlands extends into the Harbourne estuary not far short of Tin House. Following the riverside, a path leads to Middle Back Shoal and White Rock, the first a shingle bank and the second a large crag of slaty rock standing somewhat away from the shore and speckled with white and yellow lichens—and, inevitably, seabird droppings: hence, White Rock. The path then threads Kirkham Copse, where the mew of the buzzard rings loud, and its upstream extremity is the mouth of the River Harbourne. Here I have watched fishermen trawling for salmon off Langham Wood Point, where the wash from two simultaneously passing passenger vessels causes the float corks of the net to bob madly in the tributary estuary well past the '6 KNOT' sign. Twin wrecks—Tamar stone-carrying barges which can be seen at low water—once constituted a hazard to shipping off Langham Wood Point. Following the outbreak of World War II, Arthur Brook was instructed by the Admiralty to clear all navigable waters of derelict craft. So the twin barges, likely once to have carried Plymouth limestone from the Plymouth quarries to Bow Creek limekilns were consigned beam to beam to their final resting place in Harbourne mud.

The not easily motorable twists in the long, eccentric descent from the ridgeway bring it to the head of Dittisham Creek, where stands Brambletor Mill, with its brick- and stone-built launder and wooden elbow conduit constructed to supply the still remaining waterwheel; this is unusual in being a 'pitch-back' wheel that receives water just below the crest, with wooden buckets and arms, and iron rim. Nearby are two millstones (one of granite), the crown wheel with wooden cogs and part of a smaller circular stone beside the garden path. Below the mill, which, like most water-mills, is an attractive old building, a track crosses the stream and leads to private houses; in one of these, formed from two old cottages, once lived a notable personality named Dinah; hence that side (left bank) of the creek is known as Dinah's Side. Also beside the creek are four limekilns and quays. As the creek widens, the houses of Higher Dittisham appear above the right bank to mark the curve of Lower Street. At the bottom of the street the road is crossed by a stony lane squeezed between garden walls as it comes up from the beach of Dittisham Mill Creek: this is Swyre Lane. If the reader approaches the village from Cornworthy, he is advised to drive up Lower Street and park near the church, returning on foot along the street and turning into Swyre Lane down to the beach. Something of the atmosphere of old Higher Dittisham can be captured in this way.

It is also rewarding to approach the centre and Dartside areas of the village from the elevated Hemborough Post road. Descending Dittisham Hill, one passes in succession Dittisham school, the Red Lion Inn, post office and parish church—establishments of the

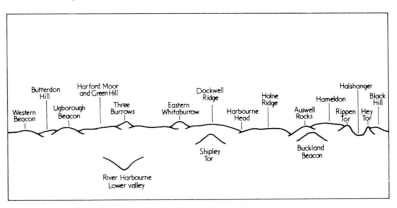

A panoramic view of Dartmoor, northward from the lay-by at the top of Dittisham Hill. Cut Hill is visible only from the superior height of Fire Beacon Hill

very essence of an English village—all standing in relief against the backcloth of the glittering Dart with its tiny white craft and the luxuriantly wooded country beyond. It is sensible to park that motor car: it can only be a liability in Dittisham's tortuous streets, which in any case are fascinating to follow on foot.

In 765 Dida or Deeda the Saxon founded his 'ham' or settlement, not, like those of his Dart country contemporaries on the hillside or top, but at the waterside. It is Didasham in the Domesday Book, Diddisham in 1230, Dyteshamme 1340 and Dytsham in 1557. From this may be realised the correct pronunciation 'Dittis-ham' rather than 'Ditti-sham', which is so often heard; like Topsham on the River Exe, it is not a 'sham' but a 'ham'. Locally, it is 'Dits'ham'.

St George's Church, built of local ashlar stone and dedicated to the saint by Bishop Grandisson on 4 October 1333, contains a beautiful late-medieval stone pulpit of Devon 'wine-glass' design, painted and gilded, bearing figures and vine-leaf decoration; a fifteenth century oak screen (no longer intact) and—a relic of an earlier church on the site in Norman times—a font of red sandstone. There are two side chapels, each with a hagioscope (squint) affording a view of the high altar, and a priest's chamber above the fine south porch. Members of the Strode family were rectors from 1583–1632.

The famous damson and Victoria-plum orchards of the parish have furnished south Devon with delectable fruits for many centuries. At one time every cottager had his plum orchard and sold his harvest at Totnes and Paignton markets, journeys necessitating portage on foot and by water of heavy baskets of plums. Older people in the parish, including the Rector, the Revd John Price, and Mr William Chapple of Hole, can remember two sisters, Mrs Allen and Mrs Fletcher, plying on the river as carriers and calling at all the quays. Their services, in constant demand, were important to the riverside communities in those days of inferior roads and were considerably stretched in plum-harvest time, when donkeys brought down the laden baskets for them to collect. The Rector and Mr Chapple also well remember the coal-fired paddle steamers which once were such a picturesque feature of the river's summertime traffic, and used to call at Dittisham Quay. Near the quay, until the war years wrought their changes, was a tavern, another Waterman's Arms, kept in 1850 by Thomas Beer, described in White's *Directory* of that year as 'land-lord, mason and ferryman'.

The tourists' mecca here, understandably, is Lower Dittisham—beach, jetty, ferry and the Ferry Boat Inn. Downstream is the Anchor Stone whereon, say the guide-books, Sir Walter Raleigh customarily sat to smoke his pipe, ostensibly without a care in the world; he would nowadays find it an uncomfortable perch, an iron stake having been driven into the rock as a warning to river traffic. After the Anchor Stone come Tippity Van, Vipers Quay and Parson's Mud, though the books are silent on these specimens of quaint nomenclature. The only explanation I can offer of Tippity Van is to say that a 'tippity' place in the West Country is a dumping ground and that there is one near here. The sun-baked stones of Vipers Quay, before our noisy mechanized times, were much favoured by basking adders, while overlooking Parson's Mud is Lord's Wood, which is surely as it should be: Parson's Mud was a rather unfruitful part of the rectory glebe and Lord's Wood belonged to the lord of the manor.

The deep valley of Balcombe Pits, where slate was quarried for building over the centuries by shallow mining, owes its name to *bal*—a mine—*combe*—a valley closed at one end—and 'pits'— hollows in the ground caused by mining. Local tradition is strong in claiming that on the hilltop above Rough Hole Point in 1620 the leader of the Pilgrim Fathers, William Brewster, mustered the entire company of their two ships and held a service to pray for God's blessing on their coming voyage and fortunes. Dartmouth, knowing beforehand of their intention—and notwithstanding a destiny twenty years later to declare for the Parliamentary cause— let it be known that Puritan extremists would not be welcome in any place of worship in the town; hence the hilltop service near Balcombe. Dissatisfaction among Christians with the early seventeenth-century government of the Church of England under James I had resulted in a growing tendency towards the simple style of Bible-inspired life and worship known as Puritanism. A group of these Bible Christians successfully petitioned the King to be allowed to found a colony on the east coast of North America in order to follow their religious rule and in 1620 seventy-eight men, twenty-four women and an unspecified number of children set sail in the *Mayflower* (180 tons) and *Speedwell* (60 tons) from Southampton, calling at Dartmouth prior to what was, for most of them, their last contact with English soil at Plymouth. Here the more widely publicised departure of the *Mayflower* took place from an old stone pier called the Causeway, demolished a few years afterwards, its site, now marked by a plaque, replaced by the Steps that have ever since born the ship's name. 'Speedwell' was a palpable misnomer for the smaller ship: leaking timbers slowed her progress from the outset and calls at Dartmouth and Plymouth were not for victualling but in order to effect repairs. At Plymouth, indeed, it became necessary to abandon *Speedwell*. Twenty of the original passengers having withdrawn, Mayflower sailed alone on 16 September with 102 persons on board, 'all being compacte togeather in one shippe, they put to sea againe with a prosperus winde', and dropped anchor in Cape Cod harbour, New England, on 21 November 1620.

Mention of manorial land and rectorial glebe leads me to say that, as Edward the Confessor presented some 3,000 acres of land in Devon to the Bishop of Exeter when Crediton was the seat of diocese (909–1050), the parish priest of Dittisham greatly benefited by the bishop's presentation to the living of that portion of the land lying within his parish, both as manor and glebe. So the incumbent became at one stroke lord of the manor and rector (a priest holding glebe-land, which a vicar does not). The Revd Price's successors have sold it off in parcels until, today, his glebe and manor consists only of one small orchard! Whether, in Norman times, a baron was given a slice of this ecclesiastical cake by a whim of the Conqueror's is not known, but below Hole Farm (see p. 43 for 'hole') is Baron's Hill, from where at point 445 may be seen a fine view of Dartmouth with the Britannia Royal Naval College pre-eminent.

The age-old fire beacon of Dittisham lies east of Foxenhole, which is beside the Hemborough Post road. It is incorrectly shown on OS maps as east of the by-road to Hole, whereas it is west of it and between that road and the major one, from which it diverges at Bosomzeal Cross. Enclosed by a ring of fir trees planted many years ago by the Raleigh estate, it is a shallow, grass-overgrown basin and provides a spectacular viewpoint. Polwhele mentions 'Fire-beacon-Hill in Ditsham parish' in his *History of Devonshire* (1747) as a tremendous viewpoint. The bold, blue-grey hills of southern Dartmoor, 12 miles to the north, range west-east 15 direct miles from Western Beacon above Ivybridge, across the great depression at the foot of the Moor of the border-country Dart, to Pinchaford Ball above Bovey Tracey. The dimension of depth takes the eye to the very heart of northern Dartmoor, where the mountainous dome of Cut Hill rises to almost 2000ft above the broad, yacht-spangled river below. The beautiful and more homespun mid-distance view is of the river, at Longstream backed by the church and houses of Stoke Gabriel, the valley of the River Harbourne from its distant head on the Moor to the hollow it has excavated at Bow Creek, ploughed fields and meadows of green, gold, russet and brown spread along its edge like so many garments laid out to dry in the summer sun, and—historically of visual significance—the castle keep at Totnes. St Mary's Church there also is visible, others being those of Holne, Broadhempston, Ashprington, Torquay St Marychurch, Dittisham and Townstal. Important inter-beacon visibility includes the destroyed beacon site above Dartmouth, Yarner—so that Dartington Hall and village could have received instant fire signals from the coast—and Western, overlooking Plymouth Sound itself.

Downstream from Dittisham Reach the river is a very busy waterway, bearing many and varied craft. At Rough Hole Point, where herons, bass and conger eel abound, is the mouth of the Old Mill Creek, the tidal foot of a hidden stream watering Old Mill Valley and fed by a series of springs and streamlets on the valley-sides, including those from Hemborough, Brown's Norton, Norton Park, New Barn, Bruckton, Downton and Lapthorn. Round the valley head runs the ridge road from Dittisham to Dartmouth where the Sportsman's Arms inn marks a crossroads of antiquity. I sat at a rustic table outside the inn on a sunny, windy May day, enjoying my pasty and ale and watching the Dartmouth road twisting away before me. It was peaceful, the only sounds being of an occasional passing car, the wind agitating the creaking inn sign and the cry of lapwing wheeling and diving over this practically treeless plateau. Eastward the land falls away to Hemborough and the depth of Old Mill Valley, while equidistant to the west are the headsprings of Barberry Water, which has cut its own scenic little valley and once supplied the leat for the waterwheel of Brambletor Mill before following a serpentine course through Dittisham Creek to the river.

Old Mill Valley is so called from the former existence of a grist mill at the head of the creek, where a narrow lane comes down from Bruckton Cross on the Hemborough Post road, passes the entrance to Chipton and reaches the valley floor below the Dartmouth reservoir. The reservoir, overshadowed by trees, looks every inch a natural tarn and can be seen from a forest path leaving the road to the right near the foot of the hill. The lane turns to follow the valley to the creek, which at normal tide limit is 13ft above sea level—that is, 1,827ft below East Dart Head. The sturdy building beside the stream, the one-time mill, has been subject to much alteration and over the original arch entrance to the mill appears a plaque that reads:

Dartmouth Corporation Water Works
Pumping Station   Erected 1908
John Brown Esq., J.P. Mayor

'Erected' as such refers to the adaptation of the building and installation of pumping and filtering plant. The old mill leat, of large capacity, is still traceable a short way up the valley where it is very overgrown, and as it twists to approach the site of the mill-pond it fringes the well-kept lawn of the waterworks. The mill must have been disused by 1841, when the *T. Appt.* gives no details and the Tithes map no plot number. Old Mill Cottage was then occupied by Richard Coombes. The waterworks people have their own name for the otherwise anonymous stream watering the valley—Downton Meadow Flow. The pumping station works only during the summer months to provide a supplementary supply to packed, holiday-time Dartmouth, whose main supply comes from the Avon reservoir above Shipley on southern Dartmoor.

Immediately below the mill the valley widens into the creek, a deep, hidden defile overhung by trees on both sides and secreting many small craft, one of them an old ferry pontoon once used on the Dartmouth Lower Ferry. This has now been put to practical, if static, use again by having a tool shed built upon the deck. In the summer of 1856 a whale made its way up the creek to Old Mill Bridge and, becoming stranded, 'was taken by some fishermen' (R. Cranford, *Up and Down the River Dart*). Now, something far larger and more damaging than any whale is trying to make its way into this naturally beautiful little creek: a scheme to create yet another marina. James Mildren wrote in the *Western Morning News* on 23 July 1980:

> The autobiography of the River Dart is literature in wildlife and singing waters. It was not, however, the prospect of listening to the pinion feathers of seabirds beating a path across the rippling estuary, but a piece of advance information. Yet another marina is being contemplated for Dartside. The project will cost £10 million and the likeliest location is just around the corner from the Britannia Royal Naval College at an inlet called Mill Creek.
>
> We now have in this country a land ethic (of preservation). Isn't the time ripe for a water ethic as well?
>
> A creek—an estuary—fulfils an ecological need in much the same way, perhaps as a church—or a cathedral—satisfies man's spiritual requirement.

The inevitable limekiln yawns from the stony hillside on the left. The lane branches right over Old Mill Bridge and up Old Mill Lane on the opposite hillside to Townstal (Dartmouth), or straight on to enter the steep tributary valley of Hole. A small car park exists about a quarter of a mile along this lane, which clings unconvincingly to the very edge of the high bank, beyond which it becomes a rough track leading to Hole and Balcombe Pits. A stream rushes steeply through the 'hole' and beneath an overgrown bridge carrying the track; here the hills are a mass of loose slate and the slopes a conifer nursery of Fountain Forestry Ltd. As the track turns towards Balcombe Pits glimpses are seen through the trees of Great Copse, Rough Hole Point and, beyond, the sheds and cranes of Philip's Noss shipyard. It has to be said that, in contrast, the modern housing estate at Townstal on the crest of the creek's south side does not beautify the scene. The dome of Balcombe Pits Hill rises above Balcombe Pits Copse.

Below the car park is a branch drive to the works of Creekside Boatyard Ltd, whose slipways for fitting out and laying up, and the installation of electronic equipment in customers' boats under the direction of Mr Stan Mitchelmore, form a busy establishment.

On the right bank are two more limekilns and the remains of

two cottages in which lime-burners lived. One of them (named Pickford) is remembered by Tom Hughes of Townstal, who was then a boy. A derelict vessel near the kilns, now practically 'fused' with the bank of the creek, was the salvage ship *Ernie Lister*. Beyond the ruined cottages, the path continues through the trees at some height above the water. It passes by an uncompleted limekiln, for which the kiln mouth was expertly hewn from the solid rock and the interior recessed above a low ledge. A short way from the kiln and now surrounded by trees is the highly intriguing ruin of Hermitage Castle, known to locals as Castle-in-the-Wood. It is mentioned by Cranford in *Up and Down the River Dart*:

> A pleasant excursion by rowing boat can be made up this Creek at high water to the "Castle in the Wood", near its extremity, which has embrasures and platform for cannon, ingeniously arranged with a half-ruined gateway and dilapidated wall, to represent the remains of a fort. It has long been unoccupied and has fallen into decay. This castle can be seen from the steamer as we pass the Creek.

This extraordinary folly is of circular construction with an internal diameter of 12ft 8in. Steps lead down to the heavily silted-up cellar as well as up to the now-vanished roof and the two intermediate storeys above the ground floor, their positions indicated by beam holes in the wall. The folly was built by Sir John Henry Seale, an active eighteenth-century landowner of Dartmouth who lived at Mount Boone, married Sarah Hayne of Lupton and in 1794 was made High Sheriff of Devon. The open parkland below the Royal Naval College, formerly fields and orchards, was converted to its present state by Seale. He was a fervent romantic, much given to the construction of expensive follies and non-functional buildings. (The lodge and bridge at the head of Old Mill Lane were his work.) So, on the south bank of Old Mill Creek he built a defensive fort to defend nothing more tangible than his own extravagant dreams. A descendant of his, Charles Seale-Hayne, was founder of the celebrated agricultural college of Seale-Hayne near Newton Abbot.

The windows of the folly tower open upon the length of the creek, commanding a view of its mouth and the east bank of Dart beyond. A lovely place in which to indulge the imagination. The

23 Royal Naval minesweeper 1040 (built at Totnes during World War II) on sea trials. The large drum mounted at the stern carried electric cable to energise a magnetic sweep of the water

24 The old cider factory of John Symons & Co at Mill Tail

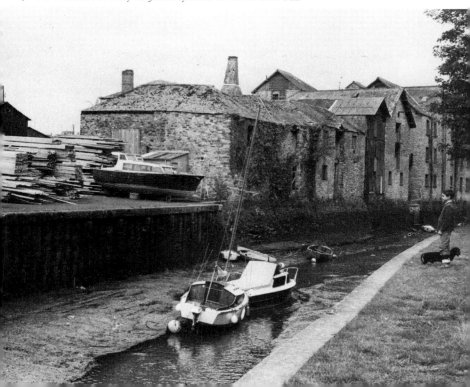

25 The three-masted schooner *Ekonom* from Russia discharging a timber consignment for E. J. Reeves at Mill Tail, Totnes. The trees in the background are on the Island. Note the laborious method of unloading, and the carter with a whip over his shoulder. (*Photo processed by Nicholas Horn, courtesy of Graham Reeves Ltd*)

26 Timber stacks at the Baltic Wharf of Graham Reeves Ltd at the Port of Totnes. The castle and church appear on either side of the mast. (*Photo Nicholas Horn, courtesy of Graham Reeves Ltd*)

folly is marked on the Tithes map of 1841 as 'Fortress and Castle Cottage' occupied at that time by Samuel Treeby. Behind the buildings (in the wood) was Gunners Garden and below them the wide opening of Old Mill Bay. From the old, low bridge, Old Mill Lane climbs the close contours of the south hillside with elbow-bends and twists, affording fine glimpses of the main valley, especially of the big curve between Vipers Quay and Rough Hole Point. The length and steepness of the climb are due to the situation of Townstal, to which it leads, 350ft above Old Mill Bridge, the fine tower of St Clement's Church dominating the scene as the lane reaches level ground—as level, that is, as any ground in Dartmouth, other than on the waterfront. Percy Russell observes in his *Dartmouth*:

> The Saxons, early in the 8th century, . . . spread over the lands which they found to be intersected not only by the creeks of the Dart, but by those of the extensive harbour of Salcombe and by the estuaries of the Avon and the Erme. Their descriptive name of all these water-hemmed lands was the South Hams.

It is fitting to reach Dartmouth by way of Townstal, which was the parent village of the waterside community far below. It was the 'Dunestal' ('homestead on a hill') of the Domesday Book, held by Walter de Douai. William Fitz Stephan, lord of the manor of 'Tunstal' in 1200, granted the church (an earlier building) to the Abbey of Torre. The present church, dedicated to St Clement in May 1318 by Bishop Stapledon, contains traces of Norman work but was badly over-restored in the nineteenth century. It is a fine church, peaceful and spacious, certainly 'of a beautiful and stately character' as the authors of the church history leaflet claim, with several interesting features, including the three beautiful arches of the nave and the lofty west arch, a piscina in each of the large transepts (where once also were altars) and an extraordinary leper squint, shaped like an eye and focussed upon the high altar from *outside* the church. Several strange old tombs in the churchyard are of nautical commemoration, having a monumental cross on a shaft entwined with anchor chain (or rope) and anchor.

On 23 January 1539 Sir William Petre, one of Thomas

Cromwell's agents for the dissolution of the monasteries, visited the wealthy Torre Abbey, round which spreads modern Torquay, when the last abbot, Simon Rede, signed the deed of surrender. Rede had already opted for the course of non-opposition and been promised the incumbency (as Vicar) of Townstal. Born at Stoke Fleming, he remained at Townstal as Vicar until his death in 1555 or 1556.

Townstal St Clement was once the parish church of—to give the town its full name—Clifton-Dartmouth-Hardness: it stands at the head of a hard 'ness' or ridge (*cf Tota's Ness*) that runs down to the great natural harbour of Dartmouth with houses clinging to its steep south side in the manner of a 'cliff town'. Only the briefest sketch can be given here of a town and port of such historic renown as Dartmouth, but there are many books available telling its story; it is impossible to better Russell's *Dartmouth* and the long entry in the gazetteer of Hoskins's *Devon*. The outstanding events of the centuries are given here in calendar form. The first three dated events are taken from the River Dart historical chart (*see Appendix C*).

Early post-Conquest The Norman 'landed gentry' appreciate the convenience of Dartmouth harbour as the best terminal for journeys between their Normandy estates and south Devon. The harbourside village grows. Duke William makes Walter de Douai responsible for the protection of the approaches to the harbour. The duke also makes a gift of Totnes to Judhael and of Stoke to Hudl the Fleming.

1099 William Rufus, hunting on Dartmoor, receives word that his dominion at Le Mans is under siege. He gathers his followers, rides to Dartmouth and embarks.

1147 **23 May** An international fleet of 164 vessels assembles in Warfleet Creek for the Second Crusade.

1154 Henry II annexes Bordeaux and wines are brought over to Dartmouth. The January wine fleet gives additional employment to the Dart fishermen.

1190 **18 May** Dartmouth provides seven ships to join the fleet of Richard Coeur de Lion at Messian for the Third Crusade. The seamen are given twelve months' wages in advance.

1192 Richard Fleming, returning from the Third Crusade, is presented by William Fitz Stephan (lord of the manor of Tunstal) with 'all

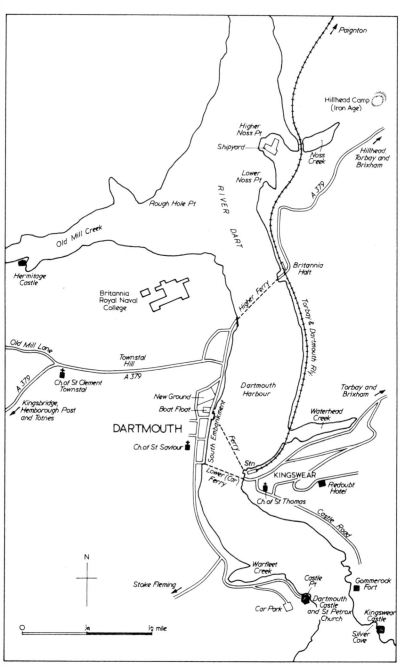

The Port of Dartmouth and Kingswear

the land of Dertmuta ... between the monastery of St Peter and the land of Stoke'. (H. W. Watkin suggests in *TDA* 61 of 1929 that the first Fleming of Stoke, if not Walter de Douai himself, established a small colony of monks to keep watch and ward; that their lamp, ever burning before the altar of St Petrox, was probably the first beacon permanently established at the mouth of the 'Derte'—as the name of the river was always written until comparatively recent times.)

1224   Dartmouth merchants co-operate in providing vessels for royal service.

1231   Richard Fitz Stephan obtains a royal grant of a weekly market and annual fair.

1275   Wine imports reach a new peak. Totnes claims a slice of the pie by levying dues.

1286   **February** Edward I visits Dartmouth. He secures its independence from Townstal by licensing the erection of a new parish church, dedicated to St Saviour, on the harbourside.

1332   Bishop Grandisson of Exeter licenses two priests to celebrate Mass in the chapel of St Petrox, within Dartmouth castle precinct. (The chapel dedicated to St Petrox is said to have existed on an ancient Christian site high above the harbour entrance. It is presumed to have been abandoned prior to the Bishop's licence.)

1341   Edward III signs a charter granting independence and borough status to 'Dertmuthe'. William Clarke becomes the first mayor.

1347   Dartmouth contributes 31 ships and 757 men to a force under Edward III for a siege of Calais.

1351   The Borough of Dartmouth returns its first MP to Westminster.

1370   Construction begins of the chapel of the Holy Trinity by licence of Bishop Brantyngham.

1372   **13 October** The chapel is consecrated by the Bishop. It is soon to become known as St Saviour's but was still referred to in 1437 registers of Bishop Lacy as 'The Chapel of the Holy Trinity of Dertemuth newly built'.

1373   Geoffrey Chaucer visits Dartmouth. He meets John Hawley, famous shipmaster of Dartmouth, merchant, privateer. Hawley is thought to be Chaucer's model for the 'shipman' in *The Canterbury Tales*. The poet writes in his Prologue:

> A SHIPMAN was ther, woninge fer by weste:
> For aught I woot, he was of Dertemouthe ...
> He knew alle the havenes, as they were,
> Fro Gootlond to the cape of Finistere,
> And every crike in Britaigne and in Spaine,
> His barge ycleped was the Maudelaine.

1377 The town is raided and partly burnt by the French.

1388 John Hawley begins the construction of a stone castle, but the work is abandoned within a short time.

1390 A royal directive is obtained ordaining that for three years 'the export of tin to foreign parts shall be from Dertemouth and from nowhere else'.

1393 John de Holand, Earl of Huntingdon, builder of Dartington Hall, becomes the proprietory lord of Dartmouth.

1408 **30 December** Death of John Hawley. He is buried at St Saviour's where he had built the chancel.

1438 Bishop Lacy grants forty days' Indulgences for the building, maintaining and repairing of the parochial chapel with the cure of St Petrox.

1474 The first documentary reference to the former signal beacon above Dartmouth harbour: 'Land between Baken parkes and Le Verebekyn'. (All traces vanished in the twentieth century when a water tower was erected on the site.)

1481 Work on Dartmouth Castle, already restarted, is supported by an annual grant of £30 by Edward IV, who directs that a defence chain be made to span the mouth of the haven. Some stone for the castle is brought down the river from Cornworthy Quarry.

1488 The great barrier chain is installed. Henry VII increases the annuity to £40.

1509–10 Bayard's Cove Castle is constructed by a directive of Henry VIII. It is an artillery fort with eleven gun ports at ground level and an upper rampart walk for the lookout.

1533 Parliament issues a decree to protect Dartmouth (and other havens) from silting up by tinners' wastes.

1536 Humphrey Gilbert, navigator and explorer, is born at (old) Greenway.

1538 Leland (page 135) visits Dartmouth. He writes of the tidal mills:

> There is only a bay filled by fluddes with salt water, driving at the ebbe 2 mills that divideth Ardenes [Hardness] from Dartmouth Town.

1550 John Davis, navigator, explorer, is born at Sandridge Barton.

1578 Sir Humphrey Gilbert assembles ships for an abortive voyage of discovery:

Ann Ager Sir Humphrey Gilbert	250 tons	126 men
Hope of Greenway Carey Ralegh	160	80
Falcon Sir Walter Raleigh	100	70
Red Lion Miles Morgan	110	53

Joined by Henry Knollys and five ships out of London.

1583 **11 June** The second expedition of Sir Humphrey Gilbert accompanied by John Gilbert and half-brother Sir Walter Raleigh: *Golden Hinde* (40 tons), *Delight* (120 tons), *Bark Ralegh* (260 tons), *Swallow, Squirrel*. The expedition is successful.

5 August The expedition of 11 June formally claims Newfoundland for Queen Elizabeth I.

9 September Sir Humphrey Gilbert dies at sea.

1588 The year of the Armada. The *Crescent* of Dartmouth engages ships of the Spanish fleet off Start Point. Archival records include an account of over twenty pages endorsed:

> 1588, the booke of all ye vittayling and al other charges bestowed upon the *Crescent* Captayne John Wilson and the *Harte* Captayne James Houston in setting them forthe to serve the Queen's Majestie under my Lord Admyral Sir Francis Drake as followyth, the first day of Maye the *Crescent* for seventy men and the *Harte* for thirty men.

The sailors, who are given four months' pay at the end of August, came from the Dart country villages of 'Ashprenton, Corneworthy, Stoke Fleming, Dytsham', as well as from places farther afield. The accounts show the thoroughness of the equipping. The first five entries are for biscuit—cost, £37 2s 10d. Next for beer—125 hogsheads at 10s 6d per hogshead; then beef and pork, some fresh, some salted. (A large proportion of the beef and pork is from Totnes—evidently the fresh.) Also, coarse and dried fish, and three barrels of butter (weighing 349lb and costing £5 10s 4d, being 4d per pound). Peas cost 3s 8d per hogshead. Then there are large quantities of wood, many pounds of candles at 5d per pound and tallow at 6s 8d per stone. (Edward Windeatt in *TDA* 12 of 1880.)

1589 66 burials of plague victims at St Saviour's Church.

1601 **18 April** The first voyage of the East India Company, commanded by John Davis of Sandridge. Capital of £72,000 is subscribed. The ships are *Red Dragon*, *Hector*, *Ascension*, *Susan* and *Guest* and there are 500 sailors. It is a prosperous voyage.

1605 John Davis is slain by Japanese pirates.

1615 124 plague victims are buried at St Saviour's.

1620 **August** The Pilgrim Father's vessels *Speedwell* and *Mayflower* lie in Dartmouth harbour for repairs to *Speedwell*.

20 August The ships sail from Bayard's Cove.

1643–4 A Royalist occupation of the town under the governor, Colonel Seymour. The governor is ordered by Sir John Pennington in Bristol to permit Captain Boone to requisition the ships then in the harbour into the King's service. Pennington proposes to send ships from Barnstaple to join the fleet at Dartmouth. Kingswear Castle is repaired. Dartmouth shore batteries and St Petrox (used as a reserve provision store for troops) are prepared for defensive action; 140 new links are made for the great chain. Royalist redoubts are constructed at Mount Ridley and Gallants Bower: the former is garrisoned by Sir Henry Gary of Cockington; the latter, an earthwork of five bastions with the main bastion faced in stone, is garrisoned by Sir Hugh Pollard. The town is nevertheless shortly to surrender to the Parliamentarians.

1646 **14 January** Dartmouth surrenders to Sir Thomas Fairfax and the Parliamentary troops, who approach via Halwell, Stoke Fleming and Dittisham, having taken Totnes on 11 January.

1663 The birth of Thomas Newcomen, a Dartmouth ironmonger and the inventor of the steam pumping engine. Several are installed in Cornish mines. Success leads other mining areas to follow, including some on the Continent. An engine is built for Pentrich Colliery, Derbyshire, in 1791, sixty-two years after the inventor's death. (It continued to work until 1918 and is now in the Science Museum, South Kensington.)

1671 **21 July** Charles II is the first English sovereign to land at Dartmouth since Edward I in 1286. The interior of St Saviour's Church is newly painted and gilded for the occasion by Christopher Lock.

1684 New Ground Quay is embanked for the first time. A small stone bridge is built to link it with the Butterwalk.

1724 Daniel Defoe visits Dartmouth. He reports that the citizens are 'great traders to Newfoundland', that Dartmouth sends out large cod-fishing fleets, and that the pilchard trade is 'hereabouts carried on with the greatest number of vessels of any port, except Falmouth'.

1725 All-metal parts are introduced into the Newcomen steam pumping engines.

1729 The death of Newcomen.

1739 Bayard's Cove gets a brick-built customs house.

1740 The two tidal mills are acquired by the town. They are leased at £61 per annum. New Ground Quay is extended, which causes the silting up of the harbour outside the mill sluices. They are abandoned by 1800.

1749 Nathaniel Symons of Harberton invents a diving machine and tests it at Dartmouth. *The Gentleman's Magazine* reports: 'he was lucky enough to come up again in 45 minutes'.

1795 Dartmouth Bank is already established. Among the extant bank notes is one dated 24 August this year for five guineas, bearing the arms of Dartmouth on a shield. Another is for £1 and shows the shipyard with two wooden-wall ships being built—a memento of the opening of the shipyard at Sandquay this year, where 'wooden wallers' are built for war with France. (The yard was eventually run by Ben Turner, who employed sixty-eight shipwrights. Thirteen men-of-war were built at Sandquay.)

1813 Ben Turner's largest man-of-war, *Dartmouth*, is launched—36 guns, 952 tons.

1819 The Warfleet Brewery is built.

1823 'Some spirited individuals set out to establish a steam packet on the Dart' (*Exeter Flying Post*). This is the basis of the future passenger service.

1832 A floating bridge is constructed to operate between Sandquay and Noss Point. The pontoon is worked by a horse treadmill. (The floating bridge continued in use until 1867.)

1838 The gross revenue of Dartmouth customs is £4,100.

1839 The customs revenue is £4,629.

1840 The first Dartmouth Regatta is attended by 'half a dozen steamers and over fifty of the finest schooners and cutters upon the coast' (local account).

1846 **20 August** Queen Victoria visits Dartmouth. The entry in the royal journal reads:

> It was thought best to give up Plymouth, and to put into that beautiful Dartmouth, and accordingly did so, in pouring rain, the deck swimming with water, and all of us with umbrellas, the children being most anxious to see everything. Notwithstanding the rain, this place is lovely, with its wooded rocks, and Church and Castle at the entrance. It puts me so much in mind of the beautiful Rhine, and its Castle, and the Lurlei.

1850 There are four sailmakers practising full-time in Dartmouth.

1858 Philip & Son commence ship-building at Sandquay.

1863 The present Warfleet Bridge is built.

30 September HMS *Britannia* is towed to a mooring off Sandquay as a training base for naval officers and cadets.

1864 **10 August** The first railway train enters Kingswear station hauled by the locomotive *Lion*.

1878–1939 Trade develops in coal-bunkering for vessels passing through the English Channel from Scandinavia to Mediterranean ports. (The ships entering the harbour used to sound their sirens and the coal barges would go out to them. The coaling men ('lumpers') and their families lived in poor waterfront cottages in slum conditions. The coal boats were unpopular with yachtsmen as the dust blew about in windy weather. At the peak of the trade, up to ten ships a day refuelled. At this time there was altogether more commerce and less pleasure-boating than in the mid-twentieth century. The conversion of vessels to oil-burning killed the bunkering trade. The coal for Torbay gas-works was imported at Kingswear and taken onwards by train.)

1891   The Natal-Durban Steamship Company, after operating a mail service between Dartmouth and Durban for some years, moved offices to Southampton because of the more convenient rail-link there.

1896   235 yachts moored in the river for the Regatta.

1902   **7 March** King Edward VII lays the foundation stone of the Britannia Royal Naval College.

1905   **14 September** The Britannia Royal Naval College is opened.

1916   **July** HMS *Britannia*, already sold as a hulk, is towed away for breaking up. The whole College assembles to watch and the band plays a last farewell.

1928   **23–26 July** The Annual Meeting of the Devonshire Association is held at Dartmouth. The Proceedings record that the President pays tribute to the inventor Newcomen.

1939   **22–23 July** King George VI, Queen Elizabeth and the two Princesses visit the Britannia Royal Naval College in the royal yacht *Victoria & Albert* (memorable for its large brass funnels). It is the yacht's last trip to Dartmouth. Prince Philip, a cadet at the Britannia Royal Naval College, is told to act as guide to the royal party. The *Victoria & Albert* is moored in Bight at Dartmouth Castle: on departure it is escorted by every boat capable of sailing out into the Channel.

August The success of the Regatta is prejudiced by the expectation of war. A destroyer traditionally comes into harbour for Regatta; on this occasion the crew are recalled from shore leave for the sudden departure of the ship. There is a general realisation that the Regatta will be the last for some years, so it is regarded as a centenary event. Large yachts come from Cowes (where the regatta is always earlier than Dartmouth's, which is by tradition the last of the season) to participate.

August A platoon of thirty men and one officer, of the Devon Regiment, is sent to Dartmouth to guard Philip's ship-building yard. Their duty lasts about two months. After war is declared, many boats arrive at the yard for conversion to naval patrol boats. The twin-screw *Campeador V* is one of these. (She was built at the yard in the previous year.)

Commander Davey, RN Rtd (for many years Master of the Dartmoor Hunt at Ivybridge and said to have gone 'like smoke over Dartmoor' in a hunt) is given command. *Campeador* is at sea for eighty-four days in ninety-three and survives the first nine months of the war unscathed. The famous naval artist Muirhead Bone hears of *Campeador* and its veteran officers and sketches them in the wardroom.

1940 **22 June** *Campeador V* is blown up by an enemy magnetic mine off the Isle of Wight. Of a crew of twenty-two, twenty perish, including the owner, Vernon MacAndrew, and Commander Davey.

1942 Night action off Nazi-occupied Cherbourg. A flotilla of four gunboats commanded by Lt Cmdr R. P. Hitchins RNVR creeps up on the enemy torpedo boats and rakes them with devastating fire. After setting two ablaze, the gunboats race away under cover of darkness and return to Dartmouth.

8 September Philip's shipyard is attacked by enemy aircraft and twenty men are killed. A ship is sunk in the harbour and the Naval College is damaged by bombing, with one staff officer killed. The staff and cadets are evacuated to Cheshire and the College is used as a training base for Combined Operations.

1943 **13 February** A German bomb is dropped on Duke Street, kills fourteen civilians and severely damages the Butterwalk. (No 6 The Butterwalk was later set up as a museum, sponsored by Percy Russell FSA. The curator in 1982 is Ralph Cawthorne.

1944 **January** American forces occupy the Naval College as their HQ. Concrete ramps are constructed for tanks and heavy vehicles to enter landing craft.

6 June Crusaders sail again! 480 vessels leave the harbour, sailing through the gap in the boom between the castles, into the Channel and across to the Normandy beaches. Russell writes of the 'grandeur of this enterprise'.

1949 **August** Colin and Stanley Smith arrive from Dartmouth, Nova Scotia, in an 18ft sloop.

1951 C. R. Milne, A. A. Milne's son 'Christopher Robin', establishes the Harbour Bookshop in Dartmouth.

April HRH Princess Margaret visits the Naval College to present prizes at the passing-out ceremony.

1954 **12 July** HRH Duke of Edinburgh visits Dartmouth to unveil a memorial on the Embankment commemorating the Allied landings in France.

1971–73 The BBC film a series for television, 'The Onedin Line', in Dartmouth.

Sailing ships brought into the harbour for filming include, apart from the *Charlotte Rhodes*, the *Sir Winston Churchill*, the Danish *Danmark*, *Als*, *Jyland* and *Artemis*. Long Wood on the river's left bank above Noss Creek becomes the New Guinea jungle.

1972 HM the Queen visits BRNC.

1979 **5 May** Annual River Dart Rowing Contest; fifty crews from throughout southern England compete over 9½-mile course Totnes–Dartmouth. Weather—snow, rain, bitterly cold. Record for course set up by Blackwall Club of London in 1975 (48 min 9 sec) remains unbroken.

The training of officers for Britain's Royal Navy has taken place at Dartmouth for almost 120 years and the whole story is told in *Royal Naval College Dartmouth—Seventy-five years in pictures* by E. L. Davies and E. J. Grove. I might add a personal note relating to the mid-fifties, when there were 500 officer students, 171 cadets and 419 midshipmen in training; they included young men from Australia, Ceylon, Malaya, New Zealand and Pakistan. I had the pleasure of guiding many of those young men over Dartmoor as a 'relaxation' period during their adventure training weekends at Ditsworthy Warren House on the southern Moor. I wonder if those delightful Saturday evenings in the old house, with supper eaten round a peat and wood fire will sound a chord in the memory of any of my naval readers.

In the summer of 1939, Prince Philip of Greece (now HRH the Duke of Edinburgh) entered the College; many years later it was the turn of his royal sons to attend and successfully complete their training—the Prince of Wales in 1971 and Prince Andrew in 1979. Britannia Royal Naval College is beyond question a splendid building nurturing a splendid tradition.

Linked closely with the function of the Naval College, if not, indeed, for a time dictating it, was the training of the forces under the command of General Dwight Eisenhower for the invasion and liberation of Nazi-occupied Europe in 1944 during World War II. The American forces arrived in the port during the autumn of 1943. Several large houses were requisitioned for their use; Nissen huts were built, as well as piers and concrete ramps—some of which are still to be seen from the river—to allow tracked and wheeled vehicles to enter landing craft, moorings being laid in the channel for 110 such vessels. Rehearsals went on by day and by night and Dartmouth, as D-Day approached, fairly buzzed with American personnel. Force U, from 'US VII Corps', embarked at Dartmouth and the 4th Division of the Corps was the first to land troops in France. U Force provided the extreme right wing of the attack, their destination being the Uire estuary at the base of the Cotentin Peninsula.

Norman Longmate gives an interesting account of the Americans' life in the English countryside in *The G.I.'s*. He writes of an officer of the 29th Division who remembered with affection 'Totnes, the Dart river, Dartington', and of a young sailor who said:

> The land rising from the Dart river is lovely, divided by hedgerows, green and beautiful. The river is so much cleaner than streams in America I have seen. We swam in it joyfully, admiring the birds perching on the buoys and learned to feel the river's channels were like our auto highways at home.

The spirit of those days—of that day, 6 June 1944—was very great. Somehow, today, it seems to have gone to ground.

The fishing harvest of the waters both fresh and salt, has for many centuries formed a vital part of Dartmouth's fortunes. Large-scale deep-sea fishing began as long ago as 1414, when men of Dartmouth fished for cod in Icelandic waters. Hoskin's *Devon* details the first recorded docking at Dartmouth as that of the *Gratias Deo* (of Dartmouth) on 8 September 1565 with 2 tons of train oil. By then the trade had greatly developed and the inshore pilchard trade was also in full swing; salt was imported from La Rochelle for use in preserving the pilchards in hogsheads, which were sold in the ports of Spain, France and England. In 1588 an embargo on the departure of fishing ships literally swept thousands of experienced mariners into the naval fleets, assembled at Plymouth and Dartmouth, to sail under Sir Francis Drake against the Spaniards.

The Dartmouth cod-fishing fleet made an annual voyage, proceeds being shared equally between the ship's owner, the victualler, and the master and crew. Preparations in port went on

during the winter months; the cost of fitting out a 100-ton ship for
forty men in late Elizabethan times, when Sir Humphrey Gilbert
opened up the Newfoundland grounds for English fishermen, was
reckoned as £300. Early in the seventeenth century much of the
Dartmouth fishermen's harvest was sold in Spain and Portugal, the
oil being brought home for soap-making. By the end of the
century, Europe was so torn by wars that the seasonal voyages had
practically ceased. Records, according to Dr W. B. Stephens in
TDA 88 of 1956, show clearly the gradual decline:

1628   Dartmouth sent eighty ships, as it did during several
        preceding and following years.

1652   Thirty-four ships.

1667   Fewer than twenty ships.

1677   Numbers slightly up, those for Dartmouth being higher than
        for any other British port.

Bounties were awarded to fishing ships in 1776 and exemption for
the crews from naval impressment. Percy Russell writes of the late
1800s:

With the eventual extinction of the sailing ship the voyages between
Dartmouth and the estates in Newfoundland and the vineyards of
Portugal ceased in 1907 after a duration of rather more than three
hundred years.

Seventy years later the value of fish landed by off-shore fishermen
of Dartmouth is recorded as £645,944, and in February 1977
planning approval was given for a fish-processing plant on the site
of an old abbatoir at Jawbones.

     Crab fishing has become quite lucrative, and Dorothy Wright of
Bovey Tracey has written a study of the subject published in *TDA*
108 of 1976. She says:

A great change has taken place in the last six years ... The boats are
bigger and faster and the catches are larger. Fishing is now in up to
30 fathoms of water and as far as, but no farther than, 20 miles out in
the Channel, from Torbay to Plymouth. The catch goes to a firm in
Paignton where it may be frozen and sent 'all over' to local shops and
hotels in the South West, to Billingsgate, to France and the Low

Countries. Some crabs are blast-frozen and go to Sweden. It is the size and quality of the shell-fish from this [Dartmouth] area that make it so outstanding.

Fishermen roam the estuary mudbanks left by the retreating tide, to retrieve crabs, especially from the bases of poles, stumps and piers.

King of the river fish is the salmon, and a brief description of the Dart salmon-fishing industry is given elsewhere. Lilley in *The South Hams* writes of 'alarming fluctuations' in the catches: in 1949, for example, 370 salmon were caught at Stoke Gabriel and in 1950 only 41.

The ancient Christian custom of asking a divine blessing on the harvests of fields and waters—the Rogationtide Ceremony—still takes place in Dartmouth. The Revd John Butler, Vicar of Dartmouth, writes:

> The ceremony opens with prayers in St Saviour's Church. Usually there is quite a large congregation made up of church people from the town, officers, lecturers and cadets from Britannia Royal Naval College and boat owners of all sorts.

Following the service everyone moves off in procession to Ferry Pontoon, singing the Dartmouth Pilgrim's Litany.

> So bless our Rogation, our asking and using
> And help us to walk in the ways of your choosing.
> Lord, hear and answer this prayer.

An appropriate feature with which to close this sketch of Dartmouth, a place of outstanding beauty, is the Church of St Saviour. St Saviour's is no mere showpiece, it is in reality a sanctuary of peace and prayer. Upon entering the building at the south door—with its elaborate ironwork (on oak) dating from 1631, depicting two beasts guarding the Tree of Life—one receives an impression of spaciousness and light. There is marvellous woodcraft in rood screen and west-end gallery— with the coats of arms of persons and families distinguished in Dartmouth's history, including Seymour, Courtenay, Drake, Charles II, Shaplegh, Hawley and Bastard— and the finest specimen in existence of a

Devon stone 'wineglass' pulpit of the late fifteenth century, painted and gilded with niches containing the royal badges of Charles II which were placed there at his Restoration in 1660. St Saviour's association with the civic growth and fortunes of the town is indicated by stalls for Mayor and Corporation, the former with two cushioned seats made in the seventeenth century—one each for his worship and wife—and the latter of *c* 1815 but skilfully turned in Jacobean style. They were moved to their present position from the chapel.

The condition of the church's interior demonstrates the loving care bestowed upon it. Only one object of interest—the painting presented to the church by William Brockeden of Totnes, 'The Raising of the Widow's Son at Nain'—is placed at a visual disadvantage. Commissioned as an altar piece for St Saviour's by Governor Arthur Howe Holdsworth of Dartmouth Castle, who became Member of Parliament for Dartmouth in 1802, it hung in its intended place for an unspecified period; eventually it was moved to the only possible alternative position, above the stairs leading to the gallery. It cannot be evaluated there, one's view of the picture being first from below, and then on ascending the stairs, at an acute angle; the frame is massive and the picture's size appears to be not less than 20ft by 14ft. Great though the undertaking was, it is difficult to escape the impression that the painter's figures lack animation and conviction.

East Bank to Kingswear

Beyond the downstream extremity of the port of Totnes an area of marsh was reclaimed towards the end of last century. Known as Shooting Marsh, it was used as a rifle practice ground before World War I when troops, flying a red flag to warn shipping, fired across the width of the river to obtain a range of 1000yd. I am told they greatly angered the occupant of Windwhistle Cottage (*see below*) by treating his chimneys as targets. The range was most unpleasant to use as, prior to the draining of the marsh, the men usually found themselves lying in water at high tide. Realistic training, no doubt! Between the wars a proper range was laid out with butts and was regularly used by the Territorial Army and, during World War II, by the Home Guard, firing .303 rifles. Used for a short time following the war, the range was eventually abandoned in the early 1950s, but is still marked on the latest OS 6in and 2½in maps. In recent years, it has been swept away in the construction of a large turning bay for cargo ships using Baltic Wharf, and a car park.

On the rising ground above the rifle range site, Weston Lane climbs to Lower and Higher Weston Farms. The latter is farmed by Mr Jim Widdicombe, who succeeded his father. In the farm fields is the high ground known as Windwhistle Hills, where Windwhistle Cottage was once occupied by a labourer at Lower Weston Farm. Now a ruin, it is perched on a hillside shelf immediately above the reclaimed Long Marsh on the river's Home Reach, from where its remaining gables are readily distinguished by a profuse growth of ivy; from the site there is a fine view of Home Reach and Totnes port.

The old 20-ton square riggers sailing up to Totnes a century ago were propelled in calm weather by pole and oar at about 1½ knots. When waiting for the tide, the crews would anchor off Parker's Barn and make a coal delivery to Windwhistle Cottage. The method of operation was unusual, the men racing each other up the 200ft hillside with coal-laden wheelbarrows! Certainly the Steer family, last occupants of the lonely dwelling, could rely on their fuel supply, which was as well, for there were nineteen children, almost as many pigs, and a score of sheep. Father Steer was obviously a man of many parts, for in addition to fathering such a family, and feeding them and his livestock, he practised locally as a 'quack veterinary'.

Above the old settlement is a group of trees planted to break the force of the whistling east winds, including five elms (now dead) and two oaks (one of great age). From the covered reservoir on the hilltop above may be seen a panoramic view beyond Totnes of the southern escarpment of Dartmoor and, in the mid-distance, Dartington, North Wood, Yarner Beacon, the tops of the higher lowland hills and Berry Pomeroy Church and Castle—meanwhile the immediate edge of the field appears to fall into the very lap of

27 'Totnes and the River Dart' by William Turner. The castle (its scale somewhat exaggerated) and the town and St Mary's Church stand out clearly. The Dartmoor Hills are represented in the background, and the penguin-like birds on the foreshore are presumably some species of wader. Two sailing barges are moored at St Peter's Quay (site of Baltic Wharf) and the buildings beyond are where the Steam Packet Inn now stands

28 The Tuckenhay paper mill of Arthur Millbourn & Co Ltd. The photograph was taken before 1910 and has been lent by Mr Jack Lynn, whose grandfather is fourth from the front in the middle row

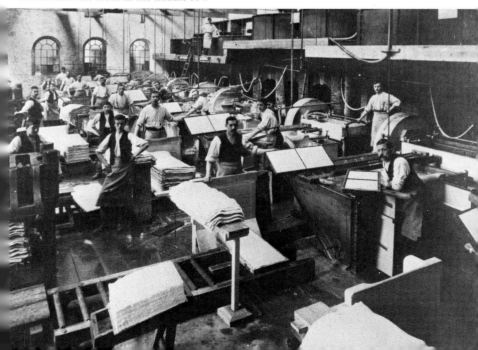

29 The coaster *Reedness* at Tuckenhay Quay in 1939. (*Photo lent by Mr David Manning*)

30 The Dart Estuary. In the foreground: Sharpham Farm fields and (right) reclaimed marsh later returned to the Duchy of Cornwall as *fundus*. In the near distance: Home Reach and (by the isolated trees on the right hillside) Windwhistle Cottage. In the mid-distance: Totnes town and St Mary's Church. On the horizon: Dartmoor, with (left to right) Yar Tor near Dartmeet, Corndon Tor (above the church tower), Corndon Down, Auswell Rocks, Buckland Beacon, Hameldon, Rippen Tor and Saddle Tor

the town. Southward is the shining Lake of Dart and the promontories separating Sharpham, Bow and Dittisham Creeks, topped by Firebeacon Hill; the nearest creek on the left bank—under the further slope of Windwhistle Hills—is Fleet Mill Creek.

Windwhistle Cottage still contains two fireplaces, a well-formed window at first-floor level, two more on the ground floor and a front doorway facing the river. Outside the north-east corner is a canopied well, now choked. It is noticeable that the north gable on this exposed side contained no window, an emphasis on the reason for its name. The large ruined outbuilding near the south gable is the barn in which the cottager kept his livestock.

The approach to the cottage is through Jim Widdicombe's fields, and only with his permission, for there is no right of way. At a time when the countryside is known to be losing some of its more attractive butterfly species, it is heartening to see that hedges on the farm have been properly trimmed rather than stripped, as too often happens: hedgerows there are in consequence extravagantly decked with wild flowers and alive with honey bees and red admiral, tortoiseshell and peacock butterflies.

The south-east slope of Windwhistle Hills is called Fleet Mill Hill, its 300ft plunge to the mill valley providing the grazing animals with unusually effective shelter. The main Totnes–Paignton road descends to Elbow Bridge in a green vale east of Weston Lane; this is the upper valley of the stream which, rising east of Berry Pomeroy village at about 400ft, occupies the Fleet Mill valley and once turned the waterwheel of the mill. Many decades have passed since corn flowed between its grinders, one of which now serves as the base of a fuel pile. The mill appears in the 1841 *T. Appt.* as 'Fleet Mills, William Widdicombe, Miller' (an ancestor of Jim Widdicombe of Higher Weston). The leat from the stream and the returning tail-race are still visible and the house has the look of a sixteenth-century building. A lane leading to Stoke Gabriel leaves Millcombe Farm, as the mill is now called, crosses the stream and climbs steeply eastward; from it after a short distance a tunnel-like packhorse lane branches right under Fleet Mill Brake and clings as an open hillside track to the side of the valley, which, below the bridge, is a tidal creek. On nearing the river the old way turns sharply right through a gateway, crosses the foot of the stream at a sluice and reaches Fleet Mill Quay. There is ancient masonry here, certainly as old as the mill itself, for corn ground at the mill was taken by packhorses along the track described, and loaded on sailing barges at the quay. Stone for the quay appears to have been obtained from the small rock outcrop above the west bank of the creek. The sluice was built for the purpose of preventing river flood-water from entering the creek, for at the upper end near the mill were lush water meadows where now bulrushes run riot; indeed, Mr W. A. Perring, the farmer at Millcombe in 1981, showed me the gateway leading to the former meadows, when the only marsh near the mill was on the verge of the road opposite and is marked on the 1841 *T. Appt.* as 'Fleet Mill Marsh'. For the same reason the mill tail-race was restricted for some way down the creek to a specially built channel and not allowed to over-swell the stream. Now the creek has returned to Nature, the rushes have taken over and the sounds of marsh birds fill the air.

Alongside Fleet Mill Quay lies the rotting hulk of the paddle steamer *Dartmouth Castle*; built for the River Dart Steamboat Company in 1904 by Philip & Son at their Noss shipyard she was one of the largest ever to ply on the river and carried passenger traffic until 1939 when the service was halted by the war emergency. Moored in the mainstream during the war and used as a hospital ship for American troops, she was eventually abandoned and removed to the quayside at Fleet Mill Creek. There the boat was stripped and secured to the quay by hawsers, with the object of allowing the hull to fill with tidal mud, so providing the quay wall with an effective buttress. This successful ruse was the work of surveyor Arthur Brook.

Between Home and Fleet Mill Reaches a ledge of rock runs across the river bed from Berry Point to the Sharpham bank; in 1935, as part of the work begun three years previously to dredge and deepen the channel, Arthur Brook ordered the ledge to be dynamited in midstream; Berry Rock, off Berry Point, is the remaining outcrop of that ledge. Hooker, in his *Synopsis Chorographical of Devon* (1714), wrote of the stone of Berry Rock:

... speciall stones very fayre and beautyfull and of estimacon whereof too do growe in the East syde of the Ryver Darte in Berry pomeroy pk.

Parker's Barn, a ruined farm among trees near the foreshore at the south foot of Fleet Mill Hill—it appears in the 1841 *T. Appt.* as 'Barn and Court: part of Higher Weston' (John Searle)—is associated with the adventure of an influential eighteenth-century local farmer of Higher Weston named Parker. Before an approaching Totnes by-election he had been heard in the town to utter threats against the townspeople's favourite parliamentary candidate. Strong preventive measures were taken by his acquaintances, who made him roaring drunk and carted him off to the old farm before the election; there they deposited him in an empty cider cask with only his head protruding, where he remained until the election was over.

Below Fleet Mill Creek and Sharpham Point is Sharpham Reach, where Ham Point intrudes its sharp nose into the channel. Interlocking with the spur of Sharpham Point it produces the picturesquely serpentine reaches that straighten out below Langham Wood Point. Under Ham Copse is a series of rocks laid along the foreshore, perhaps centuries ago. It was customary to whitewash these to aid the passage of ships by night, a custom maintained by Arthur Brook to aid navigation on the river. At the end of Ham Reach is the tree-shadowed Hackney Creek where the stream from Stoke Gabriel's holy well comes down to the river. Above and well back from the riverside are the attractive mansions known as Coombe Cross House and Aish House, from which a lane runs down the hill towards Ham Point. Aish House was built in 1820 by a Mr Jackson (it was pre-dated by Coombe Cross House, originally named Waterloo House because built in 1815), the late Georgian 'block' and façade being built on to Aish Farm, which had a rather fine circular pound house. In 1945 Victor and Helen Elmhirst moved into the house, Victor being the brother of Leonard, that Elmhirst so notable for his conception and execution of the Dartington Hall scheme. Victor Elmhirst's great interest was the aims and attainments of the Youth Hostels Association which he did much to further, and he was for several years President and Chairman of the Devon and Cornwall Council of the Association, until his death in 1958. Mrs Elmhirst employed an architect to preserve and incorporate in the house some features of the old Aish Farm, a task admirably carried out. The remaining apple crusher from the pound house now rests on the lawn near the entrance gate.

Stoke Gabriel is a place of special delight, largely because its waterfront, like that of Tuckenhay, is the shore of its own creek and secluded from the main river. The water of the creek and combe above once powered two mills. At its head is the picturesque Byter Mill (*T. Appt.* 1840, 'Biter'), now a guest house. From the lily-studded mill-pond the mill-stream drops steeply to the large waterwheel pit at one end of the millhouse, while the mainstream descends by waterfall. It is hoped in the near future to restore the fine old wheel, which last worked at the close of the nineteenth century—White's *Directory* showing Thomas Widdicombe as farmer and corn miller in 1850 and Samuel Ball in 1890. A large millstone remains in the yard and a high arch spans the entrance; engraved on the flagstones here are the words, *BYTER MILL*. Nearby is an old quarry, probably the source of stone for the building of the mill.

Below Byter Mill the combe opens into the creek, where a weir forms Mill Pool above Stoke Mouth. Here the tidal waters once worked a busy corn mill; named as 'Seamill' in the *T. Appt.*, it is included as a working mill by White in 1850, when the miller was Matthew Churchward. It is not in the 1890 edition, so must have ceased working about a century ago. Weir and sluice may still be seen at the quay, where miller's house and mill once projected into mid-creek, and his garden and linhay were on the site of the present cafe. A rare picture of the buildings appears in *Stoke Gabriel*, a well-produced booklet edited by S. F. Birch and available locally.

Mill Pool is fringed by a beach of sand and shingle, providing quite the most pleasant way of reaching the parish church, where no parking is permissible. A car may be left at the quay all day for a small charge, the parking space and lawns with flowering trees now occupying the wide foreshore where formerly the salmon fishermen used to spread their nets for inspection and repair. Follow the beach for ¼ mile and turn into the path that ascends to Church Walk and passes through a cider apple orchard below the churchyard wall.

The 'stock' or settlement beside the river with the church dedicated to the Archangel Gabriel was a Christian village before the Norman Conquest, though nothing is known of the church of those days. The present building is basically of the thirteenth century, all of it except the tower rebuilt during the fifteenth century. A medieval chancellor of Exeter Cathedral, Walter Meriet, was severely rebuked by the great 'builder' Bishop Grandisson in 1332 for:

> ... milking dry and wasting from our church and diocese all he can get hold of and giving back nothing in return, and has even allowed the buildings at Gabriel Stoke, which other chancellors erected at great expense ... to fall to the ground in decay and his poor parishioners to starve, and during all this time has neglected to repair the church and ornaments.

The sound of 'canned' church music coming from the rood loft as one enters the ancient building is perhaps not to everyone's taste; nor the ugly, plain white cross, more suited to graveyard than sanctuary and contrasting badly with the beautiful 'wine-glass' pulpit and rood screen. A wall memorial plaque commemorates Arthur Champenowne, of the Modbury branch of the family, who died on 7 November 1700, aged twenty.

At one corner of the church path near the marvellously carved north doorway is a flat piece of sandstone bearing marks of sword- or knife-sharpening—perhaps both. A fine view of Mill Pool, quay and river beyond is seen from the churchyard, where stands the great Stoke Gabriel yew tree; its spread of 90ft necessitates the use of fourteen props beneath the branches, some two or three to a branch. The vigour of the tree is astonishing; it is of very great age—perhaps ten or more centuries old—and reputed to be the oldest of its species in England. Two of the branches have felled two gravestones (now unreadable but perhaps early nineteenth century) which certainly would never have been erected there had the tree's continued growth been foreseen. It is now so huge as to be identifiable from viewpoints above the further, west bank of the river.

A cobbled walk leads from the lych gate to the Church House Inn, one of Devon's most ancient church houses, dating from 1171. There is no more pleasant place, 811 years later, in which to enjoy a ploughman's lunch and cider; if possible, visit it by walking at low tide along the beach to Church Walk. The inn's architectural features are described in *TDA* 92 of 1960, p130. Although modern by comparison, it is nice to see that the village school is still in use, its wall embellished by climbing roses.

Stoke lay on the old way from Ashprington to Paignton via the Duncannon Ferry. The lane on the Stoke side, also called Duncannon Lane, ascends the rocky hillside abruptly and it could have been no light undertaking for villagers, laden with household purchases from either Totnes or Dartmouth in the days when the river steamers called at Duncannon Quay, to make the climb to Stoke Gabriel. The 1840 *T. Appt.* shows Thomas Abbot and Henry Lake as occupants of a house and garden with orchard at the quay. They presumably were the ferrymen in those long-past days. The salmon fishermen are still to be seen laying out their nets on the little beach next to Duncannon Quay. Moored off Stoke Mouth, little used but maintained in working and seaworthy order, now the only one of its kind on Dart water, is the steam-powered, twin-screw tug, *Portwey*, built in 1927 at Belfast by Harland & Woolf.

At the head of Duncannon Lane is an attractive mansion, dating from 1798, called Mazonet. Here, tradition persists, George, Prince Regent, maintained a mistress, though how often he accomplished the tedious coach journey from London to receive her graces is not told. The *T. Appt.* of 1840 shows Richard Perrott Hulme as occupant and Henry Studdy of Waddeton Court as owner.

'For centuries Stoke Gabriel has been the centre of the Dart salmon fishing industry.' So writes Sheila Birch in *Stoke Gabriel*, and goes on to say:

It must have been the fishing that first led to a settlement here. The fishermen built houses by the creek to live in, and their descendants planted all the space between with apple trees.

The fish are netted as they come up the river, driven by mysterious compulsion to spawn in the waters where they themselves began life. The netting lasts from 15 March to 15 August, 5 days a week from 6 a.m. Monday to 6 a.m. Saturday. There are now few if any whole-time fishermen, but the salmon has for the men of the village a compulsion almost as strong as the spawning urge for the fish, and they rush home from their jobs, bolt their teas, and are off for as long as daylight and tides permit. There is a crew of 4 to a boat, to hold one end of the net at the water's edge, to row the boat, and to pay out the net in an arc to enclose the area where a fish has been spotted 'vowling', i.e. cutting a diamond-shaped wash as it swims up river. The oarsman completes the arc back to shore, and all unite to draw in the net, heavy of itself but heavier if the hoped-for salmon, from one to a record haul, are gleaming pink and silver in its folds. The days and the seasons vary as in all fishing, sometimes catches are good, sometimes haul after haul, day after day yield little save a few dabs, sticks, seaweed, and maybe a bass. The price paid for salmon has risen by leaps and bounds, so too have the fishermen's costs for boats, licences, nets, and restrictions tighten to prevent over-fishing. The fascination remains; fishing is not without its dangers, mud-banks, currents, stream fighting tide and the wind whipping both into waves, to say nothing of the wash from pleasure steamers and speed boats. Dart is a river not to be trifled with.

An old villager's memory from his youth is recorded in the *Dartington Archive*:

... the shoreman would keep hold of the ends (of the net rope). He had to be careful to keep one hand close to the ground, because otherwise the fish would escape underneath the net ... The net had cork floats on the top and lead weights on the bottom. The idea was to pay it out, so that it hung straight in the water, just like a round fence. They could tell if they had caught any fish because the corks would go up and down. Each haul took roughly 20 minutes ... The highest number of fish I ever heard of in one haul was 65 ... There used to be twelve to twenty boats that used to fish in the favourite haunts by the sandbank at the mouth of Bow Creek, at Duncannon, at Bass Rock, around by Sharpham, Galmpton and Cornworthy.

For mending their nets, both at Stoke Gabriel and Tuckenhay, the fishermen used rails about 20ft long and 3 or 4ft high and threw their nets over them. Then they would pull it towards them, mending as they went. Today, Dart salmon poaching is rife. In a recent article on the subject in the *Western Morning News*, Nick Band wrote of spear-gun poaching adding a new and frightening dimension.

It would be interesting to know what the salmon catch was in 1564, when the village was afflicted by the plague brought into Devon by ship rats, resulting in fifty-nine deaths. Lack of public—even private—hygiene in those times accelerated the spread of the disease, which was carried to humans by fleas that had sucked the rats' blood. The virus persisted in the area for several years, for at Stoke Fleming in 1557—its parish boundary reached down to the west bank at the river's mouth—forty-one people were buried from plague.

Sheila Birch lives in a pleasant, semi-detached cottage—the two are called Hoyle Cottages—outside the village. The narrow approach is Hoyle Lane, for 'Hoyle'—it was Hoyll in 1840—is a corruption of 'Holy Well'. And, in a meadow separated from the cottage by an orchard, is the ancient well, the former household supply for the Hoyle cottagers. The warm water, which steams on a frosty morning, issues through a tiny portal, with side-stones and lintel, built into the hillside, the open channel being stone-lined for a short way. The water eventually joins the Hoyle stream which, rising higher on the hillside, falls through another carefully constructed portal into the lane and creates a diminutive ford.

Above the south bank of Mill Pool rises South Down, with the private residence and grounds of that name; southward again the land rises steadily from Pighole Point to Sandridge Park, where in ornamental grounds is the mansion of Sandridge, a Regency building of 1805 designed by Nash for the second Lord Ashburton. In 1840 it was the residence of Lord Cranston. It is sometimes stated or implied that John Davis, the celebrated Elizabethan navigator, was born in an earlier house on this site; this was not so, however: Adrian Gilbert, who was born at Greenway, later lived at the Elizabethan Sandridge House and

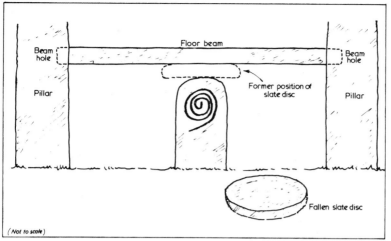

Beam hole

Floor beam

Beam hole

Pillar

Former position of slate disc

Pillar

Fallen slate disc

(Not to scale)

Detail of the pillared barn at Sandridge Barton

Davis was born at Sandridge Barton. Among Davis's achievements was the composition of a treatise of great repute on navigation, entitled *The Seamen's Secrets*.

An even older house, occupied by the de Sandridge family during the reign of Henry II, is also unlikely to have stood on the site of the Nash mansion, for a ruin of considerable size with fireplaces and an early house-type window exists behind the barton farmhouse and well below the Nash site. Although very overgrown, it is evident that this could have been a late medieval house capacious enough for a yeoman. Half a century ago, it was still roofed and in use as a cider store, for adjacent to it is the barton pound house, containing most of the mechanism of the cider press, including the great screw shaft of the press, the iron head, wooden beams and huge wooden crown wheel. Brambles and nettles shoulder-high make close inspection impossible; however, Anthony Goodson, the barton farmer, has declared his intention to clear the interior and restore what can be saved of the press. The building contains a portion of a broken granite crusher base, the remainder being near the farmhouse entrance, together with the fine granite edge-runner.

Two further ancient structures bring the number of notable outbuildings at Sandridge Barton to four. These are the shippen, built with circular pillars like North Barn at Whitestone but having solid walling, and a fine old barn used for storing hay. 'Charlie' Clarence Roper of Sandridge Cottage farmed the barton from 1937-72, and remembers two buildings, again of pillared construction, standing where Mr Goodson's new granary has been built. The hay barn consists of circular pillars with a raised floor and undercroft; its ancient roof has been replaced by one of corrugated iron. Each of the eight pillars—four rear and four front, making three bays each side—has squared beam holes in the masonry for floor supports. Some beams remain *in situ*, others have rotted away. A foot or so below the beam holes each pillar wears a stone 'collar', a disc-like projection to prevent rats from reaching the barn floor. In each bay between the pillars is a standing stone, its function presumably having been to provide inter-bay support to the floor beams, for, lying on the ground among the weeds near several of these stones are large, flat discs of slate. These I believe would have been placed on top of the stones to form staddles— stone 'mushrooms' such as often are seen supporting West Country barn floors. A highly unusual and non-functional feature of the standing stones is that each bears an identical carved design. Some have weathered badly, but the best remaining one, in the centre rear bay, shows that the design was carved to stand in relief against the face of the stone. The barn has for many years been listed as a scheduled antiquity.

The existing Sandridge Barton farmhouse is basically of mid- or late-Tudor period. Rebuilt in Georgian times, perhaps when Nash built the neighbouring mansion, it was recently restored; in removing the rendering during the course of the work, walls of pink cob were exposed, implying that the building might have been a large thatched farmhouse. Now, its white Georgian facade smiles down upon the combe and tiny Sandridge Creek below its foot, its window watching the coming and going of the Greenway Ferry, the gliding, passing sails, and sheep-dotted Dittisham fields beyond the river—with accompanying sounds of buzzards, crows and gulls over East Wood and the creek—a scene virtually unchanged since mariner John Davis gazed upon it.

Near the rear of the farmhouse is an elm tree of great age but it is now unfortunately in an advanced state of decay despite efforts it. The relic of the trunk remains to a height of 12ft and its girth is 44ft. Actually within the hollow of the tree is a stone butter-cooler and the spring that once was the barton's water supply, the water now escaping through the cider-apple orchard into the streamlet of the combe. At the foot of the combe, a track from the farm fords the streamlet and enters East Wood. Beyond the gate the way forks: left to follow the edge of the high river bank above The Cliffs and Waddeton Slipway, and right to Ladies Quay. Here is another surprise. The woodland path leads straight to an artificial cutting through rock some 20ft high to a small beach, which it approaches over steep, flat rock bedding. If ever there were a place for the clandestine landing of something or somebody, this is it. It seems significant, too, that the rock cutting is wide enough for the passage of laden pack animals. What stories do the rocks of Ladies Quay secrete? A passage in Chard's *Along the Dart* says:

> Sandridge has ... romantic tales to tell for deep in the woods there was an innocent looking mound covered with undergrowth. This hid a door and a flight of steps which led to a stone cellar, and here smugglers brought their goods on moonless nights with stockings over their donkey's feet so they made no sound as they carried kegs of wine and spirit and bales of cloth.

The convenience of the cutting as an approach to the quay was doubtless also appreciated by the Victorian ladies of Sandridge and could account for its name.

Two earthworks of different styles and periods exist on the hill slopes high on the east valley-side. The first, in the fields of Lower Well Farm above the Stoke–Waddeton road, is of notable interest and rarity in south Devon as it is of Romano-British origin. It was excavated during the summers of 1958–60 under the direction of Edward Masson Phillips FSA of Totnes. Situated on Middle Devonian limestone on the plateau of Basley Common, it is the relic of a farm of the fourth century. Mr Hugh Goodson of Waddeton, the landowner, had done some trenching at the site some years previously and discovered fragments of pottery. Discoveries during the Masson Phillips excavation included pottery of the late first and fourth centuries, the later period of the Roman Empire; eight coins of Constantine, also fourth; iron nails, grooved slates, spindle whorls, a broken quern and the bones of red deer, plainly indicating hunting.

An unusual feature was the initial construction of banks and ditches, a scheme never completed, for Masson Phillips found the ditches to have been in-filled. Perhaps, as this was originally a first-century site, the builders took for granted the need for defence against invasion by the Iron Age hut dwellers of Dartmoor, at that time seeking drier lowland sites, only to find within a short time that the emergency had passed. All walling on the site was of drystone. The occupants tended sheep or goats, cattle and pigs, and corn was grown in the small field-system adjoining. Mr E. S. Pook of Lower Well Farm must be approached for permission to vist this Romano-British farm which had its own supply spring on the plateau—its higher well, in fact.

The second earthwork is of the Iron Age; situated above the north-east corner of Cart Wood, it overlooks Noss Creek and can be approached through the fields of Hillhead Farm near Brixham Cross—with permission obtainable at the farmhouse from Mr or Mrs Ian McDade. The earthwork is a scheduled monument recorded officially as Greenway Camp; the Churston estate office, however, states that this is incorrect and it should be known as Noss Camp, the name used here. The defensive nature of the site is plain from its situation on a spur of land between Noss Creek and the tributary combe of Happy Valley. Defensive earthworks enclose the high tip of the spur between the two valleys and at the upper end, where overland approach could alone be attempted without formidable difficulties, there is a double rampart 23ft deep. The enclosed area is about 500ft long and 300ft wide, the elevation on the long axis rising from the 300ft to the 425ft contour.

It is clear that the Noss Camp site was chosen as practicably defensible against invasion by water, whether by pirates or intending immigrants. Standing in the centre, where an east-west line of oak trees has been planted across the site, one looks over the foot of Happy Valley and down into Noss Creek; the red caps of the Philip's shipyard cranes rotate weirdly above their unseen foundations and traffic on the river moves against the tranquil background of Old Mill Creek: moored at the creek mouth are the old fresh-water tank barges which were towed to the Normandy beaches in 1944 as a supply for the invasion troops; further up the creek appear the roofs of Creekside Boatyard, whilst high above the waterscape is the bald cap of OS point 557 above Balcombe Pits Hill.

The line of oak trees crossing the centre of the camp continues eastward from the fortified entrance to Shepherd's Down and the high land of Hillhead, where a prehistoric trade route is likely to have passed.

Between the two ancient encampments are three places of interest—the first two, Waddeton and Greenway, perched high above the beautiful Dittisham Reach, and the third, Galmpton Creek, at the riverside. At Waddeton Court, a handsome residence built in 1820 (at a cost of slightly over £3,000) and an ornamental, terraced garden of a century later, with flagstone terrace and creeper-hung pergola, entirely belie the antiquity of the site. Beyond the garden and fields declining to the river and the countless craft on its broad waters are Dittisham village, Quay and the Ferry Boat Inn; again above all, and an impressive point seen from here, is Fire Beacon Hill, with Cott Farm and its large silo tower occupying the hillside shelf below.

Waddeton itself, locally pronounced 'Watton'—it derives from 'Wada's *tun*'—is at the southern edge of an undulating plateau reaching northward to Torbay. At the main entrance to the Court, on the Galmpton road, is the pretty Waddeton hamlet of pink-washed cob-and-thatch cottages. Within the grounds of the Court the drive passes the private chapel before reaching the front door, where a massive apple crusher complete with edge-runner now performs a sedentary function as a roundabout in the centre of the driveway. Another huge crusher lies at the edge of the lawn overlooking Slipway Field. The chapel, with hexagonal apse, appears at first glance to be a solid Victorian edifice, but is actually a building of the mid-twelfth century, heavily restored in 1868 at the cost of much of the ancient fabric, for fragments of early English window tracery were found in a rubbish heap by Sir

Alfred Goodson, father of Mr Hugh Goodson, and rescued from oblivion by being used to border a flower bed.

Mr H. R. Watkin, writing in *TDA* 64 of 1932, gives reasons for supposing the building of the chapel to have been licensed and executed in the late 1160s for the de Wadetone family. The flower bed mentioned lies in what was, in Victorian times, a carefully tended shrub garden under one wall of the original Norman manor house, from which the entrance to the chapel was separated by only a few yards. Adjacent to the wall—and enclosing the now overgrown shrub garden—is the shell of the great hall of the manor, which was perhaps a wing of the ancient sandstone house. The outline of the ruined manor is clear to see, but the intrusion of

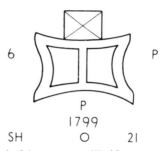

The cyphers on the barrel of the cannon at Waddeton

trees and shrubs prevents proper examination. The manor house appears to have been surrounded by a high wall and so to some extent was defensible. An imposing entrance archway in this wall was closed by huge timber doors, the large holes for the transverse door beam remaining in the masonry. Inside is a large courtyard in front of the house, while three steps on the right lead to a slightly higher level and the ruin of another building with a remaining fireplace, perhaps that of a small dower house. On the exterior of the court wall is a beautiful sundial having a slate face set in sandstone. This, which once would have been within the court, was placed there in modern times, but is unfortunately now prevented from functioning by overshadowing trees. The dial was also found in the rubbish heap by Sir Alfred Goodson.

Standing within the area of the wing of the house is a cannon bearing cyphers on the barrel. This interesting relic is one of two brought up by Mr Hugh Goodson from an old gun battery by the river at Greenway, where four cannons were mounted to defend the waters against any attempted Napoleonic invasion.

It is reasonable to suppose that both house and chapel were planned by the de Wadetone family. The precise boundary of Waddeton manor land, perhaps the cause of previous dispute, was determined by a Court Agreement. Families holding the manor were:

de Wadetone	Isabella m Martin de Fissacre *c* 1220.
de Fissacre	(meaning 'fish acre') until *c* 1390. Joan m John Maynard.
Maynard	Early fourteenth century. A daughter m William Holway.
Holway	Late fourteenth century until *c* 1565. Richard Holway 'attayned of Felonye' 1578. Mortgage passed to:
Adams	1565–1594.
Holway	William recovered mortgage 1622.
Shepherd	Nicholas purchased. Held 1632–1753.
Rogers	1754–68. Miss Rogers m Henry Studdy.
Pomeroy	1756—lease of 14 years.
Studdy	Henry, d 1840. Nephew Henry inherited. Demolished medieval manor and used material to build Court. Henry d 1905. Eldest son R. W. Studdy inherited.
Goodson	Sir Alfred purchased estate 1905; d 1940. Third son Hugh inherited.

The celebration of Mass, or the Holy Eucharist, in the family chapel has been a duty of the Vicars of Stoke Gabriel since the twelfth century.

At Waddeton slipway near the boathouse, where oak trees dip their branches so low in the water that each receding tide leaves them festooned with seaweed, are the long concrete ramps built in 1943 for embarking military landing craft. The towers seen protruding from the water were to guide returning craft; the craft, mooring between the towers would thus settle down on the ramps as the tide receded. The long, green valley seen from the river when passing Lower Gurrow Point leads down to the ramps and contains the overgrown foundations of Nissen huts; it is known at Waddeton as Slipway Field.

At the slipway is the oyster farm owned by Mr Goodson and worked by his son Anthony of Sandridge Barton. Started in 1969, it is now the supply source for high-class restaurants and hotels in the Torbay area. Young oysters are brought from grounds such as the River Fal in Cornwall, and bred on a framework of trays in

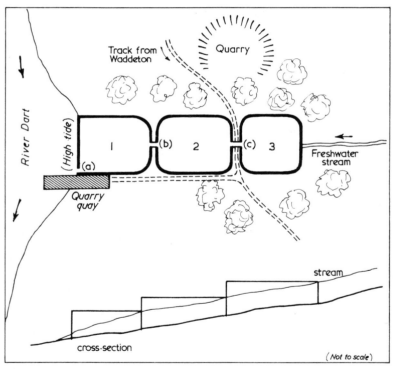

The fish trap at Waddeton. The fish entered pond 1 on the tidal water at channel (a). Progressing to ponds 2 and 3 according to the level of the tide, they were caught by means of nets dropped like curtains in front of channels (b) and (c) when the tide receded. Pond 3 was used for storing the fish, which were carp, rudd, roach, trout and salmon.

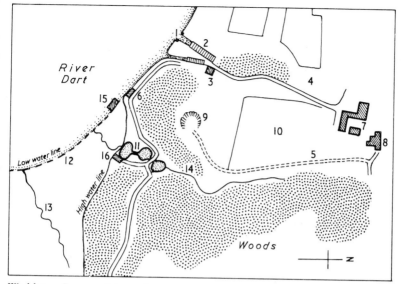

Waddeton Court and the ancient remains, as well as relics from World War II, in the grounds (from an aerial photograph).

1. Guide-towers for landing-craft
2. Slipway
3. Oyster farm
4. Slipway field
5. Ancient track from quarry to hall
6. Waddeton boathouse
7. Court (nineteenth century)
8. Chapel and manor (medieval)
9. Quarry
10. Ground called 'Torrs'
11. Fish trap
12. Tidal beach, 'The Banks'
13. Stream from Galmpton Creek
14. Stream from Waddeton Valley
15. Waddeton Quay
16. Quarry Quay

order to protect them from predatory crabs. Then, at adulthood after twelve months, they are cast into the riverside oyster beds where they lie on shingle with little or no movement. From there they can conveniently be dredged up as required, carefully cleaned, and packed for delivery.

A feature of historical interest on the Waddeton estate, not previously described, is the series of fishponds lying in an inlet at the riverside downstream from the boathouse. This was an ingenious salmon-trap engineered by the monks of Torre Abbey, to which a part of the estate was given by Isabella de Wadetone between 1275–79:

> For the welfare of her soul, of Martin (de Fissacre. deceased husband), her lord, of her children, successors and predecessors, one ferling of land in her ville of Wadetone on condition that the said Abbot and Convent, from the proceeds of the said land, keep a lamp burning for all time in the church of Torre befor the altar of the Holy Cross.

From this gift of land the monks profited greatly, its extent being from the old manor site to the foreshore, enclosures called Torrs to this day. A quarry on the north side of the inlet provided them with stone, Torrs Wood with timber, and the fish trap with river fish. The mechanics of the trap are simple but effective and the tradition of its use has been handed down from monastic times to the present day.

Downstream from Waddeton Slipway are two quays: the first, beside the fish trap, built of crudely but effectively piled stones, is Waddeton Quay, from which a path leads up to the Court; the second, more permanently built to surround an oblong dock, is in Galmpton Bay directly below the disused Waddeton Quarry. The quarry is of historical interest in being the source of stone ballast taken on board, over the centuries, by large sailing ships after discharging cargoes at Dartmouth or Totnes. The ballast was needed as a compensating weight in the hold to stabilise the ship. For this reason numerous French and Spanish ports where the ballast was unloaded have quays built from Waddeton stone. The track from quay to quarry is easily followed, when the great rock face looms through the trees on approach.

In various places in the Waddeton district are large, non-indigenous sandstone boulders of remarkable hardness, resting on the country rock of Devonian slate, which appear to have been transported by a natural agency (ice or water) from the Galmpton Common-Berry Head area. In the woods surrounding the fish trap inlet are two strange pits: one, oblong in shape, is lined with masonry; the other, a huge hole 12ft deep and 12ft across, is certainly ancient, for a yew tree some three or four centuries old has seeded in the bottom of the pit, presenting an odd spectacle. It is not possible to link these with any industrial activity and not irrational, perhaps, to regard them as smugglers' caches. To conceal the contents would have been a simple matter; smugglers were fishermen and fishermen had salmon nets. A net spread over each pit and covered with brushwood would have needed a keen-eyed exciseman indeed to unveil them.

The horseshoe curve of the river here is arrested at Greenway Quay, but at the head of the curve beside the quarry quay, and separated from it by The Banks, is Galmpton Creek. Offshore is the sandbank of Flat Owers and opposite, Lower Gurrow Point at the north-west tip of the spit of land between the river and Dittisham Mill Creek. Galmpton is a part of Churston Ferrers parish. It was 'Galmentone' in 1086, 'Galmetun juxta Bryxham' in 1209, 'Gamelton' 1231, 'Yalmeton' 1238, and 'Gaylmington' 1281: how irrational is that interpolated 'p' in Galmpton! At Warborough Common, Galmpton, several ancient roads converge; here in 1588 Sir John Gilbert of Greenway mustered 1,000 men when the arrival of the Armada had been beacon-signalled.

Galmpton Creek has been a scene of industry for many centuries. Sandstone from the Goodrington quarries was anciently brought here to be loaded on barge, including that for the tower of St Mary's Church, Totnes, in 1449, and for at least four centuries boat-building has given employment to men of Galmpton, Kingswear and Dartmouth. There was a two-way traffic, Galmpton men rowing to work at Dartmouth and vice versa, a physical feat akin to the daily walks of tin miners on Dartmoor before and after a ten-hour day in the mines. Harvey and Sanders are names of early ship-builders at Galmpton Creek; William Gibbs ran the boatyard now owned by Mr Jim Tucker, from c 1880 to the early 1900s, and built wooden sailing trawlers for the Brixham fishing fleet. During World War II wooden MTBs (motor torpedo boats) were built here by Stan Hall. Affixed to the wall in Jim Tucker's office is a small brass plate—the 'builder's plate'—which all boat-builders place in their vessels; this one reads:

MOTOR GUN BOAT 677
1942   S. HALL

and above it is a picture of the vessel on its sea trials. Jim Tucker took over the yard in 1968, and can remember the huge, gaping sawpit, now filled in, remaining from William Gibb's day, when planks were sawn from tree trunks with enormous two-handed cross-cut saws, one sawyer in the pit and the other above. Jim runs the yard in partnership with Mike Makepeace under the name Dartside Boat Park.

On the opposite, south shore of the creek, which is relatively short and has a curved quay at its head, is the Dolphin Shipyard of the Torbay Boat Construction Co Ltd. The yard is the base for the Western Lady Ferry Service between Torquay, Paignton and Brixham, all owned and managed by Mr John Perrett, who describes the firm as 'Shipbuilders and Engineers', although they rarely build now. In the field of marine engineering, for which the firm has its own foundry, a suction head was made for a dredger, for the Government of Mauritius, capable of cutting through 500 tons of coral per hour.

Downstream, Mill Point and Old Mill Farm indicate the former existence of a watermill; above, road and railway diverge when approaching the river, the former to enter Greenway Tunnel and the latter descending to Greenway Quay where a passenger-only ferry operates to Dittisham. The Quay is a picturesque place, crowded in summertime by visitors, who, when the few parking places at the Quay have been taken, leave their cars in a long string on Greenway Hill. Near the hilltop is a drive branching from the road to Greenway House, a signboard at the derelict lodge announcing that garden produce is available on certain days and times — but at the gardens, not the house. The high, sun-drenched and well-drained west-facing slopes of the valley where the gardens lie, protected from biting north and east winds, was rightly calculated, when the gardens were laid out long ago, to produce a fertile growth in return for the sower's labour.

On a level valley-side shelf below the gardens stands the ruin of what probably was an Elizabethan house; though much overgrown, one gable of the ruin reveals a small fireplace with oaken lintel. It was in this building, we may suppose, that Sir Humphrey Gilbert was born in 1537. His mother was Katherine, daughter of Sir Philip Champernowne of stannary fame. She had previously been married to Walter Ralegh Esq of Fardel Manor, Cornwood, and to them was born a son, Walter, later to become the celebrated Sir Walter Ralegh (or Raleigh). Following the death of her husband, Katherine married Otis (or Otto) Gilbert of Greenway, their children being Humphrey, Adrian and John. So it was that Sir Walter Ralegh became half-brother to the three Gilbert sons. The interpolation of the 'i' in the Ralegh family name was of a later date. Several writers, including Chard in *Along The River Dart* imply that Humphrey was born in the existing Greenway House, which was built in the 1780s when so many fine and gracious houses arose from the drawing boards of fashionable architects like Sir Robert Taylor. At all events, the Gilbert family could not have lived in Georgian Greenway; nor could Sir Walter Ralegh have stayed there in later life, as he is known to have done at old Greenway.

Humphrey Gilbert entered the service of Queen Elizabeth I as a courtier, and his personality and bravery soon earned him a knighthood. In 1570 he became a Member of Parliament for Plymouth and in 1578 realised a long-cherished hope by assembling a fleet at Dartmouth for a voyage of discovery to the New World. That this brilliant navigator and commander should have perished at sea five years before the defeat of the Spanish Armada in 1588, when he doubtless would have conducted himself with valour and distinction, was sad indeed.

It was at old Greenway that Sir John Gilbert drew up a plan for developing the fishery, but no details remain for our information. He became Sheriff of Devon in November 1573, and died at Greenway in 1596. A fine canopied memorial containing effigies of Sir John and his lady was later erected in the south transept of Exeter cathedral, beside the door leading to the Chapter House.

On 28 August 1588, the Spanish ship *Nostra Senora del Rosario* of the Armada fleet, with broken bowsprit, was towed into

Dartmouth harbour, the crew being taken off and incarcerated in the great tithe barn of Torre Abbey. Sir John Gilbert, who had inherited Greenway after his brother's death, was quick to seize an opportunity of free labour and arranged for the prisoners to come to Greenway and work on the improvement of gardens and grounds. Their work may have laid the foundations of the present-day fruitful gardens.

Mr and Mrs Anthony Hicks and several Shih-Tzu dogs are the present occupants of Greenway. Mr Hicks believes that an eighteenth-century landowner named Roope had the mansion built and sold it in 1790 to Edward Elton, who remained its owner for thirty years or more. Later in the nineteenth century it was successively owned by the Harvey and Bolitho families. During the 1920s and well into the 1930s, Charles Williams, Member of Parliament for Torquay, lived at Greenway, then owned by his wife (née Mary Bolitho); he sold the estate in 1938 to Mrs Agatha Mallowan, who had previously been married to a Colonel Christie. When her second husband was knighted she of course became Lady Mallowan and later, in recognition of her eminence as a writer, Dame Agatha Mallowan. She wrote, as she always had done, under the name of her first husband, so that the literary world had long known her as Dame Agatha Christie. Dame Agatha did not reside permanently at Greenway, preferring to use it as a summer residence. In 1967 her daughter Rosalind Hicks and husband Anthony took up residence in the house, where Dame Agatha continued to join them from time to time until her death in 1976.

Below Higher Greenway Farm the Paignton-Kingswear railway emerges from Greenway Tunnel, crosses the steep-sided little valley of Maypool Creek over Maypool Viaduct and enters Long Wood. Sir Henry Seale formed the Dartmouth & Torbay Railway Company expressly for the construction of this single line, but the geological complexities of the country rock resulted in costs soaring far above the original estimate of £90,000 to the then staggering sum of £262,000. In 1870, the line was leased to the South Devon Railway Company, which ten years later was absorbed by the Great Western Railway. Kingswear was the end of the line—though not the service. A station was built at Dartmouth, with ticket, luggage office and waiting-room facilities, for ferry passenger to and from the Kingswear trains: it was, in fact, the only station in Britain without trains. On 1 January 1973 the Dart Valley Railway Association bought the line direct from British Rail and named it the Torbay & Dartmouth Railway—a simple inversion of its first title. Below Greenway Tunnel, 495yd in length, the Long Wood stretch of the line affords tantalising glimpses through summer trees of the river, until, crossing Noss Creek on an embankment, built well up from the shore in 1921 to replace two wooden viaducts, the line takes it over a level crossing and past Britannia Halt. Here is the pier for Dartmouth Higher Ferry, operated by Dart Pleasure Craft Ltd, a paddle-driven boat for both passengers and vehicles. Hugging the estuary bank, the train crosses Isambard Brunel's Waterhead Viaduct (over Waterhead Creek) and enters Kingswear station in the very midst, as it seems, of Dartmouth harbour. Pride of the Torbay & Dartmouth Railway is ex-GWR steam locomotive 4–6–0 No 7827, *Lydham Manor*; once languishing in the Barry, South Wales steam engine graveyard, she was bought by the Association in 1970 and completely restored by late 1972.

At the mouth of Noss Creek is the busy shipyard of Philip & Sons Ltd. The Philip family came to Dartmouth from Aberdeen in 1854, and George Philip became foreman ship-builder at Kelley's yard at Sandquay, which he took over in 1858. Present head of the firm in 1981 is John Alexander Philip OBE, MINA, his company now specialising in ship repairs, marine engineering and steel fabricating. Mosley writes in *Shipping on the River Dart*:

Since the company's inception, over 1,300 craft of various types have been built for such customers as the Admiralty, War Office, Foreign Governments, the Royal Air Force, a number of harbour boards, many corporations, and numerous companies and private owners . . . Among other vessels built by this company are the *May Queen*, a 62ft passenger launch for the Creston & Turnchapel Steamboat Company; the 1924 Torpoint Ferry No 1; the *Iveston*, a coastal minesweeper; and between 1946 and 1955, 17 steel light vessels for Trinity House.

Paddle steamers built for the River Dart Steamboat Company between 1880 and 1921 included *Berry Castle*, *Totnes Castle* (two, 1896 and 1921), *Kingswear Castle* and *Compton Castle* (1914, that same veteran relic moored at Fleet Mill Quay). Her successor, a steel ship built at the yard, was moved many years ago to Kingsbridge Quay and used as a floating tea-room. In 1979 she was again moved, this time to Looe in Cornwall. The steamer was then placed in 'dry storage', pulled out of the water, that is, in the yard of Frank Curtis & Pape Bros of Looe on behalf of the purchaser, whose intention it was to restore her to working condition for passenger service on the river between Totnes and Dartmouth. So far, however, this hope has not been realised. More steamers, screw-driven, for the river followed until 1949, when the steel-clad *Berry Castle* was built. Intensive wartime work on craft conversions and fitting has already been mentioned, and since the war Philip's have built coasters, tugs and lightships, including the Goodwin lightship for Trinity House, a model of which is exhibited at the company's offices.

There is little or no ship-building now; all is repair and fitting work, often on vessels of considerable size. Steam ferry boats were needed at Dartmouth before George Philip's arrival, and the tugboat *Pilot*, built in 1852 at South Shields, was bought for the lower ferry. The iron paddle steamer *Newcomen* was shortly afterwards built especially for the service, and replaced the tug-boat. *Newcomen* was herself replaced in 1869 by a similar vessel called *Dolphin*; built by Harvey of Hale, Cornwall, this boat gave long service, being taken over by the GWR in 1901 and continuing to operate until 1908, when she was sold for scrap. The impressive new replacement was *Mew*, a twin-screw, twin-cylinder steam vessel built in 1908 by Cox of Falmouth; 90ft long, 22½ft in beam and with a displacement of 117 tons gross, she served until 1955 and was then broken up. In 1940, *Mew* had been ordered to Dover to join the Dunkirk evacuation fleet, but the initial voyage caused her boilers to overheat and she was rejected as unsafe and ordered back to Dartmouth. Following the withdrawal of *Mew*, the newly nationalised British Railways bought the motor vessels *Adrian Gilbert* and *Humphrey Gilbert* for the ferry service: they were built by Blackmore & Son of Bideford. Philip & Son of Dartmouth, meanwhile, had in 1925 and 1926 built two ferry bridges from designs by T. P. Endean, then manager of the Torpoint ferry. The first was for the Torpoint & Devonport ferry, and the second for Saltash.

The steep branch road, from the A379 Hillhead–Higher Ferry road, which descends to the mouth of Noss Creek, crosses the Torbay railway line, enters a gateway bearing Philip & Son's emblem and, before terminating at the shipyard passes the front of an impressive modern building belonging to the Reeves Group. This is Noss House, containing the computer centre which prepares all the Group's customer accounts for the south west region. There are four such centres covering Britain, this one being under the management of Mr Frank Meadows. The sophisticated equipment under his care makes possible a huge economy over old-fashioned accounting methods at individual branches, and 130,000 invoices go out to customers each month from Noss House.

At Britannia Halt is the tail of the long snake of the Hillhead road, rearing itself adroitly up the hillside to provide fine views over Noss Creek from Bridge Road. The brief remaining distance to Kingswear can be covered either by water or rail, but there is no road.

The Saxon manor 'King tun'—'the farm of the king'—later held by the Norman de Vasci family and recorded as Kingston Vasci, is the probable origin of Kingswear, the king having a water mill and weir, of which remains still exist, at Waterhead: hence, 'King's Weir'. The 1841 *T. Appt.* names Waterhead Mill and Waterhead Creek, the map showing the mill positioned across the stream. But as neither number nor details appear in the apportionment the mill must even then have been long disused. With the changed conditions brought about by Norman invasion and administration, the dwellers of Kingston Vasci, like those of Townstal on the west side, chose to move down to the riverside to trade and to build cottages there. The new riverside settlement inherited the old name, which appears in documents as 'Kingswere' (1170), 'Kingeswerr' (1200), 'Kyngiswere juxte

Dertemouth' (1340) and 'Kyngesware' (1445). The villagers built their church shortly after the assassination of Archbishop Thomas Becket at Canterbury in 1170, dedicating it to that archiepiscopal martyr, on land granted for the purpose by William and Juliana de Vasci. The church is likely to have been built as a chapel for continental pilgrims landing here on their way to the shrine of St Thomas at Canterbury. It continued as a chapel of ease to St Mary's Brixham until 1837, when Kingswear became an autonomous ecclesiastical parish. The building was in a thoroughly decrepit condition by the end of the eighteenth century, and plans were made to rebuild it soon after it received parochial status; the work was completed in 1847, which accounts for its Victorian aspect both inside and out (cf Waddeton Chapel), with exception of the ancient tower.

Below the church is the Square, containing the town well, and the district named Kittery. The outcrop of rock above the town was originally Kite Tor, eyrie of the kite, and mentioned in various documents as 'Kittitor' and 'Kyttor'—the latter in 1500. The spread of the tiny medieval town on the cramped site under the declivity gave rise to a labyrinth of passages and archways long since swept away when the Yacht Club (1881) and certain houses were built, and the grounds of Kittery Court laid out. Percy Russell writes in TDA 85 of 1953:

> In Elizabethan times, when the port of Dartmouth was a thriving base for scores of ships engaged in the Atlantic trade, the whole area south of Kingswear Church was a close built huddle of merchants' houses, warehouses and wharves. Great must have been the congestion at busy times of the year, such as the end of February, when the first fleet destined for Newfoundland was making ready to sail. It was this crowded little port which was the forerunner of Kittery, the oldest township in the state of Maine.

A ferry was recorded as operating between Kittery Quay and Dartmouth as long ago as 1365 (Close Rolls of that year), a monopoly acquired at that time by William Carey. Robert Colyns is mentioned as ferryman two centuries later (1558). The traveller Leland used the ferry in 1540 and wrote: 'I ferried over to Kingswear. This town standeth at a pointlet (Kittery Point) into the haven.' When it became customary for wheeled vehicles to use the ferry, from the late eighteenth century onward, the old Kittery slipway was abandoned in favour of the wider one leading into the Square. The large slipway now in use there was constructed by the Great Western Railway Company. White's *Directory* of 1850 records only one shipbuilder in Kingswear, named Edward Alford.

At Kingswear we are again in Champernowne country, for Gawen, son of Sir Arthur Champernowne who had been Vice-Admiral of the West, held the Castle of Gommerock and property at Kingswear. Russell writes in the *TDA*:

> High above Kittery were the archery butts, with the track now called Castle Road, but the principal road to the mouth of the river, now damaged by landslips, was the lane immediately above the Kittery houses, now marked as Beacon Road. The term Beacon is of interest because the large house of that name was built and titled in 1845, nineteen years before the harbour light was set up in the tower below it. This implies that some earlier guiding light fire had been lit at that point, possibly in very early times.

Mouth of Dart

The tight, congested township of Kingswear is huddled on Dart's last eastern declivity, with streets and houses 'All to one side, like Kingswear folk' as the old saying goes. Delightful though it is, one has a sense of relief and freedom in escaping down the broad waterway of Dart to the river's opening to view the defensive bastions of a former age which make it visually so remarkable: Kingswear Castle, Gommerock Fort, Dartmouth Castle and the torpedo jetty in Silver Cove.

To begin on the west side with Dart's last creek: the war fleets of the Middle Ages assembled in Warfleet Creek—hence its name—and Queen Elizabeth I's Channel Squadron used it as their anchorage. At the top of the creek, where a good head of water was available, a large mill was built by Governor Holdsworth after the Napoleonic Wars. The *T. Appt.* of 1841 gives Joseph Hobbs as 'Flour Miller', the map showing the mill as a small building south of the large brewery already existing, and worked by John Baker & Brother. The present Warfleet Bridge was built across the creek in 1863 to replace on earlier structure (shown on the ancient maps *see plate 22*). The town accounts of 1643 contain a claim by Mistress Margaret Burgin for erecting a fortification above 'Warfleet Mill' called 'Strathay Fort'. This, like the strong, round Paradise Tower, has now vanished; the latter, which once stood above the north side of the creek, was demolished in 1855.

The brewery was owned by Bartlett's Breweries for some years prior to World War II, its produce being advertised by the jingle—'The Barley Wine of the English Rhine'. Becoming a munitions store during the war years, the building was purchased shortly afterwards by Dartmouth Pottery Ltd, whose major output is in earthenware vases, tableware, and bowls, including the 'Gurgling Fish Jug' and the 'Dartmouth Swan'. The pottery is marketed throughout the United Kingdom and exported to Holland, the USA, South America, West Indies and Australia. The clay, like that for Buckfastleigh Blue comes from the Bovey beds of Watts, Blake & Bearne, as well as from red beds in North Devon.

From Warfleet Creek the road passes above the once busy Warfleet 'Lime Kilns Coal and Quay' (*T. Appt.* 1841) and One Gun Point, to terminate at Castle Point, where Dartmouth Castle and St Petrox Church make so striking an addition to the scenery. The castle was preceded by an older, unfinished building on a nearby site, of which the curtain wall still remains and is marked on the *T. Appt.* of 1841 as Garrison Rampart. An interesting and detailed account of the building and equipping of the castle is on sale at the ticket office, and the following are a few items from the town accounts conerning its construction and maintenance:

Item pd for byndyng and Stokkying of two grete murderers (guns) and reparying of the chambyr	£4. 0.0.
Item pd for two dosyn of hyrdylls [hurdles] for scafolds	8.0.
Item pd for 5 botes of Cornworthy stone	1.11.8.
45 qrs of lime per the qr 1/–	2. 5.0.
2 botes of Cornworthy stone	10.0.

Were I to provide a list of the ten features most representative of
Dart country, this castle would be one of them. To begin with, its
situation is striking and memorable. Then the building itself
contains so much of historical interest: the basement, hewn from
the solid rock and with seven gun-ports to seaward; the ground-
floor museum, the openings for musket fire, and the timber-framed
opening through which, over a pulley, passed the great barrier
chain that lay across the harbour entrance in times of war; the first
floor with garderobe, windows, fireplace and oven, the quarters of
the castle garrison; the huge beams above it and the roof
battlements on corbels. An extraordinary effect, too, comes from
looking through the battlements into the stained-glass windows of
St Petrox, seemingly just at arm's length away.

Sabine Baring Gould wrote in his *Lives of the British Saints*, 'Saint
Petroc (or Petrox at Dartmouth and in Pembrokeshire) has left a
deeper impression in the West of England than any other saint.'
Tradition claims that St Petrock established a monastic cell at the
river's mouth, where the monks may have maintained a guiding
light for shipping. It first receives documentary mention clarifying
its site in 1192 as the 'monastery of St Peter'—though it is not clear
why a dedication to the great Apostle came to supplant that to the
missionary saint, and 'St Peter' could possibly be a mistake by a
scribe for 'Petrox'. At all events, Petrock was reinstated and by
1332 two priests were nominated by the Bishop of Exeter to
celebrate Mass in the chapel. The rocky foreshore below the chapel
was ideally suited to the building of a defensive castle at the water's
edge, hence the unusual 'twinning' of church and castle after John
Hawley's abortive plan had been realised as too distant to secure a
satisfactory range on vessels in midstream. There are indications
(in documentary sources) that the chapel was enlarged and kept in
good repair until, in 1641, it was rebuilt and a 20ft spire added to
the new tower. It was later used as a provision store for the castle
garrison during the Civil War. Remarkably, it suffered little or no
damage and the disappearance of the spire must be attributed to
later years—perhaps in the early nineteenth century when the
building lapsed into disrepair—for it appears in a water-colour of
1839 by Miss C. B. Hunt, pupil of Samuel Prout, a noted

architectural artist of that time. The picture hangs in Dartmouth Museum.

On entering St Petrox one receives an impression of a weather-beaten outpost of the Faith. Water laps at the very base of its crenellated churchyard wall, and windows are larger than might be expected in a building subjected to the winds and storms of Start Bay. It is perched only a few feet above the restless waters of the bay and is open to the sounds of men and Nature from river and sea. Percy Russell, Historian Emeritus of the Dartmouth scene, wrote in *The Story of St Petrox Church* (obtainable in the church) that it is:

> ... used for services on the fine summer evenings from Whitsun until the end of August, when returning Dartmothians and visitors love to meet in this hallowed building for a service. The bells ring out their message of welcome across the water to passing shipping.

South of Warfleet Bridge, the castle road throws off a branch, right, to a small car park above Sugary Cove. It is satisfying to stop short of this, park in one of the spaces indicated along the branch road and walk towards the cove. Passing above the tops of the two opposing castle towers, there comes a moment when there is still a river below, next a moment when it is there no longer, but only the waves of Start Bay. That is the Mouth of Dart, the end of the river; it is as sudden as that.

The attractions of Sugary Cove, Compass Cove, Compass Hill, Deadman's Cove and Ladies' Cove can have no place here; they are beyond Dart. But crowning the high, wooded slopes above all is the Royalist redoubt named Gallants Bower, once directly concerned with the defence of river mouth, harbour and town. In the Patent Roll of 23 June 1463 (3 Edward IV) is this passage:

> ... the ... township of Southtoundertemouth shall henceforth be annexed to the said borough of Cliftondertemouth hardenasse, in consideration that the burgesses keep watches against invaders on the confines of the township and beyond at a place called Galions Boure.

The earthwork is now, in 1982, profusely overgrown, making

movement difficult in summertime when, of course, most visitors make the climb to the summit. A signpost placed above the higher seat, directing the walker to the authentic site on the right, would be helpful. As it is, one cannot look down to the harbour, only to the river mouth and Kingswear Castle beyond; looking across to the Day Mark Tower, and northward to Beacon Parks and the Naval College is easier but hardly so relevant to the ancient purpose of the fort.

Inside the earthwork is a wall over 20ft thick reinforcing the innermost rampart and remains of masonry 7ft high, doubtless part of a building that perhaps had a lean-to-roof. This would have provided shelter for the unfortunate garrison which, commanded by Sir Hugh Pollard, was fated to be on the hilltop during the bitter January of 1656. The view of the Bight, harbour and Warfleet Creek was obviously of bird's-eye clarity before the fort became overgrown, for it occupies a completely commanding position. The declivity east to the river is extremely steep. Cranford comments in *Up and Down the River Dart* that: 'The hill called Gallants Bower was formerly used as a Beacon Station in times of danger.'

Views across the river mouth from the higher seat on Gallants Bower include the sites of four more harbour-mouth defences; the Mouth of Dart over the ages has increasingly bristled with fortifications, though not all, of course, were in simultaneous use. As one fell into disuse another would take its place, an eventuality seen in three stages on the Kingswear side. The first fortification down-river, and oldest, is the oddly named, secluded ruin of Gommerock Fort. It is unfortunately not possible to date this fortified dwelling, but it appears to be of not later than fourteenth-century origin, and possibly thirteenth. It was certainly still habitable in 1591 when it was the property of the Champernownes; its earliest documentary reference is in a deed of 1580, where it is described as a 'castelle', and in another document of 1590 was the 'old Castelle of Kingswear'—'old' castle because already superseded as a harbour-mouth defence by the new Kingswear Castle. Russell's description in *TDA* 85 of 1963 is precise:

In plan it is a rectangle 36ft by 27. The length of the building runs up the slope of the hill so steeply that the rock floor of the upper part is reached by a stone stair of six steps from that of the lower part. The upper walls, which appear to be separated from the hill slope above them by a rock-hewn ditch, are surmounted by a rampart walk and parapet, and so give meaning to the description of the place as a castle.

The *T. Appt.* of 1841 shows the site of the fort as 'Gommerock Waste' and the wood as 'Gommerock Brake', all in the ownership of Arthur Howe Holdsworth, Governor of Dartmouth Castle.

No mention appears in Russell's paper of two unusual features, one functional, the other sentimental. The first is the largest baking oven I have ever seen. It consists of a circular chamber with portal, 3ft 2in high and 9½ft in diameter. In front of this is an in-filled, stone-lined pit which may have been the castle well and would, of course, have been covered. These interesting objects are within the shell of what apparently was the castle kitchen. The walls of the old fort are now surrounded by the trees of a copse and on one wall near the path from the roadside gate is the second feature—no fewer than seventeen memorial tablets to pet animals of the 1930s. From the castle entrance, which faces seaward, steps lead down the cliffside to a narrow platform, still high above the water, in which several rows of shallow beam holes have been cut. Here, presumably, preparations once began to build a stronger tower opposite Dartmouth Castle, its intended function ultimately fulfilled by Kingswear Castle. Below the platform, and exactly opposite the port constructed in the wall of Dartmouth Castle for the passage of the great barrier chain, is, in Russell's words, 'a great slanting slit just above high watermark, about 10ft high and 5oft through, enabling a chain to be secured to the main body of the cliff itself'. Gommerock Castle, or Fort, is approached by a track leaving Castle Road as it ascends a short hill on approaching Kingswear Court. This is not a public right of way.

Beyond Kingswear Court is Kingswear Castle, the private residence of Sir Frederick Bennett, present Member of Parliament for Torbay. Erected in 1491–1502, it cost £68 19s 0½d. It contains internally splayed embrasures on the ground floor through which artillery could fire on enemy ships approaching the Narrows. Its square tower almost duplicates that of Dartmouth Castle, but its exposed position led Sir John Gilbert of Greenway in 1578 to advise that the castle needed 'four pieces of ordnance royal' which should be brass, 'for the breath of the sea will consume quickly iron ordnance, for the fort stands wholly open to the breath of the sea'.

As a harbour-mouth defence the castle was strategically less effective than that of Dartmouth, and although manned in times of trouble until the end of the Civil War, it was then abandoned, and was described by Colonel Lully when carrying out a survey of coastal defences in 1717, as 'useless and irreparable'. A century and a half later in 1855, Charles Seale-Hayne, owner of much land on both sides of the river including that on which Kingswear Castle stands, repaired the old fort, added a stone gallery leading to a new, small tower 'embellished with the arms of his family and their kin' (Russell) and furnished it as a summer residence.

Sir Frederick Bennett kindly allowed me to explore the castle, where, from the roof of the tower, I saw a rare view of Dartmouth Castle, St Petrox Church and the ancient curtain wall, the Narrows, the Bight, Southtown and the overlooking stronghold of Gallants Bower, while almost at my feet was Silver Cove.

Thick plate-glass windows have been fitted to the gun embrasures in what is now the lounge, traditionally known as the 'guardroom'. The undercroft windows also have exterior wooden shutters, which it is imperative to close when storms generate heavy seas. A combination of high tide and storm can cause waves to crash against the castle rock with such appalling force that the water leaps right over the tower to fall at the front door (on the landward side); there, proof of this violent phenomenon, is a large grating to prevent water entering the building. The castle is, regrettably, not open to the public, but privacy is important in such a small residence.

Below Kingswear Court and reached by a long flight of now treacherous steps is Silver Cove. Here is another summer folly, a sham castle built by the late Sir Thomas Leonard of Kingswear Court during or shortly after World War I. Now disused, the 'castle' consists of a round tower, squat and battlemented, standing on a rocky shelf just above the waterline. Admiral Sir Frank Hopkins of Kingswear can remember the tower being built when he was a child. The site was seized upon by the War Office at the beginning of World War II as suitable for a missile base for the protection of the Narrows—history thus repeating itself over at least seven centuries. A large, low shed was constructed, with concrete roof, directly below a perpendicular cliff face—which shows unusually contorted strata as evidence of the violence of primeval land upheaval here—and a wide concrete bridge to span a small inlet next to the cove, where Sir Thomas Leonard had a small footbridge. The round tower was used as a store and the new shed equipped to secrete three torpedo tubes and a large winch (which still remains). This new coastal defence post was to guard against surprise attack, but it would be true to say that 'never a shot was fired in anger'. At the foot of the cliff behind the concrete bridge is a cavern, its mouth provided with a huge granite portal with keystone; rowing boats and launches were able to enter here given the right tides and water conditions.

High above this rugged piece of coastline, with its three disused river-mouth defences, is Mount Ridley, where now stands the pleasant Redoubt Hotel, a former Victorian residence on the site of another Civil War redoubt; built and garrisoned by Royalist Sir Henry Cary of Cockington, it provides a magnificent view of river mouth and harbour such as once was commanded by Gallants Bower, directly opposite over the water.

How different these viewpoints might have looked today had it not been for certain zealous watchdogs who have been concerned, not like those of old with seaborne vandals, but, with land vandals that seek to commercialise anything beautiful! An early conservator of the land was Charles Seale-Hayne, who was responsible not only for re-afforesting the Kingswear slopes between 1850 and 1880, but succeeded also in persuading neighbouring landowners to adopt the same measure. The riverside lands had for centuries been owned by a few aristocratic families, but during the 1850s the pattern changed and parcels of land increasingly were sold to smallholders. In 1905 a speculator bought the hill of Gallants Bower and planned to fell all trees and

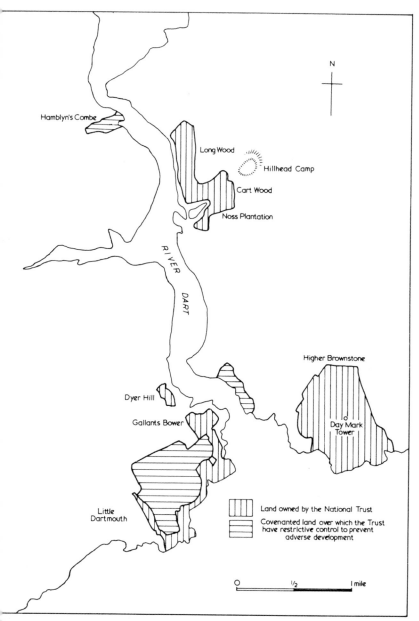

he National Trust around the Dart Estuary

lay out the ground in eighty-five building plots. The fierce opposition encountered by this man forced him to withdraw his plan.

It was in the early post-World War II days that Brigadier William Hine-Haycock of Kittery Court, Kingswear—historian Percy Russell had been a close friend of his parents—stepped into the conservation picture as contemporary watchdog, and this book cannot close without paying tribute to his work. Without it, houses, bungalows, villas and concrete access roads would by now disfigure the magnificent, sea-fiord approaches to the mouth of England's most beautiful river. As a Committee member of the National Trust William Hine-Haycock has been directly responsible for purchasing for the nation such outstanding areas of natural beauty as Little Dartmouth (1970), Dyers Hill (1973), Gallants Bower (1975) and Higher Brownstone (1979). If you spread out a map of the estuary you may visualise what might have been were it not for the Trust holdings. Brigadier Hine-Haycock launched 'Enterprise Dart' in 1974 for the conservation of the estuary, the appeal receipts now standing, in 1981, at £90,000. 'Please help save our coast' is the justifiable cry on the appeal leaflet, '£100,000 urgently needed to purchase, maintain and provide access to unspoilt coast from Torbay to Salcombe'.

Higher Brownstone Farm has 300 acres of land and in two of its fields are objects of interest. One is a prehistoric burial barrow, opened in 1932 by Mr J. Watkins and found to contain a kistvaen and charred bones. It has since been largely ploughed down and is now inconspicuous. Notably conspicuous in contrast is the second feature: it stands in a field bordering a lane through the farmlands (and therefore private) on Down End, the highest point overlooking the harbour approach. It is the remarkable Day Mark Tower. Built in 1866 by the Peninsula & Oriental Steam Navigation Co (otherwise 'P&O') as a navigational guide and landmark, it can be seen from over 20 miles out at sea—a quarter of the way, that is, between Dartmouth and the French coast. The site was chosen as the first piece of English land sighted by P&O passengers returning from the Far East. The great beacon was taken over by Trinity House in 1870, the site being leased to them for 1,000 years at one shilling (five new pence) per year.

The tower resembles a huge chimney stack, but is much wider; its pillars rise from large, flat slate foundations and its upper portion forms an octagon. Southern Dartmoor appears in the hazy distance, Fire Beacon Hill rises boldly to the north-west, Townstal Church (topped now by new housing estates) and Beacon Parks water-tower stand in the mid-distance, while the restless sea appears as countless miles of sheet silver.

Day Mark Tower on a clear day is a good place to stand and reflect on the story contained in these pages, and I cannot provide a better *finale* than the closing prayer from the Dartmouth Pilgrim's Litany. The current of the words, like that of the historic River Dart, flows from inland lake and stream to sea, and calls for the divine blessing:

> ... on this and all waters, springs, and brooks, lakes and wells, small and great rivers and the great outer seas.

A river, like history—indeed, like life itself—moves ever onward: a living thing gathering from its tributaries enrichment, sometimes defilement, until, in the final unalterable form in which its current has shaped its course, it joins the boundless sea.

APPENDICES

A. LIST OF INDUSTRIES, ARTS, CRAFTS AND ACTIVITIES

The many activities on the banks of the Dart through the ages are listed here in the order of their description in the text, with page numbers. Figures in italics are plate numbers.

The Moorland Dart
Cutting of peat passes through highland blanket bog, 17, 25
Cutting of peat as fuel for lowland markets, 18
Medieval tin-streaming, 19–20
Mesolithic flint tool and weapon making, 21
Manufacture of gunpowder for quarries and mines, 21–2
Formation of medieval trading tracks and construction of clapper bridges, 22–3
Twentieth-century Government afforestation, 23
Range-farming of cattle, ponies and sheep, 24, 28
Eighteenth-century water supply leat for Devonport Dockyard, 26
Aerial ropeway for transport of timber during World War I, 28
Medieval tinners' blowing houses for smelting and processing of tin ore, 29, 151, *1*
Rabbit warrening for supply of local markets, 30

The Border-Country Dart
Pre-Industrial Revolution mining for iron, 47–8
Mining during Industrial Revolution: copper, 56–7, *3*
Mining during Industrial Revolution: tin, 49–50
Country hotel embracing true country life, 50
Organised recreational activities under qualified instructors: camping; swimming; canoeing; life-saving; climbing; scuba-diving; snorkelling; map-reading; pony trekking; caving; lightweight camping; archery; orienteering; environmental studies; photography; and first aid, 55

B. ABBREVIATIONS USED IN THE TEXT

LTA   Land Tax Assessment
A Tax was first levied on land in 1692. It included real estate, offices, personal property and a duty on mining royalties. Assessment became increasingly difficult as time went on and by the mid-eighteenth century the tax was levied on land only. It was abolished in 1914.

T. Appt.   Tithes Apportionment
Tithe payments were made compulsory in AD 787. In origin, a tithe was the tenth part of the yearly produce of land and in early times was payable to the Church through the bishops. With the establishment of the parochial system by the Normans, tithes became due to the rector of a parish. Many parishes, with the rectories, were held by monasteries, and after the Dissolution were invariably granted to laymen who were termed 'lay impropriators' and as such were entitled to receive tithes. This was the origin of the holding by a layman of the gift of a parochial benefice, or 'living'. The Tithes Act of 1836 commuted tithe payments to an annual rent charge, and a further Act of 1836 dissolved the charge, substituting annuities for sixty years.

TDA   Transactions of the Devonshire Association
The Association was formed in 1862 for 'the advancement of Science, Literature and Art', and publishes annually information of county interest contributed by members in the form of papers read at meetings and data sent to the 'Recorders' in the various fields (entomology, folklore, dialect, geology, history, natural history etc).

8 Henry VIII
This usage denotes (in this case) the eighth year of the reign of Henry VIII.

C. RECOMMENDED MAPS AND CHART

For the course of the river from its source to Dartmouth and Kingswear, see the OS 1in:1 mile Tourist Map of Dartmoor. For the reaches in greater detail, use the OS 1/25:000 Second Series (2½in:1 mile), as follows:

Parts	Map	
1	SX68/78	Chagford
1,2	SX67/77	Widecombe
2,3	SX66/76	Ashburton and Buckfastleigh
3,4	SX86/96	Totnes
4	SX85/95	Dartmouth

Also recommended is the *Historical Chart of Navigable Dart*, Part IV ('The River Dart in Devon, England') Research by Sqdn Ldr G. H. W. Glenn DFC, design by John Gillett, Peterborough. It is distributed by the Mayflower Gift Shop, Dartmouth, and is obtainable in bookshops in Dart country and Torbay.

D. SECTION OF AN IMAGINARY BONE CAVE

By A. J. Sutcliffe of the British Museum (Natural History). (See page 69.)
Reprinted from Studies in Speleology, Vol 2, Part 2 (July 1970).

The shortly to be opened Pleistocene hall of the Fossil Mammal Gallery of the British Museum (Natural History) contains a semi-pictorial coloured section of an imaginary bone cave. A more diagrammatic version [see figure] also appears in the Introduction to Cave Palaeontology exhibit at the Pengelly Centre.

The section is intended to introduce the caver (who may from time to time encounter bones during the course of his explorations) and the non-specialist (whose knowledge of bone caves may be limited to having heard, during a visit to a commercial show cave, that the bones found there had been carried underground by a torrent) to some of the complexities of bone cave sedimentation, commonly investigated by the cave palaeontologist.

The section shows how, in general, the lowest deposits in a cave are the earliest; those above later, but that deposits may be discontinuous or disturbed, so that their relationship is not always easy to interpret. The earliest deposit shown (1a) is a river-terrace deposit laid down on the hill above the cave at a time when a river was flowing at level I and the entire cave lay beneath the water table. While this deposit was being laid down cave formation was still taking place under phreatic conditions and insoluble residue from the limestone was settling on the cave floor (1b).

Valley downcutting then caused the river to fall to a lower level, II, draining all but the lowest part of the cave. A vadose stream flowing out of the cave laid down sand and silt (2) in its bed. Animal remains sometimes occur in such deposits, but are uncommon. Further valley deepening caused the river to fall again, leaving the cave dry and causing layer 2 to be truncated by erosion at the cave mouth. A layer of flowstone (3) then accumulated on the floor of the inner part of the cave. Carnivorous animals, entering the cave, left the débris of their food and other remains (4a). Man, sheltering at the cave mouth, left the ashes of his fires (4b).

A rock fall (5) then opened a shaft in the cave roof and another layer of flowstone (6) formed. Earth and rock fragments and the remains of animals which had fallen into the cave by accident formed a talus cone (7), as in Joint Mitnor Cave, beneath the shaft, which finally became completely filled with sediment (8).

A human body (9) was then buried in the cave floor, disturbing deposits 2, 3 and 4, but subsequently being covered by part of another rock fall (10) and by further flowstone associated with stalagmites and

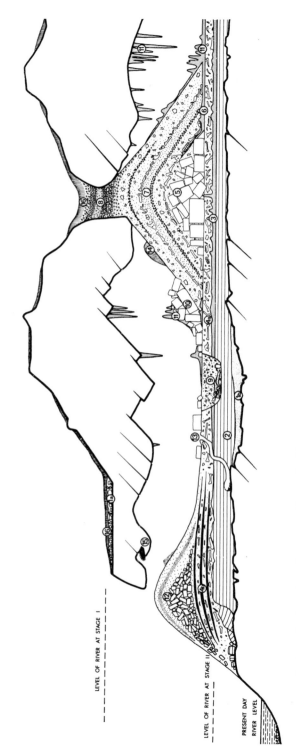

LEVEL OF RIVER AT STAGE I

LEVEL OF RIVER AT STAGE II

PRESENT DAY
RIVER LEVEL

Section of an imaginary bone cave. Drawn by Una M. K. Sutcliffe

stalactites (11). A talus cone at the cave mouth (12) accumulated directly upon layer 4 but cannot be related to layers 5-11 of the cave interior, because it is isolated from them.

A burrowing animal dug a burrow (13), deflected by flowstone layer 3, in the cave floor, throwing up fossil bones from depth onto the surface and subsequently dying in the burrow. A pile of bat dung (14) accumulated beneath a bat roost inside the cave and a pile of rodent bones beneath a nest of birds of prey (15) at the cave mouth. A layer of soil (16) formed on the hill top above the cave.

Consideration of deposits such as those shown in the section emphasizes some of the problems associated with reconstructing the sequence of events leading to their accumulation. Only careful examination of the burial (9) can show that it is later than deposit (4), which is at the same level. Similarly the bones of the burrowing animal, which has died in the burrow (13) are surrounded by deposits of layer 2 and (unless the burrow is carefully cleaned out before 2-4 are excavated) could be thought to be older than is really the case. A further hazard lies in the excavation of layer 7 since the divisions are sloping and finds from them will become mixed if this deposit is excavated in horizontal layers.

The excavation of a bone-cave must be treated like a dissection; each horizontal layer, each talus cone, each burial, each burrow being examined separately, if the full history of the deposits is to be successfully reconstructed. The excavation of bone caves is not justified unless full attention can be paid to such detail and the excavation results can be published subsequently.

ACKNOWLEDGEMENT

Grateful acknowledgement is made to J. Simons, whose excellent paper on cave formation and sedimentation provided many of the ideas for the section.

REFERENCE

SIMONS, J., 1965. Some basic principles of cave formation and methods of sedimentation. *Newsl. of the Cave Explor. Group. E. Africa,* 3: 2-20.

E. THE TRIAL OF CAPTAIN EDWARD GOULD

This account of the case R. v. Gould, *heard in Exeter in 1768, is taken from* Devonshire Characters *by S. Baring-Gould.*

Edward Gould, of Pridhamsleigh, died in 1736, and as he was the last of the elder branch of the family, he left all his lands in Staverton, Ashburton, Holne, Widdecombe-on-the-Moor, and Chudleigh to William Drake Gould, of Lew Trenchard, the representative of the next branch, who was then a minor. This William Drake Gould died in 1766, and all his estates devolved on his only son Edward, born in 1740. Edward was a spendthrift and a gambler. One evening he had been playing late and deep, and had lost every guinea he had about him. Then he rode off, put a black mask over his face, and waylaid the man who had won the money off him, and on his appearance, challenged him to deliver. The gentleman recognized him and incautiously exclaimed, 'Oh! Edward Gould, I did not think this of you!'

'You know me, do you?' was his reply, and Edward shot him dead. Then he rode to Pridhamsleigh, reversed his horse's shoes, and sped across Dartmoor to Lew Trenchard.

Now there had been a witness, a man who had seen Edward take up his position, and who, believing him to be a highwayman, had secreted himself and waited an opportunity to effect his escape. Edward Gould was tried for the murder. Dunning was engaged to defend him. It was essential to weaken or destroy the testimony of the witness. On the day of the trial he cross-questioned this same witness sharply.

'How can you be sure that the man on the horse was Mr. Gould,' asked Dunning 'when, as you say, it was past midnight?'

'Sir, the full moon shone on him. I recognized his horse. I knew his coat. Besides, when he had shot the other he removed the mask.'

'The full moon was shining, you assert?'

'Yes, your honour. I saw his face by the clear moonlight.'

'Pass me a calendar,' said the judge. 'Who has got a calendar?'

At that time almanacs were not so plentiful as they are now. As it happened, no one present possessed one. Then Dunning said, standing up:—

'My lord, I had one yesterday, and put it, I believe, in my overcoat pocket. If your lordship will send an apparitor into the ante-room to search my pocket, it may be found.'

The calendar was produced. There was no moon on the night of the murder. The evidence against the prisoner broke down, and he was acquitted.

Dunning on the previous day had purchased an almanac, removed the sheets containing among others the month and those preceding and following it, and had had the calendar reprinted, altering the moons so that there might be none on the night in question.

This was considered at the time a clever and sharp bit of practice of Mr. Dunning; it occurred to no one that it was immoral.

BIBLIOGRAPHY

Band, Nick, Article on salmon poaching (*Western Morning News*, October 1980)

Baring-Gould, Revd Sabine, *A Book of Dartmoor* (Methuen, 1900)

——*Devonshire Characters* (John Lane, The Bodley Head, 1908)

——*Further Reminiscences* (John Lane, The Bodley Head, 1929)

Binney, Marcus, 'Sharpham House' (*Country Life*, July 1967)

Birch, Sheila, *Stoke Gabriel* (Mitcham, undated)

Booker, Frank, *Industrial Archaeology of the Tamar Valley* (David & Charles, 1971)

——*Buckfast Abbey Chronicle*, Vol 10 (Buckfast Abbey, 1940)

Burr, Revd B. G. W., *The Parish Church of St Thomas of Canterbury, Kingswear* (undated)

Burton, S. H., *Devon Villages* (Robert Hale, 1973)

Chard, Judy, *Along the Dart* (Bossiney Books, 1979)

Cook, G. H., *The English Medieval Parish Church* (Phoenix House, 1954)

Cranford, R., *Up and Down the River Dart* (published privately, undated)

Crossing, William, *The Ancient Stone Crosses of Dartmoor* (J. G. Commin, 1902)

——*From a Dartmoor Cot* (Homeland Association, 1906)

——*Guide to Dartmoor* (*Western Morning News*, 1909; 1912 edition reprinted, David & Charles, 1965)

Davies, E. L., and Grove, E. J., *The Royal Naval College, Dartmouth: Seventy-five Years in Pictures* (Gieves & Hawkes, 1980)

Devonshire Association, Transactions of the (1862–1981)

Dines, H. G., *The Metalliferous Mining Region of South-West England* (HMSO, 1956)

Emery, Anthony, *Dartington Hall* (Clarendon Press, 1970)

English Place Name Society, The, *English Place Names*, Vol 8 (Cambridge University Press, 1931)

Green, J. F. N., 'The History of the River Dart, Devon' (*Proceedings of the Geological Association*, Vol 60, 1949)

Gunnell, Elizabeth, *Totnes* (Bossiney Books, 1979)

Hemery, Eric, *High Dartmoor: Land and People* (Robert Hale, 1982)

Hooker, John Vowell, *Synopsis Chorographical of Devon* (British Museum, Harleian MS 5827, 1600)

Hoskins, W. G., *Devon* (Collins, 1954; new edition, David & Charles, 1972)

Isham, K., Article on limekilns (*Western Morning News*, 16 December 1966)

Kingdom, A., *The Ashburton Branch* (Oxford Publishing Co, 1977)

Longmate, Norman, *The G.I.s* (Hutchinson, 1975)

Mellor & Kidel *Dartington Rural Archive* (Dartington Hall Trust, 1978)

Mildren, James, Article on proposed marina (*Western Morning News*, 23 July 1980)

Mining Journal, The (issues 1858–1862)

Moseley, Brian, *Shipping on the River Dart* (published privately, 1968)

Page, J. W. Lloyd, *An Exploration of Dartmoor and its Antiquities* (Seeley & Co, 1889)

Perkins, John, *Geology Explained in South and East Devon* (David & Charles, 1971)

Purcell, William, *Onward Christian Soldier* (Longmans, Green & Co, 1957)

Risdon, Tristram, *The Chorographical Description or Survey of the County of Devon* (1714; third edition, Rees & Curtis, 1820)

Rowe, Revd Samuel, *A Perambulation of the Royal and Ancient Forest of Dartmoor & the Venville Precincts* (J. B. Rowe, 1848)

Russell, Percy, *Dartmouth* (Batsford, 1950)

——*The Good Town of Totnes* (Devonshire Association, 1963)

Seymour, Deryck, *Torre Abbey* (published privately, 1977)

——'South-West England', *British Regional Geology* (third edition, HMSO, 1975)

Stéphan, Dom John, OSB, *Buckfast Abbey: A Short History & Guide* (Buckfast Abbey, 1955)

Torquay Natural History Society, Transactions of the, Vol 13 (1959–62)

Vancouver, Charles, *A General View of the Agriculture of the County of Devon* (Board of Agriculture, 1808)

Willey, Margaret, *The South Hams* (Robert Hale, 1955)

Wilson, John W., *Alluvial Tin at Colston, Buckfastleigh* (undated pamphlet)

ACKNOWLEDGEMENTS

My thanks are due to the following for their co-operation:

Mr & Mrs N. Amherst; Mr & Mrs Maurice Ash

Nick Band; Miss J. A. Bell; Sir Frederick Bennett MP; Marcus Binney; Miss Sheila Birch; Mrs E. Bishop; Revd J. Bishop; Frank Booker; Britannia Royal Naval College; Arthur Brook; Mr & Mrs K. Bromage; Garth Bromley; Buckfast Plating Co; Buckfast Pottery Ltd; Revd J. Butler

Revd C. A. Cardale; R. Cawthorne; A Chaffe; William Chapple; A. Coaker; Jack Connabear; Sam Cox; Creekside Boatyard Ltd; Curtis & Pape Bros Ltd

Dartington Hall Trust; Dartington Litho; Dartington Solar Quest; Dartington Tweeds Ltd; Dartington Woodlands Ltd; Dart Pleasure Craft; Dart Valley Railway Association; Dartmouth Pottery Ltd; Dartmouth Town Council; Julian David; E. L. Davies; R. Davies; Mr & Mrs E. Drew

J. Elliot; Mr & Mrs Elliott; Mrs H. Elmhirst; Anthony Emery; Mrs Audrey Erskine; Richard Evans

Fountain Forestry Ltd

Ian Glendenning; Anthony Goodson; Hugh Goodson; J. D. Graham; T. Greaves; E. J. Grove

Peter Hannaford; C & T Harris (Calne) Ltd; Percy Haywood; Mr & Mrs Anthony Hicks; Raymond Hill; Mr & Mrs Hillhouse; Brigadier W. Hine-Haycock DL; D. J. Hitchcock; Honnor Marine Ltd; Robin Hood; John Hooper; Admiral Sir Frank Hopkins; Miss G. Hoyte; Tom Hughes

Miss B. M. Jewell; Mrs S. Johnson; H. Jonas

Bro Adam Kerhle OSB; Anthony Kingdom; Stewart Kington

Mrs Margaret Lambert; Mrs Avril Longman; Jack Lynn

Mike Makepeace; David Manning; Mrs Marshall; J. Matters; Jack May; Mr & Mrs Ian McDade; Frank Meadows; M. J. Messenger; James Mildren; Miss E. J. Mitchell; Stan Mitchelmore; Revd J. E. Morris; Mrs Mullender

Miss Susan Pearce; Pepe & Son; W. A. Perring; John Perrett; D. Perryman; Philip & Son Ltd; Edward Masson Phillips; R. A. Pilkington; E. S. Pook; Revd John Price

Edgar Reed; Graham Reeves Ltd; Lieut Cdr P. H. G. Richardson RN; S. E. Rigold; 'Charlie' Clarence Roper; Miss Alison Rose

P. Simpson; S. V. J. Simpson; R. C. Scrivener; Mrs Sheilagh Shore; Dom Leo Smith OSB, PhD, Abbot of Buckfast; Staverton Contracting Group; Staverton Joinery; Dr Anthony Sutcliffe; Mrs Una Sutcliffe

Torbay Boat Construction Co Ltd; *Totnes Gazette*; Totnes Town Council; Miss Patricia Townsend; Jim Tucker

W. F. Vallance

Tom Wakenham; Donald Warren; John Watson; John Westall; P. Wheeler; Jim Widdicombe; R. J. Williams; John W. Wilson; R. J. Wilson; Mrs Dorothy Wright; J. H. Woodward; G. E. Wyatt

In particular I acknowledge gratefully the practical and critical help of my wife Pauline during the compilation of the book, of my daughter Francesca in small and tedious tasks, and of my son Gabriel in field work.

INDEX

Communal activities and past and present industrial establishments are listed in Appendix A and do not appear in this index.

Royal personages appear under, respectively, Kings, Queens, Princes and Princess. See under Bishops of Exeter, Bridges, Churches, Ferry services and Inns for individual names in these categories.

Figures in *italics* are plate numbers.

OF RELATED INTEREST

DEVON
W. G. Hoskins
216 × 138mm (8½ × 5⅜in) 12pp b/w photographs, 6 figures & maps

CROSSING'S GUIDE TO DARTMOOR
184 × 122mm (7¼ × 4¾in) Maps & illustrations throughout

WORTH'S DARTMOOR
Edited by G. M. Spooner & F. S. Russell
222 × 154mm (8¾ × 6⅛in) 94pp b/w photographs, diagrams & maps

DARTMOOR A New Study
Crispin Gill
209 × 148mm (8¼ × 5¼in) 24pp b/w photographs, several maps and sketches

WALKING WEST COUNTRY RAILWAYS
Christopher Somerville
216 × 138mm (8¼ × 5⅜in) 24 b/w photographs, several maps and sketches

A REGIONAL HISTORY OF THE RAILWAYS OF GREAT BRITAIN Vol 1 The West Country
David St John Thomas
216 × 138mm (8½ × 5⅜in) 20pp b/w photographs, 12 line illustrations & 1 folding map

THE INDUSTRIAL ARCHAEOLOGY OF THE TAMAR VALLEY
Frank Booker
210 × 148mm (8¼ × 5¾in) 52 b/w photographs, maps & diagrams

DEVON SHIPWRECKS
Richard Larn
216 × 138mm (8½ × 5⅜in) b/w photographs, maps & diagrams